D1507322

# Political Crime: Ideology and Criminality

### Frank E. Hagan
Mercyhurst College

**Allyn and Bacon**
Boston • London • Toronto • Sydney • Tokyo • Singapore

MERCYHURST COLLEGE
HAMMERMILL LIBRARY
ERIE, PA 16546-0001

*Vice President, Social Science:* Karen Hanson
*Series Editorial Assistant:* Jennifer Jacobson
*Marketing Manager:* Karon Bowers
*Composition and Prepress Buyer:* Linda Cox
*Manufacturing Buyer:* Megan Cochran
*Cover Administrator:* Suzanne Harbison
*Editorial-Production Service:* Shepherd, Inc.

Copyright © 1997 by Allyn & Bacon
A Simon & Schuster Company
Needham Heights, MA 02194

All rights reserved. No part of the material protected by this copyright notice may be reproduced or utilized in any form or by any means, electronic or mechanical, including photocopying, recording, or by any information storage and retrieval system, without the written permission of the copyright owner.

**Library of Congress Cataloging-in-Publication Data**

Hagan, Frank E.
    Political crime: ideology and criminality / by Frank E. Hagan.
      p.  cm.
    Includes bibliographical references and indexes.
    ISBN 0-02-348993-6
    1. Political crimes and offenses.   2. Crime—Political aspects.
  3. Ideology.   I. Title.
  HV6254.H24   1997
  364.1'31—dc20                     96–14638
                                    CIP

Printed in the United States of America

10  9  8  7  6  5  4  3  2  1     01  00  99  98  97  96

# Brief Contents

# Contents

# *Preface*

*Political Crime: Ideology and Criminality* is intended to serve the need for an up-to-date general, primary, or secondary text for upper-level and graduate courses in criminology/criminal justice, sociology, and political science/policy studies. While the author would like to pay homage to all of the excellent specialized works on specific types of political crime (for example, books on terrorism or state crime), the attempt here is not to duplicate the coverage of these works. Instead, the author hopes to provide a general introduction to the full range of political crime which I feel has not been done since Proal's *Political Crime* [1898] (1973) or Stephen Schafer's *The Political Criminal* (1974). In other words on any given topic the more detailed coverage of specific topics elsewhere will be cited, but an overview of the entire spectrum of political criminality will be the intention of this book.

Two broad divisions of subject matter are covered: crime by government and crime against government. The former includes war crimes, violations of human rights, illegal secret police operations, genocide and ethnic cleansing, crime by police, as well as illegal surveillance, disruption, and experiments. Coverage of crimes against government will include protest and dissent, activities of social movements, espionage, assassinations, political whistleblowing, and domestic and international terrorism.

Chapter 1 will serve as an introduction to political crime, crime committed for ideological purposes. The concepts of "crime by government" and "crime against government" are discussed. Legal aspects of political crime are examined including the Nuremberg precedent, war crimes, and the Universal Declaration of Human Rights. The problematic nature of enforcing international law is also examined. In Chapter 2, crimes by government such as secret police operations, human rights violations, and genocide are scrutinized, while Chapter 3 focuses on crimes of the

Reagan and Bush era. This includes the Iran-Contra conspiracy as well as Iraqgate (the Banco Lavora case). The latter involved the secretive financing of Iraqi leader Saddam Hussein's military with United States agricultural loan subsidies.

Crimes against government involving illegal protest and dissent are the subject of Chapter 4. Civil disobedience, whistleblowing, as well as activities of social movements are explored. This includes the civil rights, labor, antiwar, sanctuary, pro-life/pro-choice, and other social movements. Chapter 5 looks at crime against government by assassins and spies. James Clarke's notion of the "pathological myth" of assassins as well as his typology are discussed. Treason, the only crime included in the United States Constitution, is also described as is the author's typology of spies. Cases such as the Ames Spy case, the Falcon and the Snowman, the Walker Spy Ring, and Edwin Wilson's "false flag" operation are detailed.

International terrorism is the subject of Chapter 6. A brief history of terrorism from the assassins of Persia to the Battle for Algiers to the downing of Pan Am 103 is presented. Also discussed are types of international terrorist groups as well as myths regarding terrorism. Among the groups examined are Hamas, Islamic Jihad, Hezbollah, the Provisional Irish Republic Army, Basque ETA as well as state-sponsored groups. The bombings of the World Trade Center by Islamic fundamentalist fanatics as well as the Oklahoma City federal building by right-wing extremists punctuate the growing concern with domestic terrorism in the United States which is the subject of Chapter 7. Among the groups examined are various separatist as well as leftist and rightist groups including Puerto Rican independence groups, neo-Nazi hate groups, as well as those identified with militia groups, and with "identity theology" such as the Order, the Covenant, Sword and the Arm of the Lord.

The final chapter looks at social control and political crime. The motivations of political criminals such as *raison d'etat* and use of the doctrine of sovereign immunity are detailed. The future of efforts to control terrorism is viewed as dependent on divergence in international ideology. Political criminal activity is often symptomatic of unmet needs in society and of new demands for change and, depending on the response, may generate new political criminals either in the form of bell-ringers of change or overzealous guardians of the gates.

The author would like to thank Karen Hanson, senior editor at Allyn and Bacon, Jennifer Jacobson, production editor, Kelly Bechen, project editor, and Lynn Steines for their editing and production. Finally I would like to thank my wife MaryAnn whose patient efforts in typing and editing and whose moral support made completion of this project possible. I dedicate this work to MaryAnn and our daughter, Shannon.

*F. E. H.*

*1*

# Introduction

*Political passions have bathed the earth in blood;*
*kings, emperors, aristocracies, democracies,*
*republics, all governments have resorted to murder*
*out of political considerations, these from love of*
*power, those from hatred of royalty and aristocracy,*
*in one case from fear, in another from fanaticism.*
*—LOUIS PROAL,* POLITICAL CRIME *[1898], 1973, p. 28*

*The tree of liberty must be refreshed from time to*
*time with the blood of patriots and tyrants.*
*—THOMAS JEFFERSON, "LETTER TO WILLIAM*
*STEVENS SMITH," 1787, IN* MORLEY AND
EVERETT, *1965, p. 191*

Evil often gilds itself with an ideological gloss. Throughout history more harm has been done to human beings in the name of God, country, or cause by the religious zealot, the "true believer," the patriot, or the rebel than by all the usual purveyors of crimes of passion or greed.

## Ideology

The twentieth century and particularly the post-World War II period had been described as the "age of ideology," a period characterized by a war of words and ideas in which even the purpose of warfare was viewed as an attempt "to win the hearts and minds of the people." *Ideology* refers to distinctive belief systems, ideas, and abstract ideals that are perceived as providing the true meaning of life. Communism, capitalism, fascism, Islam, Judaism, Christianity, fundamentalism, and the like

1

all may represent political, religious, or economic belief systems that provide to their adherents an underlying meaning and purpose to life. The post-Cold War era, which was at first heralded as a postmodern "end to ideology" era (Bell, 1964), instead offered a rediscovery of forgotten ethnic, religious, and other enmities and inspired new political crime in countries such as Bosnia and Rwanda.

Schafer (1971, 1974) referred to political criminals as convictional criminals, those who are convinced of the truth and justification of their own beliefs (Schafer, 1977, p. 138). The actual crimes committed by political criminals may be traditional crimes such as kidnapping, assassination, blackmail, or robbery. It is not the crimes themselves that distinguish political criminals but rather their motivations, their views of crime as a necessary means to a higher ideological goal. Some political criminals, particularly human rights advocates, have committed no crime but have merely expressed their political views in authoritarian or totalitarian societies that forbid such expression or criticism. Even in free societies civil disobedience may be viewed with suspicion and subject to repression.

*Political crime* refers to criminal activity committed for ideological purposes (Hagan, 1994). Rather than being motivated by private greed or passion, such offenders believe they are following a higher conscience or morality that supersedes present society and its laws. Such political criminals may possess social-political reasons (Robin Hood), moral-ethical motivations (antiabortion activists), religious beliefs (Martin Luther), scientific theories (Copernicus, Galileo), or political causes (Nathan Hale, Benedict Arnold) (Schafer, 1974). Such crime may take one of two forms: crime by government or crime against the government.

Crimes by government include violations of human rights, civil liberties, and constitutional privileges as well as illegal behavior that occurs in the process of enforcing the law or maintaining the status quo. Writers such as Barak (1991) and Chambliss (1989) preferred the term "state crime," whereas Turk (1969) used "political policing" and Friedrichs (1992) suggested the concept of "governmental crime" as terms to describe some of this behavior. Secret police violations, human rights abuses, genocide, crimes by police as well as illegal surveillance, disruption, and experiments are just some of the examples of governmental crime to be discussed in this chapter.

Crimes against the government may range from protests, illegal demonstrations, and strikes to espionage, political whistle-blowing, assassination, and terrorism. "One person's terrorist is another's patriot" is a common expression that argues for the relative nature of such political crime. In revolutions, the victors' beliefs become the status quo and the victors inherit the power and privilege by which to brand the acts of their enemies as criminal.

There is a surprising paucity of literature on political crime in criminology (Hagan, 1986; Martin, Haran, and Romano, 1988; and Martin and Romano, 1992). Fewer than twelve works in the field appear to have specifically addressed this issue (see Barak, 1991; Ingraham, 1979; Kelman and Hamilton, 1988; Kittrie and Wedlock, 1986; Proal, 1973; Roebuck and Weeber, 1978; Schafer, 1974; Schur, 1980;

Tunnell, 1993; and Turk, 1982). Political crimes may be committed by or against the government, but governments or government officials seldom acknowledge their own lawlessness. Sagarin (1973, p. xiv) noted that political crime includes the tyrant as well as the assassin. At the close of World War II Hitler was not around to be prosecuted along with his fellow Nazis for war crimes, unlike Emperor Hirohito of Japan. In the name of expediency of postwar reconstruction, the Allies ignored the emperor's complicity in war crimes—what Bergamini (1971, p. 1) called Japan's "Imperial Conspiracy." The allies were acknowledging the sacredness of the powerful or the "doctrine of sovereign immunity" in which authorities of the state cannot be held responsible for wrongdoing:

> *The Emperor is sacred and inviolable (Constitution, Article 3). He cannot be removed from the Throne for any reason, and he is not to be held responsible for overstepping the limitations of law in the exercise of his sovereignty. All responsibility for the exercise of his sovereignty must be assumed by the Ministers of State and other organs. Thus, no criticism can be directed against the Emperor, but only against the instruments of his sovereignty. Laws are not to be applied to the Emperor as a principle especially criminal laws, for no court of law can try the Emperor himself and he is not subject to any law (Japan Yearbook, 1944, 1971, p. 1).*

## Political Crime and the Law

Although some would argue that all crimes are political (Chambliss and Seidman, 1971; Quinney, 1970), since crime is a creature of criminal law that is politically defined, the usage of the term "political crime" will be restricted in this book to a more specific meaning:  crimes committed for ideological purposes.

In the United States, various laws are or have been intended to protect the government from the clear and present or probable danger of disruption or overthrow, such as the Alien and Sedition Act, the Espionage Act, the Voorhis Act, the Smith Act, the Internal Security Act, and the McCarran-Walter Act. The 1940 Voorhis Act required registration of agents of foreign powers, while the Smith Act (1940), which was later struck down by the Supreme Court, outlawed advocating the overthrow of the government. The Internal Security Act (McCarran Act) called for registration of communists and communist-front organizations, whereas the McCarran-Walter Act (1952) provided for deportation of aliens who espouse or have associates who espouse disloyal beliefs (Clinard and Quinney, 1974, p. 155).

Authoritarian countries and theocratic states possess criminal laws forbidding propaganda against the state, complaining about social conditions to foreigners, and attempting to publish works that are not authorized by the state. Many of these laws and their enforcement bear an uncanny resemblance to those in George

Orwell's *1984* (1971) and to his descriptions of the Minitrue (Ministry of Truth) in which thought criminals become political criminals or enemies of the state. In the nineties the government of Iran issued a death warrant against author Salman Rushdie (1989) who, because of his book *The Satanic Verses*, was accused of blaspheming Muhammad.

Under Anglo-American law, political crime and political criminals are not recognized as such and are handled under traditional or nonpolitical laws. Anglo-American criminal law considers intent, but not motive. The motive, whether good or bad, has no bearing on guilt. Sagarin (1973, p. ix) pointed out: "At one time it was against the law in some parts of this country to preach freedom and abolition of slavery to slaves, or even to free men; it was often against the law to organize into trade unions; at various times political parties have been driven underground and their leaders jailed."

Kittrie and Wedlock in *The Tree of Liberty* (1986) give examples of political criminality in American history:

- The Peter Zenger trial of 1735 for false, scandalous, and seditious libel, which established the "freedom of the press" doctrine
- The "crime of being black or Indian," for example, the "Trail of Tears" of the Cherokee Nation, the Abolitionists, the underground railroad, and the harboring of fugitive slaves
- Subjugation of blacks through terrorism
- Genocide against Indians
- Voter registration drives and Freedom Rides during the Civil Rights struggle
- Imprisonment of Japanese Americans (Nisei) in internment camps during World War II
- Antiwar protests, burning draft cards and records
- Arson, bombing, and other violations against abortion clinics
- "Sanctuary activists" hiding Central Americans they consider to be political refugees

## The Nuremberg Principle

After World War II, the victorious Allies held a trial and convicted Nazi war criminals at Nuremberg. This conviction represented the first time that defeated war leaders were held responsible in an international legal arena for activities that were legal, even encouraged, by their governments at the time they were committed. Defenses such as "I was just following orders" were rejected and considered unjustifiable explanations for Nazi atrocities. Kelman and Hamilton (1988) referred to this as an example of a "crime of obedience." Offenses defined by the international tribunal included war crimes and crimes against humanity (Smith, 1977; Maser, 1979; and Nuremberg Principle, 1970, p. 78).

### War Crimes

War crimes (violations of law or customs of war) include, but are not limited to; (1) murder, ill treatment, or deportation for slave labor or for any other purpose of civilian population of or in occupied territory; (2) murder or ill treatment of prisoners of war or persons on the high seas; (3) killings of hostages; (4) plunder of public or private property; (5) wanton destruction of villages, towns, or cities; or (6) devastation not justified by military necessity.

### Crimes against Humanity

Crimes against humanity include murder, extermination, enslavement, deportation, and other inhumane acts committed against any civilian population before or during the war, or persecutions on political, racial, or religious grounds, whether or not in violation of the domestic law of the country where perpetrated.

## The Universal Declaration of Human Rights

Human rights is a concept stemming from the period of Enlightenment in Western society and appears in documents such as the Magna Carta, the English Bill of Rights, the American Declaration of Independence, the French Declaration of the Rights of Man and of the Citizen, and the United Nations Universal Declaration of Human Rights (1948). All of these documents support the notion of inalienable rights and freedoms that supersede those of government.

Adopted unanimously by the U.N. General Assembly on December 10, 1948, the Universal Declaration of Human Rights is a proclamation, but not a treaty or international agreement. The basic elements of these human rights consist of three principles: integrity of persons, basic human needs, and civil and political liberties. Integrity of persons is addressed in the following articles of the Universal Declaration (1948):

Article 3: Everyone has the right to life, liberty, and security of persons.

Article 5: No one shall be subjected to torture or to cruel, inhuman, or degrading treatment or punishment.

Article 9: No one shall be subjected to arbitrary arrest, detention, or exile.

Article 10: Everyone is entitled in full equality to a fair and public hearing by an independent and impartial tribunal, in the determination of his rights and obligations and of any criminal charges against him.

Basic human needs are addressed specifically in the following articles:

Article 25: (1) Everyone has the right to a standard of living adequate for the health and well-being of himself and of his family, including food, clothing, housing, and medical care and necessary social services, and the right to security in the event of unemployment, sickness, disability, widowhood, old age, or other lack of livelihood in circumstances beyond his control. (2) Motherhood and childhood are entitled to special care and assistance. All children, whether born in or out of wedlock, shall enjoy the same social protection.

Article 26: Everyone has the right to education. Education shall be free, at least in the elementary and fundamental stages. Elementary education shall be compulsory. Technical and professional education shall be made generally available and higher education shall be equally accessible to all on the basis of merit.

Articles of the Universal Declaration dealing with civil and political liberties include:

Article 13: (1) Everyone has the right to freedom of movement and residence within the borders of each state. (2) Everyone has the right to leave any country, including his own, and to return to his country.

Article 19: Everyone has the right to freedom of opinion and expression; this right includes freedom to hold opinions without interference and to seek, receive, and impart information and ideas through any media and regardless of frontiers.

Article 20: (1) Everyone has the right to freedom of peaceful assembly and association. (2) No one may be compelled to belong to an association.

Article 21: (1) Everyone has the right to take part in the government of his country, directly through freely chosen representatives. (2) Everyone has the right of equal access to public service in his country. (3) The will of the people shall be the basis of the authority of government; this will be expressed in periodic and genuine elections which shall be by universal and equal suffrage and shall be held by secret vote or by equivalent free voting procedures (Congressional Research Service, 1978).

As revised, "Respect for Human Rights" as set forth in the Universal Declaration of Human Rights contains the following:

Section 1. Respect for Integrity of Person, including freedom from:

**a.** Political or other extrajudicial killing
**b.** Politically motivated disappearance
**c.** Torture and other cruel, inhuman, or degrading treatment or punishment
**d.** Arbitrary arrest, detention, or exile
**e.** Denial of fair public trial
**f.** Arbitrary interference with privacy, family, home, or correspondence

Section 2. Respect for Civil Liberties, including:

**a.** Freedom of speech and press
**b.** Freedom of peaceful assembly and association
**c.** Freedom of religion
**d.** Freedom of movement within the country, foreign travel, emigration, and repatriation

Section 3. Respect for Political Rights; The Right of Citizens to Change Their Government.

Section 4. Governmental Attitude Regarding International and Nongovernmental Investigation of Alleged Violations of Human Rights.

Section 5. Discrimination Based on Race, Sex, Religion, Disability, Language, or Social Status.

Section 6. Worker Rights.

**a.** The right of association
**b.** The right to organize and bargain collectively
**c.** Prohibition of forced or compulsory labor
**d.** Minimum age for the employment of children
**e.** Acceptable conditions of work (U.S. State Department, 1994)

Exhibit 1.1 at the end of this chapter discusses the purpose and methodology of the U.S. State Department's human rights reports which are issued annually.

## *International Law*

Much political criminality is international in nature. Theoretically, it falls under the jurisdiction of (1) international law, which covers diplomatic and commercial customs between nations, (2) agreements such as treaties that are drafted in international conventions, and (3) international courts such as the International Court of Justice, which was sponsored by the United Nations. Using precedents (past decisions), customs, and general principles of law, international law is theoretically binding on any signatories to international treaties, although it may also through custom be held to be binding on those who have not ratified the treaties. The Geneva Convention of 1929 regulating wartime conduct serves as an example.

The Geneva Conventions are another attempt to establish rules regarding the waging of war in a humane manner. Four Geneva Conventions have been signed, the 1949 agreements having 164 signatories. The International Committee of the Red Cross has been agreed upon as the monitoring organization. While disputes between nations are handled by the International Court of Justice in the Netherlands, actual war crime prosecutions have traditionally taken place under the laws of individual nations. The Nuremberg trials were a special case of an ad hoc procedure. Some examples of convention rules include protection of civilians, shipwrecked sailors, and prisoners of war (POWs). POWs are to be treated humanely and protected from intimidation and torture. Under questioning they are required only to give their name, rank, date of birth, and military identification number and they are to be moved from combat zones while in captivity (Barrett, 1991, A3).

Although international bodies past or present, such as the World Court, the League of Nations, and the United Nations have the facade of law, they lack the power to enforce their decisions (Kidder, 1983, p. 34). The closest entities to international police organizations are U.N. police units, which are intended to temporarily block hostile armies, or Interpol, which is a criminal intelligence-sharing organization with membership primarily composed of the Western democracies and former British Commonwealth nations. Although U.N. policing actions have had some success, the degree of success depends on the cooperation of contending bodies. In Bosnia, for example, the Serbs made a mockery out of U.N. policing activity by practicing the worst atrocities since the Nazi holocaust. Essentially, international law lacks teeth—the authority and power to ensure compliance. The end of the Cold War has considerably improved the prospect for international cooperation in enforcing international law and sanctions. U.N. actions in forcing Iraq to withdraw from Kuwait in 1991 serve as one such example. On the other hand, the ineffectiveness of U.N. actions in Bosnia and Somalia illustrates that cooperation is not always forthcoming.

In 1993 the U.N. General Assembly unanimously condemned the military rulers of Myanmar (Burma) for human rights violations. The same year this body adopted critical human rights resolutions on Iraq, Iran, Cuba, Sudan, and the former Yugoslavia. The adoption of a resolution against Myanmar was seen as a victory for Western nations' views of the universality of human rights. Earlier that year at a world conference on human rights in Vienna, China and other Asian nations argued that every culture has a different view of human freedoms (Lewis, 1993b) and that the U.N. was imposing Western cultural norms on Asia. In essence it was their view that human rights is a Western cultural concept that does not apply in non-Western, newly developing countries.

The human rights movement is primarily a post-World War II phenomenon and has met with some success due to thousands of volunteers working in monitoring groups. While China and other Asian nations argued that the universality of human rights standards is a Western concept, a meeting in 1993 in Bangkok of over 100 nongovernmental groups including Asian countries responded that the protection of the rights of women, children, and refugees was universal. Pressure from human rights groups has forced even despotic regimes to be embarrassed by negative international publicity. But as late as 1988, Amnesty International estimated that of the 135 countries on which it had information, half imprisoned people for their ideas, over a third used torture, and many kidnapped and murdered their citizens. Included in the abused are human rights monitors themselves, hundreds of whom have been murdered, tortured, beaten, and harassed (Satchell, 1988, p. 31). Figure 1.1 lists the various international human rights conventions that have been signed by most of the world's nations.

In forthcoming chapters we will explore political crime and political criminals, areas that test the waters of societal change while at the same time threatening the very

**A.** Convention to Suppress the Slave Trade and Slavery of September 25, 1926, is amended by the Protocol of December 7, 1953.
**B.** Convention Concerning Forced Labor of June 28, 1930 (ILO Convention 29).
**C.** Convention Concerning Freedom of Association and Protection of the Right to Organize of July 9, 1948 (ILO Convention 87).
**D.** Convention on the Prevention and Punishment of the Crime of Genocide of December 9, 1948.
**E.** Convention Concerning the Application of the Principles of the Right to Organize and Bargain Collectively of July 1, 1949 (ILO Convention 98).
**F.** Geneva Convention Relative to the Treatment of Prisoners of War of August 2, 1949.
**G.** Geneva Convention Relative to the Protection of Civilian Persons in Time of War of August 12, 1949.
**H.** Convention for the Suppression of the Traffic in Persons and of the Exploitation of the Prostitution of Others of March 21, 1950.
**I.** European Convention for the Protection of Human Rights and Fundamental Freedoms of November 4. 1950.
**J.** Convention on the Political Rights of Women of March 31, 1953.
**K.** Supplementary Convention on the Abolition of Slavery, the Slave Trade, and Institutions and Practices Similar to Slavery of September 7, 1956.
**L.** Convention Concerning the Abolition of Forced Labor of June 25, 1957 (ILO Convention 105).
**M.** International Convention on the Elimination of All Forms of Racial Discrimination of December 21, 1965.
**N.** International Covenant on Civil and Political Rights of December 16, 1966.
**O.** International covenant on Economic, Social and Cultural Rights of December 6, 1966.
**P.** Protocol Relating to the Status of Refugees of January 31, 1967.
**Q.** American Convention on Human Rights of November 22, 1969.
**R.** Convention Concerning Minimum Age for Admission to Employment of June 26, 1973 (ILO Convention 138).
**S.** Protocol Additional to the Geneva Convention of August 12, 1949, and Relating to the Protection of Victims of International Armed Conflicts (Protocol I), of June 8, 1977).
**T.** Protocol Additional to the Geneva Conventions of August 12, 1949, and Relating to the Protection of Victims of Non-International Armed Conflicts (Protocol II), of June 8, 1977.
**U.** Convention on the elimination of All forms of Discrimination Against Women of December 18, 1979.
**V.** Convention Against Torture and Other Cruel, Inhuman or Degrading Treatment or Punishment of December 10, 1984.
**W.** Convention on the Rights of the Child of November 20, 1989.

---

**FIGURE 1.1   International Human Rights Conventions**

Source: U.S. State Department. Country Reports on Human Rights Practices for 1993. Washington, D.C.: Government Printing Office, February, 1994.

---

existence of future societies. Louis Proal's book *Political Crime* (1898), written approximately a century ago, has held up remarkably well in defining the turf of political crime of the then upcoming twentieth century. What unknown horrors lie in wait in the twenty-first century, and how well will social scientists be able to isolate, define, and explain the critical variables associated with them? Philosopher George Santayana has indicated that those who fail to learn the lessons of history are condemned to repeat them. Political terrorists or despots of the twenty-first century may not offer a second chance.

---

**EXHIBIT 1.1    State Department Country Reports
on Human Rights Practices**

*Notes on Preparation of the Reports*

The annual Country Reports on Human Rights Practices are based upon all information available to the United States Government. Sources include American officials, officials of foreign governments, private citizens, victims of human rights abuse, congressional studies, intelligence information, press reports, international organizations, and nongovernmental organizations concerned with human rights. We are particularly appreciative of, and make reference in most reports to, the role of nongovernmental human rights organizations, ranging from groups in a single country to major organizations that concern themselves with human rights matters in larger geographic regions or over the entire world. While much of the information we use is already public, information on particular abuses frequently cannot be attributed, for obvious reasons, to specific sources.

The reports by law must be submitted to Congress by January 31. To comply, United States diplomatic missions are given guidance in September for submission of draft reports in October, which are updated by year's end as necessary. Contributions are received from appropriate offices in the Department of State, and a final draft is prepared under the coordination of the Bureau of Human Rights and Humanitarian Affairs. Because of the preparation time required, it is possible that developments in the latter part of the year may not be fully reflected; moreover, reports from some of the nongovernmental organizations are

for periods ending well before the end of the year. We make every effort to include reference to major events or significant changes in trends.

We have attempted to make these country reports as comprehensive as space will allow, while taking care to make them objective and as uniform as possible in both scope and quality of coverage. We have given particular attention to attaining a high standard of consistency despite the multiplicity of sources and the obvious problems related to varying degrees of access to information, structural differences in political and social systems, and trends in world opinion regarding human rights practices in specific countries.

It is often difficult to evaluate the credibility of reports of human rights abuses. With the exception of some terrorist groups, most opposition groups and certainly most governments deny that they commit human rights abuses and often go to great lengths to cover up any evidence of such acts. There are often few eyewitnesses to specific abuses, and they frequently are intimidated or otherwise prevented from reporting what they know. On the other hand, individuals and groups opposed to a particular government sometimes have powerful incentives to exaggerate or fabricate abuses, and some governments similarly distort or exaggerate abuses attributed to opposition groups. We have made every effort to identify those groups (e.g., government forces, terrorists, etc.) that are believed, based on

Source: U.S. State Department. Country Reports on Human Rights Practices for 1993. Washington, D.C.: Government Printing Office, 1994, pp. xx–xix, 1399–1402.

**EXHIBIT 1.1**  *Continued*

all the evidence available, to have committed human rights abuses. Where credible evidence is lacking, we have tried to indicate why. Many governments that profess to oppose human rights abuses in fact secretly order or tacitly condone them or simply lack the will or the ability to control those responsible for them. Consequently, in judging a government's policy, it is important to look beyond statements of policy or intent in order to examine what in fact a government has done to prevent human rights abuses, including the extent to which it investigates, tries, and appropriately punishes those who commit such abuses. We continue to make every effort to do that in these reports.

There is a conceptual difficulty in applying a single standard of evaluation to societies with differing cultural and legal traditions. There is also a problem of perspective in discussing countries that face differing political and economic realities, which must be taken into account in describing the human rights environment. Rather than viewing a country in isolation, these reports take as their point of department the world as it is and then seek to apply a consistent approach in assessing each country's human rights situation. While we have tried to make each report self-contained by including enough background information to place the human rights situation in context, readers who need to delve more deeply may wish to consult other sources, including previous country reports.

To increase uniformity, the introductory section of each report contains a brief setting, indicating how the country is governed and providing the context for examining the country's human rights performance. A description of the political framework and the role of security and law enforcement agencies with respect to human rights is followed by a brief characterization of the economy. The setting concludes with an overview of human rights developments in the year under review, mentioning specific areas (e.g., torture, freedom of speech and press) in which abuses occurred.

There are two format changes in this year's report. Public law 103–87, enacted on September 30, 1993, requires that the reports include "an examination of the discrimination against people with disabilities," including whether the government has enacted legislation or otherwise mandated provision of accessibility to public buildings. As a result, the heading of Section 5 has been changed to: "Discrimination Based on Race, Sex, Religion, Disability, Language, or Social Status," and the topic is discussed in each report. The second change is the use of subtitles in Section 5 to make that section more readable and to enable readers searching for information on discrimination against specific groups to find it more readily. We have continued the effort from previous years to expand reporting on the human rights of women, children and indigenous people. We discuss in the appropriate section of the report any abuses that are targeted specifically against women (e.g., rape or other violence perpetrated by governmental or organized opposition forces, or legal restrictions on freedom of movement). Socioeconomic discrimination; societal violence against women, children or minority group members; and the efforts,

*Continued*

**EXHIBIT 1.1** *Continued*

if any, of governments to combat these problems continue to be discussed in Section 5.

The following notes on specific categories of the report are not meant to be comprehensive descriptions of each category but to provide definitions of key terms used in the reports and to explain the organization of material within the format:

*Political and Other Extrajudicial Killing.*—Includes killings in which there is evidence of government instigation without due process of law, or of political motivation by government instigation without due process of law, or of political motivation by government or by opposition groups; also covers extrajudicial killings (e.g., deliberate and illegal use of lethal force by the police, security forces, or other agents of the State whether against criminal suspects or others or deaths in official custody resulting from unnatural causes or under suspicious circumstances); excludes combat deaths and killings by common criminals, if the likelihood of political motivation can be ruled out (see also Section 1.g.).

*Disappearance.*—Covers unresolved cases in which political motivation appears likely and in which the victims have not been found or perpetrators have not been identified; cases eventually classed as political killings are covered in the above category, those eventually identified as arrest or detention are covered under "Arbitrary Arrest, Detention, or Exile."

*Torture and Other Cruel, Inhuman, or Degrading Treatment or Punishment.*—Torture is here defined as an extremely severe form of cruel, inhuman, or degrading treatment or punishment, committed by or at the instigation of government forces or opposition groups, with specific intent to cause extremely severe pain or suffering, whether mental or physical. Discussion concentrates on actual practices, not on whether they fit any precise definition, and includes use of physical and other force that may fall short of torture but which is cruel, inhuman, or degrading.

*Arbitrary Arrest, Detention, or Exile.*—Covers cases in which detainees, including political detainees, are held in official custody without charges or, if charged, are denied a public preliminary judicial hearing within a reasonable period.

*Denial of Fair Public Trial.*—Described the court system and evaluates whether there is an independent judiciary and whether trials are both fair and public (failure to hold any trial is noted in the category above); includes discussion of "political prisoners" (political detainees are covered above), defined as those imprisoned for essentially political beliefs or nonviolent acts of dissent or expression, regardless of the actual charge.

*Arbitrary Interference with Privacy, Family, Home, or Correspondence.*—Discusses the "passive" right of the individual to noninterference by the State; includes the right to receive foreign publications, for example, while the right to publish is discussed under "Freedom of Speech and Press"; includes the right to be free from coercive population control measures, including coerced abortion and involuntary sterilization but does not include cultural or traditional practices, such as female genital mutilation, which are addressed in Section 5.

**EXHIBIT 1.1**  *Continued*

*Use of Excessive Force and Violations of Humanitarian Law in Internal Conflicts.*—Includes indiscriminate, non-selective killings arising from excessive use of force, e.g., by police in putting down demonstrations (deliberate, targeted killing would be discussed in Section 1.a.). Also includes abuses against civilian noncombatants. For reports in which use of this section would be inappropriate, i.e., in which there is no significant internal conflict, use of excessive force by security forces is discussed in Section 1.a. if it results in killings or in Section 1.c. if it does not.

*Freedom of Speech and Press.*—Evaluates whether these freedoms exist and describes any direct or indirect restrictions. Includes discussion of academic freedom.

*Freedom of Peaceful Assembly and Association.*—Evaluates the ability of individuals and groups (including political parties) to exercise these freedoms. Includes the ability of trade associations, professional bodies, and similar groups to maintain relations or affiliate with recognized international bodies in their fields. The right of labor to associate and to organize and bargain collectively is discussed under Section 6, Worker Rights (see Appendix B).

*Freedom of Religion.*—Includes the freedom to publish religious documents in foreign languages; addresses the treatment of foreign clergy and whether religious belief affects membership in a ruling party or a career in government.

*Freedom of Movement Within the Country, Foreign Travel, Emigration, and Repatriation.*—Includes discussion of forced resettlement; "refugees" may refer to persons displaced by civil strife or natural disaster as well as persons who are "refugees" within the meaning of the Refugee Act of 1980, i.e., persons with a "well-founded fear of persecution" in their country of origin or, if stateless, in their country of habitual residence, on account of race, religion, nationality, membership in a particular social group, or political opinion.

*Respect for Political Rights: The Right of Citizens to Change Their Government.*—Discusses the extent to which citizens have freedom of political choice and can change the laws and officials that govern them; assesses whether elections are free and fair.

*Governmental Attitude Regarding International and Nongovernmental Investigation of Alleged Violations of Human Rights.*—Discusses whether the government permits the free functioning of local human rights groups (including the right to investigate and publish their findings on alleged human rights abuses) and whether they are subject to reprisal by government or other forces. Also discusses whether the government grants access to and cooperates with outside entities (including foreign human rights organizations, international organizations, and foreign governments) interested in human rights developments in the country.

*Discrimination Based on Race, Sex, Religion, Disability, Language, or Social Status.*—This year, every report contains a subheading on Women, Children, and People With Disabilities. As appropriate, some reports also include subheadings on Indigenous People, National/Racial/Ethnic Minorities, and

*Continued*

**EXHIBIT 1.1**   *Continued*

Religious Minorities. Discrimination against groups not fitting one of the above subheadings is discussed in the introductory paragraphs of Section 5. In this section we address discrimination and abuses not discussed elsewhere in the report instigated or condoned by the government, and, where not condoned, efforts by the government to counter them. This includes restricted access to employment, housing, education, or to other economic, social, or cultural opportunities. (Abuses by government or opposition forces, such as killing, torture and other violence, or restriction or voting rights or free speech targeted against specific groups would be discussed under the appropriate preceding sections.) Government tolerance of societal violence or other abuse against women, e.g., "dowry deaths" and wife beating, is discussed in this section. Female genital mutilation (circumcision), because it is most often performed on children, is discussed under that subheading.

*Worker Rights.*—See Appendix B.

### Appendix B.—Reporting on Worker Rights

The Generalized System of Preferences Renewal Act of 1984 requires reporting on worker rights in GSP beneficiary countries. It states that internationally recognized worker rights include "(A) the right of association; (B) the right to organize and bargain collectively (C) a prohibition on the use of any form of forced or compulsory labor; (D) a minimum age for the employment of children; and (E) acceptable conditions of work with respect to minimum wages, hours of work and occupational safety and health." All five aspects of worker rights are discussed in a final section under the heading "Worker Rights." The discussion of worker rights considers not only laws and regulations but also their practical implementation, taking into account the following additional guidelines:

A. "The right of association" has been defined by the International Labor Organization (ILO) to include the right of workers and employers to establish and join organization of their own choosing without previous authorization; to draw up their own constitutions and rules, elect their representatives, and formulate their programs; to join in confederations and affiliate with international organizations; and to be protected against dissolution or suspension by administrative authority.

The right of association includes the right of workers to strike. While strikes may be restricted in essential services (i.e., those services the interruption of which would endanger the life, personal safety, or health of a significant portion of the population) and in the public sector, these restrictions must be offset by adequate guarantees to safeguard the interests of the workers concerned (e.g., machinery for mediation and arbitration; due process; and the right to judicial review of all legal actions). Reporting on restrictions affecting the ability of workers to strike generally includes information on any procedures that may exist for safeguarding workers' interests.

B. "The right to organize and bargain collectively" includes the right of workers to be represented in negotiating

**EXHIBIT 1.1**   *Continued*

the prevention and settlement of disputes with employers; the right to protection against interference; and the right to protection against acts of antiunion discrimination. Governments should promote machinery for voluntary negotiations between employers and workers and their organizations. Reporting on the right to organize and bargain collectively includes descriptions of the extent to which collective bargaining takes place and the extent to which unions, both in law and practice, are effectively protected against antiunion discrimination.

C. "Forced or compulsory labor" is defined as work or service exacted from any person under the menace of penalty and for which the person has not volunteered. "Work or service" does not apply in instances in which obligations are imposed to undergo education or training. "Menace of penalty" includes loss of rights or privileges as well as penal sanctions. The ILO has exempted the following from its definition of forced labor: compulsory military service, normal civic obligations, certain forms of prison labor, emergencies, and minor communal services. Forced labor should not be used as a means of (1) mobilizing and using labor for purposes of economic development; (2) racial, social, national, or religious discrimination; (3) political coercion or education, or as a punishment for holding or expressing political views or views ideologically opposed to the established political, social, economic system; (4) labor discipline; or (5) as a punishment for having participated in strikes. Constitutional provisions concerning the obligation of citizens to work do not violate this right

so long as they do not take the form of legal obligations enforced by sanctions and are consistent with the principle of "freely chosen employment."

D. "Minimum age for employment of children" concerns the effective abolition of child labor by raising the minimum age for employment to a level consistent with the fullest physical and mental development of young people. In addition, young people should not be employed in hazardous conditions or at night.

E. "Acceptable conditions of work" refers to the establishment and maintenance of machinery, adapted to national conditions, that provides for minimum working standards, i.e., wages that provide a decent living for workers and their families; working hours that do not exceed 48 hours per week, with a full 24-hour rest day; a specified annual paid holiday; and minimum conditions for the protection of the safety and health of workers. Differences in levels of economic development are taken into account in the formulation of internationally recognized labor standards. For example, many ILO standards concerning working conditions permit flexibility in their scope and coverage. They may also permit countries a wide choice in their implementation, including progressive implementation, by enabling countries to accept a standard in part or subject to specified exceptions. Countries are expected to take steps over time to achieve the higher levels specified in such standards. It should be understood, however, that this flexibility applies only to internationally recognized standards

*Continued*

**EXHIBIT 1.1**  *Continued*

concerning working conditions. No flexibility is permitted concerning the acceptance of the basic principles contained in human rights standards, i.e., freedom of association, the right to organize and bargain collectively, the prohibition of forced labor, and the absence of discrimination.

### 1993 Human Rights Reports

#### Why the Reports Are Prepared

This report is submitted to the Congress by the Department of State in compliance with sections 116(d)(1) and 502B(b) of the Foreign Assistance Act of 1961 (FAA), as amended, and Section 505(c) of the Trade Act of 1974, as amended. As stated in Section 116(d)(1) of the FAA: "The Secretary of State shall transmit to the Speaker of the House of Representatives and the Committee on Foreign Relations of the Senate, by January 31 of each year, a full and complete report regarding the status of internationally recognized human rights, within the meaning of subsection (A) in countries that received assistance under this part, and (B) in all other foreign countries which are members of the United Nations and which are not otherwise the subject of a human rights report under this Act." We have also included reports on the few countries which do not fall into the categories established by these statutes and which thus are not covered by the Congressional requirement.

The idea that the United States has a responsibility to speak out on behalf of internationally recognized human rights standards was formalized in the 1970's. In 1976 Congress enacted legislation creating a Coordinator of Human Rights in the U.S. Department of State, a position later upgraded to Assistant Secretary. Congress also wrote into law formal requirements that U.S. foreign and trade policy take into account countries' human rights and worker rights performance and that country reports be submitted to Congress annually. When the reports were first produced in 1977, which at the time covered only countries receiving U.S. aid, 82 were compiled and published; this year, there are 193 reports.

#### How the Reports Are Prepared

The human rights reports reflect a year of dedicated effort by hundreds of State Department and other U.S. Government employees. In August 1993, the Secretary of State issued a directive which further strengthened the human rights structure in our embassies. All sections in each embassy were asked to contribute information and to corroborate reports of violations. New efforts were made to link mission programming to the advancement of human rights and democracy.

Our embassies, which prepared the initial drafts of the reports, gathered information throughout the year from a variety of sources, including contacts across the political spectrum, government officials, jurists, military sources, journalists, human rights monitors, academics, and labor union members. Gathering information can be hazardous. Foreign Service Officers often go to great lengths, under trying and sometimes, dangerous conditions, to investigate reported human rights violations, stand up for individuals, and monitor elections.

**EXHIBIT 1.1**   *Continued*

The draft reports were then sent from each embassy to Washington, where they were carefully reviewed by the Bureau of Human Rights and Humanitarian Affairs, in cooperation with other relevant offices in the State Department. As they corroborated, analyzed, and edited the reports, Department officers drew on their own additional sources of information. These included reports by and consultations with U.S. and other human rights groups, foreign government officials, representatives from the United Nations and other international and regional organizations and institutions, and experts from academia and the media. Officers also consulted with experts on worker rights issues, refugee issues, military and police issues, exile issues, women's rights issues, and legal matters. The goal was to ensure that all relevant information was included and that assessments were as objective, thorough, and fair as possible. The report will be used as a resource in making decisions on U.S. foreign policy, training, and aid allocations. It also will serve as a basis for valuable dialog and program planning on ways in which the United States can work with foreign governments and private groups to improve human rights observance worldwide.

The Country Reports on Human Rights cover internationally recognized individual, political, civil, and worker rights, as set forth in the Universal Declaration of Human Rights. These rights include freedom from torture or other cruel, inhuman, or degrading treatment or punishment; from prolonged detention without charges; from disappearance due to abduction or clandestine detention; and from other flagrant violations

concerning life, liberty, and the security of the person. Individuals have the inalienable right to change their government by peaceful means and to enjoy such civil liberties as freedom of expression, assembly, religion, and movement, without discrimination based on race, national origin, or sex. Free societies also require free trade unions. The reports assess key internationally recognized worker rights, including the right of association; the right to organize and bargain collectively; prohibition of forced or compulsory labor; minimum age for employment of children; and acceptable conditions of work.

*The 1993 Reports*

The 1993 Report describes a world far short of the vision we and other countries hold for it. Around the globe, people who by right are born free and with dignity too often suffer the cruelties of authorities who deprive them of their rights in order to perpetuate their own power. Yet again in 1993, children too often were denied their birthright in countries ruled by dictators or rent by armed conflict, where bullets, torture, arbitrary detention, rape, disappearances, and other abuses were used to silence those who struggle for political freedom; to crush those whose ethnicity, gender, race or religion mark them for discrimination; or to frighten and mistreat those who have no defenses. The United Nations' Charter affirms the "dignity and worth of the human person." In too many places in 1993, however, human dignity was assaulted; violence was perpetuated with impunity; those responsible for massive violations of

*Continued*

**EXHIBIT 1.1**  *Continued*

human rights went unpunished; and political repression went unchecked.

This year, we draw particular attention to several trends evident from the 1993 reports. Armed conflict posed the most significant risk to human rights. In contrast, the historic handshake between Prime Minister Yitzhak Rabin of Israel and Palestine Liberation Organization (PLO) Chairman Yassir Arafat, the Nobel Prize-winning efforts of African Nationalist Congress (ANC) leader Nelson Mandela and President F.W. de Klerk in South Africa to enfranchise all citizens, and the peace process in El Salvador exemplify movement toward reconciliation in places where it once seemed impossible.

This polarity between violence and reconciliation was typical of a year in which democracy and human rights were marked both by progress and backsliding. The process of democracy moved forward in Cambodia, where successful elections were held, but backwards in Haiti, where the military continued to obstruct the return of President Aristide. At the same time, human rights abuses continued around the world. Of particular concern to us in 1993 were torture, arbitrary detention, impunity for perpetrators of abuse, and the trampling on the rights of women, children, indigenous people, and workers in many parts of the world.

Yet, in 1993, we also witnessed positive trends. Countries working together in the United Nations, the Conference on Security and Cooperation in Europe (CSCE), the Organization of American States (OAS), and the Organization of African Unity (OAU) supported new democracies, mediated conflicts, and took steps to hold each other accountable for human rights abuses. Around the world, grassroots movements to promote human rights and democracy spread, as people claimed their inalienable rights and demanded accountability from their governments.

*I. Armed Conflict*

In Bosnia, Sudan, Burundi, Somalia, Angola, Iraq, Azerbaijan, Georgia, and elsewhere, armed conflict led to massive numbers of civilian deaths, refugee flows, and human rights abuses. Many of the conflicts were stimulated by irresponsible political leaders who placed on people's fears.

In many parts of the former Yugoslavia, the carnage continues. In 1993 as in 1992, all nationalities were victimized, and there were numerous violations of the Geneva Conventions. Bosnian Serb armed forces, supported by Belgrade and by Serbian paramilitary counterparts, persisted in their program of "ethnic cleansing," including laying siege to cities, indiscriminately shelling civilian inhabitants, raping and executing noncombatants, and interfering with humanitarian aid deliveries. The warfare continued relentlessly through 1993, with Bosnian government and Croat forces also committing egregious abuses.

In Sudan, both the Government and the Sudanese People's Liberation Army (SPLA) engaged in widespread human rights abuses, including torture, forced displacement, and massacres of civilians.

In Somalia, although massive starvation was averted by international humanitarian efforts, most Somalis remained beyond the rule and protection of recognized law and social order.

**EXHIBIT 1.1**    *Continued*

In Iraq, Saddam Hussein's regime continued its flagrant abuses of human rights by conducting military operations against civilians, including burning and razing villages, and forcing people to abandon their homes, particularly Shi'a Arabs living in the wetlands of southern Iraq.

In Azerbaijan, the continuing conflict over Nagorno-Karabakh gave rise to human rights abuses by all sides.

In the Georgian province of Abkhazia, Abkhaz separatists launched a reign of terror after a successful offensive gave them control of the province. Many Georgian civilians and troops were subjected to torture and summary execution.

## II. Reconciliation

In the face of such bloodshed, 1993 was also a year in which some countries, against all odds, moved toward reconciliation. In 1964, Nelson Mandela of South Africa wrote:

"I have fought against white domination, and I have fought against black domination. I have cherished the ideal of a democratic and free society in which all persons will live together in harmony and with equal opportunities. It is an ideal which I hope to live for and achieve."

Thirty years later, Nelson Mandela and F.W. de Klerk have led their country toward that ideal.

In the Middle East, there was also progress toward peace. On a warm September day in Washington, the world witnessed an historic handshake between Prime Minister Yitzhak Rabin and PLO leader Yassir Arafat that stretched across

years of conflict. In that moment, two men joined together their people's hopes for peace.

In El Salvador, once racked by civil war, the U.N. Truth Commission completed its investigations of human rights violations of the past decade and recommended specific actions to further the reconciliation process.

In Mozambique, while there have been many setbacks in the process of political reconciliation, implementation of the 1992 peace accords continued, giving Mozambicans increasingly greater protection from human rights abuses and opportunities for greater enjoyment of civil and political rights.

Although human rights violations continued in these countries, progress is being made.

## III. Democracy

In 1993, democracy continued to capture the imagination of people around the globe. There were both advances and setbacks.

In Cambodia, following the largest United Nations peacekeeping effort ever undertaken, 90 percent of voters participated in free and fair elections in May—the first in decades—thus providing the opportunity for long-term democratic evolution. The remainder of the 370,000 Cambodian refugees who had been living mostly along the Thai-Cambodian border were voluntarily repatriated under the direction of the U.N. High Commissioner for Refugees (UNHCR).

By contrast, in Haiti the military continued to obstruct the return of democratically elected President Aristide. Right-wing thugs closely allied with the

*Continued*

**EXHIBIT 1.1** *Continued*

military assassinated the legitimately appointed Justice Minister and conducted many other killings targeted against specific individuals.

In Guatemala, President Jorge Serrano was peacefully and constitutionally dismissed after he had suspended several sections of the Constitution and dissolved Congress and the Supreme and Constitutional Courts. When Congress reconvened, it elected as President Ramiro de Leon Carpio, the former Human Rights Ombudsman.

In Russia, democratic parliamentary elections were held for the second time in the country's history. Despite this, and continuing progress in the areas of civil and political rights, there were setbacks, most notably during the violent constitutional crisis in October.

In Burma, military authorities continued to refuse to implement the results of the May 1990 elections that rejected their rule.

In Nigeria, the military overturned the results of an election, dissolved all democratic institutions, and now rules the country by decree.

In Burundi, the nation's first democratically elected president was assassinated, and a bloody conflict followed.

The starting point of democratic government is the right of citizens, through free and fair elections, to choose their government. Elections are not the sum total of democracy, of course, but they are a foundation. Democracy also requires establishing civil societies, where people can participate fully in the democratic process. The rule of law, civilian control of the military, an independent judiciary, free media, and the rights of people to free speech, association, and assembly are essential elements of democratic societies.

### IV. Torture, Arbitrary Detention, and the Impunity of Abusers

Major violations of human rights occurred not only in war-torn countries. Human rights abuses also remained widespread in countries in which violators were not held accountable. When violators can commit human rights abuses with impunity, abuses multiply.

In Iran, the Government continued to torture and execute people summarily and to restrict the freedoms of speech, press, assembly, and association. Minority religious groups, including the Baha'is, faced systematic repression.

North Korea remains one of the most repressive countries of the world. The Government treats individual rights as potentially subversive of the goals of the State and the party.

In Burma, the autocratic military regime reinforces its power with a pervasive security apparatus. People are arrested arbitrarily and prisoners are abused. Citizens are denied basic political rights and the rights of free speech and assembly.

Zaire is undergoing its worst human rights crisis since the end of the civil war in the 1960's. The Mobutu regime was responsible for massive human rights violations, including extrajudicial killings, unlawful detections, ethnic violence, torture, and disappearances.

In China, fundamental human rights provided for in the Chinese Constitution frequently are ignored in practice, and challenges to the Communist Party's political authority are often dealt with harshly and arbitrarily. China took some

**EXHIBIT 1.1**   *Continued*

positive but limited steps in human rights areas, including releasing prominent political prisoners. Hundreds, perhaps thousands, of political prisoners, however, remained under detention or in prison. Reports of physical abuse persisted, including torture by police and prison officials. This was especially the case in politically restive and minority-populated regions such as Tibet. In November, China announced that it would give positive consideration to a request from the International Committee of the Red Cross to visit China.

In Peru, the terrorist activities of the Shining Path declined following the capture of its leader in 1992. The number of extrajudicial killings and disappearances instigated or condoned by the Government also fell. Nonetheless, human rights violations continued and serious due process questions arose concerning the military trials of civilians.

In Cuba, the Government does not permit domestic or international human rights groups to function legally. Human rights activists and political dissidents are systematically harassed, beaten, and otherwise abused by police and security officials.

In Turkey, both the Government and the Kurdistan Workers Party (PKK) terrorist forces committed human rights violations, including torture.

In Egypt, torture and other human rights violations continued. In a positive development, the country's Supreme Court acquitted 25 defendants in cases in which confessions were extracted under torture.

In Indonesia, extrajudicial arrests and detections, as well as torture of those in custody, continued. In East Timor, no significant progress was noted in the accounting for those missing from the November 1991 shooting incident in Dili.

*V. The Rights of Women*

We have paid special attention in 1993 to the problem of rampant discrimination against women. Physical abuse is the most obvious example. In many African countries, the practice of female genital mutilation continued. In Pakistan, many women in police custody are subjected to sexual or physical violence. On several continents, women and girls sold into prostitution. In many Gulf countries, domestic servants from Southeast Asia are forced to work excessively long hours and are sometimes physically and sexually abused. In Bangladesh and India, dowry deaths continue. Marital rape in many countries is not recognized as a crime, and women raped or beaten at home often have no recourse. That female life is not valued as much as male life is apparent in countries such as China where it is reported that more female fetuses than male are aborted.

In addition to physical abuse, the political, civil and legal rights of women are often denied. In 1993 women throughout the world were subjected to onerous and discriminatory restrictions of such fundamental freedoms as voting, marriage, travel, testifying in court, inheriting and owning property, and obtaining custody of children. All too often, women and girls find that their access to education, employment, health care, and even food is limited because of their gender.

*Continued*

**EXHIBIT 1.1**   *Continued*

## VI. Worker Rights

In far too many countries, the freedom of workers to associate, which is the paramount right on which trade unions base their ability to bargain collectively, defend their members' grievances, and protect them from unfair and unsafe working conditions, falls well short of the standards elaborated by the International Labor Organization (ILO). Restrictions on freedom of association abound. They range from outright and total government control of all forms of worker organizations to webs of legislation so complicated that full compliance is virtually impossible, giving authorities excuses to intervene at will.

In 1993, the practice of forced labor continued, as did the abuse of expatriate workers, particularly domestics. Slavery still exists in some countries, particularly in Mauritania and Sudan. Given the rising concern about the impact of international trade on worker rights standards, this year's reports focus more sharply on the presence of child labor in export industries and on minimum wage and occupational safety standards. Our reports document a number of serious bonded and child labor problems, particularly in South Asia and North Africa.

## VII. Accountability

In the face of widespread human rights violations, the impunity of violators and absence of the rule of law, some progress was made at the international level in 1993 to develop new global institutions to promote human rights accountability.

In February the United Nations created a War Crimes Tribunal to prosecute those responsible for gross violations of human rights in much of the former Yugoslavia. By year's end, all judges had been sworn in.

In December, following the recommendation of the World Conference on Human Rights in Vienna in June, the U.N. General Assembly established the office of High Commissioner for Human Rights with a mandate to remove obstacles to citizens' full enjoyment of basic human rights.

The World Conference also recommended establishing a Special Rapporteur on Violence Against Women. The Human Rights Commission will take up this project in 1994.

Meanwhile, the U.N. Human Rights Center had rapporteurs assess conditions in countries such as Burma, Iraq and Cuba, where human rights are largely disregarded. Other bodies, such as the Committee Against Torture, monitored compliance with U.N. treaties and conventions.

The Conference on Security and Cooperation in Europe (CSCE) has been a significant force in holding countries accountable for adherence to human rights standards. In September the CSCE held a review conference to assess each participating state's progress in implementing its "human dimension" commitments, including to human rights, fundamental freedoms, and the rule of law. The CSCE has also been active in mediating disputes, particularly through the work of its High Commissioner for National Minorities. In Latvia and Estonia, CSCE and other international factfinding missions looked into allegations of human rights abuses. While finding no systematic violations, they urged these governments to adopt an inclusive approach to citizenship and alien

**EXHIBIT 1.1** *Continued*

rights and assure the equitable and nondiscriminatory treatment of ethnic Russians living in their countries. Both Latvia and Estonia have accepted the establishment of CSCE missions to help improve intercommunal relations.

The Organization of African Unity (OAU) assisted in meditation efforts in Burundi that have helped move that country toward a resolution of its constitutional and humanitarian crisis.

The Organization of American States (OAS) played an important role in defending human rights and due process, notably in Nicaragua.

*VIII. Grassroots Movement for Human Rights and Democracy*

The willingness of nations to begin to hold each other accountable for human rights abuses is a reflection of the work of individuals to hold their own governments accountable. Around the world in 1993, grassroots movements supported the spread of human rights, freedom, and democracy. This commitment of people, acting through nongovernmental organizations, is reflected in the final Declaration of the World Conference on Human Rights held in June in Vienna, that the individual—and not the state—is at the center of development. Moreover, underdevelopment can never justify human rights abuses. There is indeed an important linkage among human rights and the full participation of individuals in their own political system create the necessary context for development to take place.

Human rights will not be protected without the constant vigilance of courageous individuals who promote human rights, document abuses, and hold their

governments to account. These sentinels for human rights engender hope. Amidst the abuse of 1993, there is another story, that of countless men and women who stood up and said "No!" No to injustice, no to tyranny, no to torture, and no to censorship. We salute those who are working against great odds to advance human rights and democracy:

- Monique Mujawamariya who works in Rwanda and Burundi, and those like her whose bodies bear the scars of thugs as the price of documenting human rights violations;
- Mansour Kikhiya of Libya, and all the "disappeared" who have been abducted because of their human rights work;
- Liu Gang who sits in jail in China, and all who are imprisoned for peaceful expression of their views;
- Sebastian Arcos of Cuba, and all who refuse to be silent when others are being abused;
- Aung San Suu Kyi, in her fifth year of house arrest in Burma, and all who work for freedom at the price of their own liberty;
- The staff of the Sarajevo daily newspaper, Oslobodjenje, and all who work for a free press and who demonstrate that Serb and Croat, Muslim and Jew, can work and live side by side in peace.

We salute these people, and the tens of thousands of courageous human rights workers around the world.

The year 1993 was a difficult one for human rights, a year in which setbacks outweighed advances in some parts of the world. Paradoxically, it was also a

*Continued*

**EXHIBIT 1.1** *Continued*

year in which the daily struggle for human rights at global, national, and local levels received more attention than ever before, a year in which the world-wide grassroots movement for human rights and democratic change gathered momentum. The year saw the community of nations reaffirm its commitment to the protection and promotion of human rights at the World Conference on Human Rights in Vienna on the 45th anniversary of the Universal Declaration of Human Rights. The force of this movement was captured by Eleanor Roosevelt in an address to the United Nations in 1958:

"Where, after all, do universal human rights begin? In small places, close to home—so close and so small that they cannot be seen on any maps of the world. Yet, they are the world of the individual person; the neighborhood he lives in; the school or college he attends; the factory, farm or office where he works. Such are the places where every man, woman and child seeks equal justice, equal opportunity, equal dignity without discrimination. Unless these rights have meaning there, they have little meaning anywhere. Without concerned citizen action to uphold them close to home, we shall look in vain for progress in the larger world."

John Shattuck,
*Assistant Secretary of State*
*for Human Rights*
*and Humanitarian Affairs.*

# 2

---

# *Crime by Government: Secret Police, Human Rights, and Genocide*

> *The only thing necessary for the triumph of evil is for good men to do nothing.*
> —*EDMUND BURKE*

> *Power corrupts, absolute power corrupts absolutely.*
> —*LORD ACTON*

Crime by government involves crimes or violations of human rights committed for ideological reasons by government officials or their agents. Such government political criminals are motivated not by self-interest but by a dedication to a particular belief system, a conviction that they are defending the status quo or preserving the existing system. Since many such violations are not formally recognized or enforced by the criminal law within most states, the concept of political crime by government is more a sociological than a political entity. Friedrichs (1992, pp. 26–27) prefers the term "governmental crime," which he defines as:

> *The broad, all-encompassing term for a range of illegal and demonstrably harmful activities carried out from within or in association with, governmental status. . . . They [governmental crimes] are committed within a governmental context, and facilitated by governmental power.*

As indicated previously, Barak (1991) prefers the term "state crime," whereas Chambliss (1988b) calls these behaviors "state-organized crimes." At times, it is difficult to determine whether crimes by government officials are ideological or occupational crimes (personally benefiting the offender either in terms of power or monetary reward). The Watergate events were primarily an example of occupational crime, though Nixon and his accomplices claimed the offenses were committed in order to preserve national security. In fact, most such offenses are inspired by both ideology and the desire for personal benefit.

## *Secret Police*

All countries require some type of secret police for clandestine intelligence gathering and internal security. Plate and Darvi (1981, p. 8) define secret police as "official or semiofficial organs of government. They are units of the internal security police of the state, with the mandate to suppress all serious, threatening political opposition to the government in power." Their mandate is to control all political activity within (and sometimes even beyond) the borders of the nation-state. Often involved in the extraordinary means of illegal surveillance, searches, detention, and arrest, secret police, as a matter of practice, may violate or border on violating human rights.

In authoritarian regimes the effectiveness of secret police in deterring illegitimate violence (crime in the streets) occurs through legitimate secret police such as Hitler's Gestapo, Stalin's OGPU (later KGB), and Haiti's Tonton Macoutes, and practices such as midnight raids, tortures, and disappearances which were notorious, frightening, and brutally effective.

Austin Turk (1982) prefers the term "political policing" to refer to secret police operations. Turk (1982, pp. 238–239) provides a number of illustrations of political policing:

- Assassination of political figures
- "Geneva offenses" such as germ warfare, letter bombs, or use of cattle prods in order to torture political prisoners
- The torture of political prisoners, such as those listed by Amnesty International
- Character assassination, which involves intimidation through innuendo
- Intervention in conventional politics, such as the FBI campaign against Martin Luther King, Jr.
- Violations of civil or human rights, for example, from illegal surveillance to mental institutionalization of political dissidents in the former USSR
- Economic or political harassment of dissident groups
- Use of "agents provocateurs," informants, and spies in order to manipulate public institutions
- Subversion of economic or other institutions, for example, the overthrow of the Chilean government of Salvador Allende by the Central Intelligence Agency

---

**EXHIBIT 2.1     In the Name of the Father:**
**The Guildford Four**

In 1993 a film entitled *In the Name of the Father* portrayed the case of the "Guildford Four," three young Irishmen and a young Irishwoman who had served 15 years in British prisons having been falsely convicted of a terrorist bombing of a pub in Guildford, near London, in which five were killed and fifty were wounded. They were convicted due to coerced confessions under interrogation after being held incommunicado, deprived of sleep and food, beaten and threatened. Without any other evidence, the accused signed confession letters prepared by the Royal Ulster Constabulary. One of the four, Paul Hill (husband of the late Robert Kennedy's daughter, Courtney), also signed a confession under duress admitting to the murder of Brian Shaw, a British soldier who had been tortured and killed by the IRA.

Faced with mounting incidents of terrorism, the British had resorted to increasing suspensions of civil liberties in order to bring matters under control. In 1989 at an appeals trial the Guildford Four were suddenly released when their defense lawyer produced a 1977 police file which was marked "Not to Be Shown to the Defense," in which it was clear that the police knew they had arrested the wrong parties. Paul Hill was still being held responsible and convicted of the Shaw murder despite the fact that the case also was based solely on a coerced confession (Styron, 1994; Darnton, 1994).

---

Some additional tactics available to state agents of social control to suppress a social movement (Baylor, 1990; Marx, 1979) include:

- Litigation against the movement or leaders
- Administrative harassment
- Disinformation campaigns
- Wiretaps and other electronic surveillance methods
- The use of informants and agents provocateurs
- Support of counter or alternative groups
- Bad jacketing or snitch jacketing (falsely accusing innocent individuals of being informants or "snitches")
- Police response, including force

Many of these tactics involve the state officially encouraging its agents to commit crime (Marx, 1990). The criminological study of such crimes by government has been far less a topic of research than similar crimes against the government in part due to a lack of funding for the former (Longmire, 1988).

The lack of criminological attention to governmental crime is also due to the lack of access to the politically powerful, the ability of elites to cover up their crimes, the broad scope and complexity of such crimes, as well as ideological resistance to the notion of government officials as criminals (Friedrichs, 1992, p. 8a). As an example of crime by government, Exhibit 2.1 reports on the false imprisonment of four Irish political prisoners for 15 years by Great Britain.

## Human Rights Violations

The most dramatic example of crimes by government is the pervasive international violation of human rights. Thousands of "political prisoners"—individuals who have committed no crimes other than their espousal of political ideas—are tortured, murdered, or abandoned throughout the world. Due to governmental secrecy it is difficult to gain an accurate estimate of such prisoners, although human rights organizations such as Amnesty International provide rough figures. Authoritarian and totalitarian regimes of the Left and Right are the least tolerant of political dissent and are thus the biggest violators. These countries most resemble that described in George Orwell's *1984,* in which the state is preeminent.

While Savak (the Iranian secret police) under the shah was a brutal force, in the subsequent theocracy of Khomeini and his successors in Iran, over 60,000 political prisoners have been held and over 25,000 executed including members of the Baha'i religion, who were systematically exterminated. In 1990 members of the People's Mojahedin (a rival political party) claimed that over 90,000 had been executed and 150,000 tortured (Anderson and Van Atta, 1990). Torture is routinely practiced on detainees in order to extract confessions as are beatings, floggings, suspension by limbs, and mock executions. Thefts are punished by amputations, in accordance with Islamic law. The death penalty is given for acts ranging from adultery and repeated lesbianism to wine drinking (Elias, 1986). Beginning in 1975, the Pol Pot regime in Cambodia embarked on a system of mass genocide that destroyed a large portion of that small nation's population. In Latin America right-wing governments and private government-related "death squads" kidnapped and/or tortured and murdered individuals who they felt threatened the state. Amnesty International estimated that ninety-eight countries practiced torture during the eighties, primarily as a tool for repression rather than to extract information (Satchell, 1988, p. 38). Concern has been raised that, as a result of international attention focused on the plight of political prisoners, many governments turned to execution of dissidents (Whitaker *et al.,* 1983, p. 52), assuming that the dead tell no tales.

In the former South Africa, racist policies of apartheid (racial separation) and their enforcement led to systematic violations of the human rights of black and "colored" South Africans by the white government. A former member of the South African police "murder unit" admitted to being a commander of an elite undercover unit that tracked and killed black activists such as members of the African National Congress ("The Secrets," 1989). In Ethiopia, Somalia, and Sudan, starvation of civilian populations was used as a political weapon.

## Massacre at Tiananmen Square

The raw, naked power of the state to exercise its political power against popular will was illustrated by the Chinese government's crackdown on the democracy movement in May 1990. Thousands who took to the streets to protest authoritarian rule were massacred by their own troops. Additionally, more than a thousand had been killed or arrested. (Some of the latter were executed after being tried.) The Chinese government obviously had not forgotten Chairman Mao's axiom, "Power comes from the barrel of a gun."

In 1975 the Harkin Human Rights Amendments required that U.S. foreign economic and military aid be dependent on the certification of satisfactory human rights records of recipient countries. The linking of human rights and foreign policy can have beneficial results in prodding abusive countries to improve their policies. American human rights demands in South Africa, Eastern Europe, and in Latin America have improved the political climates in previously offensive regimes. In 1994 the Clinton administration continued this human rights approach to foreign and economic policy, but discovered limits (Sciolino, 1994). Having threatened economic sanctions against China unless it expanded human rights and ceased persecuting political prisoners, the Clinton administration backed off, fearing the rupture of a very delicate Sino-American detente. The hope was that, rather than severing relations, a continuing prodding would accomplish a liberalizing policy and encourage the emerging moderates and reformers in China.

Some of the booming trade and exports from China were the products of forced labor. In 1994 China's forced labor prison camps may have represented the world's largest engine of political repression, with estimates of as many as ten million inmates. A number of these were political prisoners. Harry Wu (1994, p. A15), a former inmate in one of China's gulags, explains how he was arbitrarily thrown into labor camps in 1960 without a trial, and spent 19 years in captivity. While merely a student condemning the Russian invasion of Hungary in 1956, he was labeled a "counter revolutionary rightist" by Mao Zedong's then political campaign leader Deng Ziaoping, the leader of the Communist Party in the 1990s. He was repeatedly mistreated, tortured, and nearly starved to death. Disowned by his own family who feared government persecution, he learned to survive by eating rats, snakes, or just about anything in order to stay alive. He indicates (ibid., 1994, p. A15), "These ordinary people, among them workers and religious believers are still locked away as political prisoners, along with common criminals they are forced to work or starve, a practice which violates international law and basic decency."

In June 1995, Harry Wu, now an American citizen, was arrested by the People's Republic of China as he attempted to legally reenter the country. He was convicted of espionage and returned to the United States. He had been continually criticizing and revealing China's human rights violations.

## Genocide

Armed troops, some of them former neighbors, first surrounded the town of Vlasenica. Tanks were stationed at strategic positions which made it impossible to leave the town. Beatings, random arrests, rape, and reprisal killings became common followed by systematic eviction and slaughter. A camp was prepared in a former military depot called Susica and it was surrounded with barbed wire. Civilians—men, women, and children—were removed from the town and concentrated in the camp. Individuals, a total of about 3,000, were executed every night at the command of a military leader. These activities describe not the work of Hitler or Stalin in the thirties, but of the Serbs and Bosnian Serbs in 1992 (Cohen, 1994). Susica was a Serbian concentration camp being used for the ethnic cleansing (removal) of Muslims from Serb-controlled areas of Bosnia and Herzegovina. The attack on Vlasenica's Muslim population was under the direction of a unit of the Yugoslav army and Major Mile Jacimovic. What all of this illustrates is genocide and its most recent version: "ethnic cleansing." This involved the systematic use of violence and terror to scare a population into removing itself from a territory. Exhibit 2.2, found at the end of this chapter, describes such activities.

Genocide, the mass destruction or annihilation of populations, is the ultimate example of violence and political crime by government. The term was coined by jurist Raphael Lemkin (1944), who defined genocide as the destruction of a nation or of an ethnic group. Genocide has a long history, from the Crusades, Roman persecutions, Genghis Khan, and medieval pogroms against European Jews to the massacres of the present century. Kuper (1981, pp. 17–18) notes that modern totalitarian ideologies replaced religious justifications for genocide:

> *The major examples of the genocidal potentialities of these ideologies in our day are provided by the Nazi regime with its conception of a brave new world of racially tolerated and ordered societies under German hegemony; the Soviet regime, under Stalin, with the Gulag Archipelago receiving, as a sort of "rubbish bin of history," the successive blood sacrifices of the communist utopia; and the recent Pol Pot regime in Cambodia, freely and righteously exterminating in total dedication to a starkly elemental blueprint for living. . . . It is a massive toll of genocidal conflict, if one adds to the civil wars of decolonization, the destruction of scapegoat groups, and the ideological, ethnic and religious massacres. And it is a particularly threatening scourge of our day and age, facilitated by international concern for the protection of the sovereign rights of the state, by international intervention in the arming of contending sections, and by United Nations de facto condonation, which serves as a screen for genocide.*

In the late eighties as part of the Iran-Iraq War, Iraq used chemical weapons on civilians as well as on the Iranian military, even though this practice had been prohibited by international conventions since the 1925 Geneva Protocol.

Condemnation of political crime may be compromised for other political reasons. In July 1987 the French government convicted Klaus Barbie, "the butcher of Lyons," of crimes against humanity he had committed as a gestapo (SS) commander during World War II. He was responsible for the torture, death, and deportation to concentration camps of thousands of Jews and Resistance fighters. Barbie had been hidden from the French after the war by the Americans, who had used him for intelligence purposes (Misner, 1987). Similar charges were levied against former U.N. secretary-general and Austrian president Kurt Waldheim. It was charged that Waldheim, while a young German lieutenant in the Balkans during World War II, was an accomplice to war crimes. Investigations of Waldheim's involvement were inconclusive, although the charges did little to prevent Austrians from electing him president.

Activities at Japanese Unit 731 during World War II were covered up by the U.S. government itself after the war in order to protect as well as obtain germ warfare secrets from former Japanese war criminals. This camp located in then-occupied China was the scene of horrifying experiments such as dissection of living human beings without anesthesia and other uses of Allied POWs as human guinea pigs.

In the early nineties Brazilian business people employed "death squads" to execute poor street children. In 1989 alone 445 children were murdered as a means of eliminating street crime ("Death Squads," 1991).

In November 1993 the United Nations set up a war crimes tribunal to begin compiling evidence against war criminals in mainly Serb-run camps in Bosnia. Of particular note in the policy of "ethnic cleansing" was the use of rape as a political weapon. By January 1993 the Women's Rights Project of Human Rights Watch estimated that 20,000 Muslim women had been raped since fighting began in April 1992. Mass rapes were used as a strategy of war and did not represent simple individual transgressions.

Unlike the last war crime trial at Nuremberg (1945–1949) the Yugoslavian war crime trials possessed neither the suspects in custody nor a clear documentary proof of guilt. Former U.N. High Commissioner for Refugees Sadruddin Aga Khan (1994) expressed the view that the tribunal was a monumental whitewash of Serbian and Croatian leaders in the interest of political expediency; namely, to keep them at the negotiating table. In order to attempt to bring an end to the conflict, likely, peace agreements will include the provision that each side (Croatians and Serbians) will prosecute their own. Despite Khan's belief, in 1995 the tribunal found a number of Bosnian Serb leaders guilty as charged of war crimes and crimes against humanity.

A latent (unanticipated consequence) function of the end of the cold war is that it has resuscitated long-suppressed ethnic, tribal, and religious rivalries that had been held in check or had been subordinated under previous superpower umbrellas (Moynihan, 1993). Beginning in the nineties, particularly with the United States' aborted intervention in Somalia, the United Nations and developed nations have been reluctant to intervene particularly in third-world nations unless a very clear and compelling national interest was apparent. Such was the case in 1994 in the African nation of Rwanda. Four centuries of tribal hatred exploded in a blood lust, civil war between Hutu and Tutsi tribes. Anarchy reigned as gangs of drunken Hutu men with machetes ruled the streets and hacked to death thousands of men, women, and children. Estimated casualties were between 200,000 and 500,000. Developed nations may have hesitated calling these horrendous acts genocide, because they would have been legally bound to do something about it as signatories to the U.N. Convention for the Prevention of Genocide (Des Forges, 1994).

## Pol Pot's Genocide

Massive genocide did not end with Hitler's holocaust in Europe. Pol Pot's Khmer Rouge regime in Cambodia in the late seventies practiced unbelievable horrors on their own people. Imagine a country ruled by the Charles Manson family, and you could picture the raw terror generated by Angka (the organization of Khmer Rouge) in Cambodia. Of all the Cambodian refugees who fled the country after its invasion by Vietnam, the most devastated were Khmer Rouge refugees ("Cambodia," 1979). In an effort to create a radically new society overnight, the Angka had tortured, terrorized, and murdered their subjects to the point that many exhibited zombielike behavior devoid of many normal human emotions. Occupation by Vietnam in the eighties brought a temporary halt to Khmer Rouge atrocities. But by the early nineties, after the Vietnamese pullout, a new coalition government was formed in Cambodia with the Khmer Rouge as one of the parties.

The 1948 U.N. Convention on Genocide defined genocide as a crime (Kuper, 1981, p. 19):

> *In the present Convention, genocide means any of the following acts committed with intent to destroy, in whole or in part, a national, ethnical, racial or religious group, as such:*
>
> a. *Killing members of the group;*
> b. *Causing serious bodily or mental harm to members of the group;*
> c. *Deliberately inflicting on the group conditions of life calculated to bring about its physical destruction in whole or in part;*
> d. *Imposing measures intended to prevent births within the group;*
> e. *Forcibly transferring children of the group to another group.*

Despite this, the United Nations has been less than firm in condemning or acting against genocide, whether it be committed by the Pol Pot regime in Cambodia, Idi Amin's Uganda, Khomeini's Iran, or the Serbs in Bosnia.

## Crimes by Police

Democratic societies require the government not only to enforce the law but also to obey the law itself. In the United States, the government is held accountable to certain constitutional guarantees of individual rights such as freedom of speech, due process, and the right to privacy. Sometimes, however, federal and local law enforcement agencies are more interested in bureaucratic efficiency than in proper law enforcement and have ignored and violated these rights (see Henderson and Simon, 1994; and Lieberman, 1984). Jerome Skolnick, in his book entitled *The Politics of Protest: The Skolnick Report to the National Commission on the Causes and Prevention of Violence* (1969, p. xxv) which analyzed U.S. violence in the sixties, indicated:

> *Police response to mass protest has often resulted in an escalation of conflict, hostility, and violence. The police violence during the Democratic National Convention in Chicago (1968) was not a unique phenomenon. We have found numerous other instances where violence had been initiated or exacerbated by police actions and attitudes, although violence also has been avoided by judicious planning and supervision.*

Before the success of the civil rights struggle, local and state officials in the southern United States systematically violated federal law in maintenance of a racist, caste system. Murders, lynchings, beatings, and institutionalized denial of constitutional guarantees were all committed in the name of "law and order." It was to the destruction of this de jure discrimination that the civil rights movement was directed.

In 1991 televised coverage of a bystander's videotape of the beating by Los Angeles police officers of Rodney King and the subsequent court decision that the police were not guilty led to the deadliest urban riots in the United States this century. While three or four officers had beaten King, eleven others looked on; and the first court decision in light of the videotape struck most of the American public and particularly blacks as unfair. Many black citizens had at the time complained of police harassment and disrespect, much of it associated with aggressive proactive patrol as part of the "war on drugs." Other abuses by government officials may include illegal surveillance of citizens, disruption of democratic process, and secret experiments with unknowing subjects.

## Illegal Surveillance, Disruption, and Experiments

### Operation CHAOS

During the student protest period of the sixties, President Johnson directed the Central Intelligence Agency (CIA) to investigate and determine whether foreign elements had infiltrated protest activity. This program, Operation CHAOS, involved the surveillance activities of domestic groups and violated the CIA's initial charter, the National Security Act, which clearly excluded its activities from the domestic arena. Pressure for the expansion of activities was ordered by both President Johnson and later Nixon. Operation CHAOS and a related Project 2 planted agents in radical groups and collected 13,000 different files. The Rockefeller commission (1975) investigated the impropriety of the CIA's encroaching on the domestic field of espionage, sabotage, and provocation and found that the CIA and FBI in its operation Cointelpro committed 238 break-ins (black bag jobs) and later attempted to destroy records of such activities.

## Cointelpro

Abuse of power by intelligence agencies was further illustrated in hearings conducted by the U.S. Select Committee to Study Government Operations (1979), which revealed that civil rights organizations had been investigated for over a 25-year period in order to uncover possible communist influences (Karmen, 1974, in Thomas and Hepburn, 1983, p. 280):

> *Dr. Martin Luther King, Jr., was harassed by anonymous letters, his telephone was tapped, his speaking engagements were disrupted by false fire alarms—all as a strategy to discredit him and his organization. In addition it is apparent that the FBI and various state police departments used agents provocateurs to infiltrate dissenting groups, radicalize the members, secure the weapons and explosives necessary for violent confrontations, and plan the target of attacks as a means to discredit dissident groups.*

In Cointelpro, the FBI's counterintelligence program to harass and disrupt legitimate political activity such as the Socialist Worker's Party and various black nationalist groups, the FBI employed "snitch jacketing" in which false letters were used accusing people of being informants in order to foment internal warfare (Blackstock, 1976, p. 9). Separating ideologically motivated actions from personal corruption and vendetta is difficult, as is illustrated in examinations of J. Edgar Hoover's personal files, some of which were released in the 1980s under the Freedom of Information Act. In nearly 50 years in office Hoover kept personal files on the personal lives of public figures, particularly those whom he happened to dislike. Eleanor Roosevelt, John and Robert Kennedy, and Martin Luther King, Jr., were just a few of the political figures who were the subject of scrutiny. In addition to surveillance on Dr. King, it is alleged that the FBI sent threatening letters and a tape to Coretta King regarding her husband's enjoying a sexual tryst (Garrow, 1981). Below are the contents of a note sent to Dr. King, by the FBI 34 days before he was to receive the Nobel Peace Prize. It suggests that he should commit suicide (Blackstock, 1976):

> *King, there is only one thing left for you to do. You know what it is. You have just 34 days in which to do it. (This exact number has been selected for a specific reason). It has definite practical significance. You are done. There is but one way out for you.*

## Political Assassination

Assassination of foreign leaders or domestic opponents may be sanctioned by government officials as a means of preserving the state. Under the apartheid system, South Africa's intelligence service waged a secret war against the then-outlawed African National Congress (ANC). A "counterterrorist" group which ended in 1982 tracked and killed activists inside South Africa and ran missions against ANC exiles in other countries ("The Secrets," 1989). In another example, the former East German secret police, the Stasi, murdered defectors who were living in the West. In the 1960s U.S. intelligence targeted Fidel Castro in Operation Mongoose, as well as was implicated in the assassination of President Diem in South Vietnam, and was alleged to have been involved in the murders of Allende (Chile) and Lumumba (the Congo).

## The Search for the Manchurian Candidate

*Those whom God wishes to destroy he first makes mad.*

—Euripedes

In 1958 Richard Condon published a novel (later made into a movie) entitled *The Manchurian Candidate*. In a plot that takes place during the Korean War, a character named Raymond Shaw and a U.S. army squad returned after having been missing behind enemy lines. Members of the squad praised Shaw's heroism in saving them from the enemy, and he received the Congressional Medal of Honor. In reality, Shaw and his squad were "brainwashed" or "hypnotized-programmed" by the communist Chinese. Asking Shaw to play solitaire until the queen of diamonds appeared would trigger Shaw into zombielike obedience. His own mother (a Chinese communist "mole" or spy) was his operator, and the plan was for Shaw to function as an assassin of the presidential nominee, thus propelling his father, the vice presidential nominee, into the Oval Office.

Condon's theme captivated the Western intelligence community, as had the "Moscow show trials" of the period, in which dissidents were paraded before television cameras and, as if in a trance, admitted treasonous activities against the state (Scheflin and Opton, 1978, p. 437). Cold War propagandist Edward Hunter (1951) coined the term "brainwashing" to describe what was happening, although it is very likely that he popularized the concept as part of his job with the CIA (Scheflin and Opton, 1978, p. 226).

On November 28, 1953, Frank Olson, a civilian employee of the U.S. Army, jumped to his death from the tenth floor window of his New York City hotel room; and the CIA stated at the time that he had become mentally unbalanced. Over 20 years later during the Rockefeller commission (1975) hearings on CIA activities, government documents revealed the actual facts of the incident, which had been hidden from Olson's own guilt-ridden widow and family for over two decades. As part of the secret CIA Project Bluebird, which involved mind control research, the agency secretly drugged unsuspecting citizens and employees. Olson unknowingly had been slipped a very heavy dosage of LSD and had a "bad trip" (a psychotomimetic reaction that mimics psychosis). When Olson killed himself, the CIA lied and smeared Olson's reputation in the process (Marks, 1979). When the facts were revealed many years later, the White House issued an apology to the Olson family along with $750,000. But this was just one in a series of bizarre mind control, field experiments conducted by the CIA, using as subjects unsuspecting private citizens.

Scheflin and Opton (1978, p. 225) maintain that the brainwashing concept which precipitated many of these experiments was a myth and that the alleged communist methods differed little from common police interrogation practices.

> *That the CIA was able to take an old form of torture, dress it up with a lurid name and convince the public that a new technique for mind subversion was being practiced by the Communist nations, is a propaganda coup of stunning proportion. . . .*
>
> *There was absolutely no basis in fact to allege that the "communists" had started "brain warfare." It is not entirely impossible that the "brainwashing" scare was created by the CIA because it wanted to do mind-control research and considered that the safest way to get authorization was to allege that the Soviets had done it first.*

Using code names such as Bluebird, Artichoke, and MKULTRA, the CIA, FBI, and military in the 1950s experimented with various behavioral control devices and interrogation techniques, including ESP (extrasensory perception), drugs, polygraphs, hypnosis, shock therapy, surgery, and radiation. This involved secret experiments on unknowing citizens and, when harm took place, a cover-up. The U.S. Army in the fifties and sixties conducted outdoor tests of poisonous bacteria (serratia), which can cause pneumonia. Due to these bacteriological warfare tests, one hospital reported twelve cases of serratia pneumonia and one death (Cousins, 1979; Simon and Eitzen, 1993, p. 265). A Canadian teenager seeking medical treatment for an arthritic leg was subjected to LSD, electroshock therapy, and forced to listen to hours of taped messages including one repeating, "You killed your mother," as part of a series of bizarre experiments financed by the CIA and conducted by a former president of the American Psychiatric Association. Over 100 Canadians from 1957 to 1961 were unknowing guinea pigs, causing them much psychiatric harm. In 1988 the CIA agreed to pay damages to victims of the experiment—$750,000 to be shared by eight of the victims (Witt, 1988, p. 2A).

## American Nuclear Guinea Pigs

In 1986 the House Energy and Commerce Subcommittee discovered that federal agencies had conducted experiments on U.S. citizens, including injecting them with plutonium, radium, and uranium over a 30-year period beginning in the mid-1940s. This included elderly adults being fed radium or thorium from a Nevada test site at MIT, inmates receiving x rays to their testes, and open-air fallout tests (Lawrence, 1988).

In December 1993 U.S. Energy Secretary Hazel O'Leary was so upset regarding the details of these sinister experiments that she went public with previously secret information. Together with congressional investigations and investigative journalistic reports it was revealed that these experiments included:

- Oregon and Washington inmates whose testes were radiated and who were also given vasectomies to avoid fathering mutants;
- The Hanford Nuclear Facility (Richland, Washington) experimentally released a huge cloud of radioactive iodine 131 that drifted over three states and had thousands of times more radiation than that emitted by the 1979 Three Mile Island accident in Pennsylvania;
- Between 1945 and 1947, eighteen hospital patients were given injections of plutonium without their permission. Some doses were ninety-eight times the levels believed safe at the time;
- In the late fifties the CIA hired prostitutes in Greenwich Village, NY, and San Francisco to slip LSD to their customers and observed them from behind two-way mirrors (Watson *et al.,* 1993);
- Forty students at a Massachusetts state school for the mentally retarded and handicapped were told they were joining a science club and were fed minute doses of radioactive materials by Harvard and MIT researchers ("2 Tell," 1994).

Similar behavior was exhibited by the former Soviet Union during the Cold War which, in order to rival the superpower status of the United States, resulted in vast areas of the country being treated as a nuclear dump and a victim of ecocide. Dozens of ad hoc nuclear dumps were created, seeping radioactivity. A senior health official in the Semipalatinsk region (the main Soviet nuclear test site) charges: "We were turned into human guinea pigs for these experiments. They kept telling us that it was for the good of the people, the Communist party, the future. The individual never counted for anything in the system" (Dobbs, 1993, p. 13). Ironically, much of this bizarre experimentation was unnecessary because reports of the "Manchurian Candidate" were much exaggerated and it turns out that the Russian superiority in the Cold War was a myth.

## Veil

In the 1980s then-Director of the Central Intelligence Agency William Casey executed a domestic-propaganda campaign to promote support for the Nicaraguan contras as well as discredit domestic opposition to U.S. Central American policy. This program risked violating an executive order forbidding CIA involvement in American politics. Much of the operation was run "off-the-shelf" (secretly and independently), involving operatives such as Oliver North or former CIA officials and not current employees of the agency. According to Bob Woodward, author of *Veil: The Secret War of the CIA: 1981–1987* (1987), "Veil" was the code word for all covert action in the later Reagan administration. According to the General Accounting Office this domestic covert operation, which was begun in August 1983, involved secret propaganda activities such as members of the National Security Council ghostwriting Op-Ed columns for the *New York Times* and the *Washington Post* and planting stories on *NBC News* while pretending that the information came from contra sources (Jacoby and Parry, 1987, p. 36). This violated federal law against using public funds for domestic propaganda purposes. There was also a campaign to discredit U.S. opponents of the contras. Although much of this operation had been run by Oliver North, a marine lieutenant colonel detailed to the National Security Council, using private funds, Casey himself had met with members of Congress and shared classified information ("disinformation") on the Sandinistas (the Marxist regime in Nicaragua). According to Republican Senator David Durenberger, the outrageous report portrayed any member of Congress who voted against contra aid as a "stooge of communism" (ibid.). Such domestic intrigue was not limited to the CIA.

## The CISPES Investigation

From 1981 to 1985 more than 100 individuals and groups that opposed Reagan administration policies in Central America were investigated by the FBI. Believing that CISPES (the Committee in Solidarity with the People of El Salvador) was a communist front for Central American Marxists, the investigation involved photographing rallies, collecting license plate numbers, tailing college students, and using informants. Although CISPES admitted providing humanitarian aid to areas controlled by El Salvadoran rebels, there was no evidence that it was aiding guerilla military operations (Jacoby, Sandza, and Parry, 1988, p. 29). Although the original investigation may have been justified as routine, it apparently got out of hand and began to resemble harassment of dissenters' constitutional rights. Of particular importance in the discovery of this operation was the fact that harassment of legitimate, nonviolent dissenting groups by intelligence agencies had obviously not ended with the death of J. Edgar Hoover.

## Torture

In her book *The Politics of Cruelty: An Essay on the Literature of Political Imprisonment,* Kate Millett (1994) describes how nations use torture as a conscious policy, as a method of rule to engender fear, as a general condition. She defines torture as:

> *Any act by which severe pain or suffering whether physical or mental, is intentionally inflicted by or at the instigation of a public official on*

*a person for such purposes as obtaining from him or a third person information or confession, punishing him for an act he has committed or is suspected of having committed, or intimidating him or other persons (ibid., p. 13).*

Although torture as a part of the process of criminal law was abolished throughout Europe by the 1870s it continued to be unofficially and secretively used for political crime, particularly against suspected subversives. Millett (ibid., p. 15) claimed that torture in the 1990s was practiced on a global scale greater than during the Spanish Inquisition.

In 1975 the U.N. General Assembly adopted the Declaration on the Protection of All Persons from Being Subjected to Torture and Other Cruel and Inhuman or Degrading Treatment or Punishment. Believing that a declaration was not sufficient, in 1977 the U.N. General Assembly asked the Commission on Human Rights to elaborate a draft convention on torture. This was developed and adopted by the General Assembly in 1984. Basic elements of the U.N. Convention Against Torture include:

- All signatory countries are required to criminalize acts of torture under their criminal law.
- No exceptional circumstances or justification for torture is recognized and torture-induced evidence is inadmissible in criminal trials.
- All participating countries agree to a system of universal jurisdiction and to either prosecute or extradite torturers.
- Each state will take effective legislative, administrative, and judicial measures to prosecute and investigate torturers.
- Cruel, inhuman, and degrading treatment will be prevented.
- Victims of torture have a right to compensation.
- The convention may be used as a grounds for extradition of alleged torturers to stand trial.

Ironically, most of the offending nations are signatories to the U.N. Convention Against Torture.

Roman law permitted the torture of barbarians but not citizens of Rome. "Its doctrine of torture influenced strongly two revivals of torture that the Western world has experienced—those of the thirteenth and twentieth century" (Peters, 1985, p. 98). About 1,000 years after Roman practice, the Inquisition restored torture as part of canon law from the time of Pope Innocent IV in 1252 until the Enlightenment in Spain in the nineteenth century. The twentieth century found the secretive reappearance of torture under special power acts that usually "temporarily" suspended constitutional rights under martial law and other emergency provisions and provided extraordinary "detention statutes" (Millett, 1994, p. 99). The French in Algeria and the British in Ireland both used such powers and practices in an attempt to hold the last outposts of empire. "Interrogation centers were set up and civil liberties suspended; confessions were frequently the result of tortures" (ibid., p. 101). Torture became institutionalized as a deliberate policy or strategy of intimidation.

In speaking of the use of torture in national security states in Latin America, Millett (1994, p. 252) points out:

> *Somehow the official version is always a lie, and even the most informative reports fail to produce results. Because if a trial ever takes place, the court fails to convict: the witnesses come forward, the bodies are exhumed and analyzed for evidence of torture by experts, yet somehow the military always escapes unscathed. Somehow the national security state maintains its immunity; it is such a general phenomenon now, such a widespread ideology so essential to the military element and its unchallenged power in the society of the region and its neocolonial mission, that, like a colony of bacteria temporarily in remission, it simply relocates and continues to operate with impunity.*

In the Middle East, Iraq and Iran in particular have been singled out for violations of human rights and use of torture. During the Iran-Iraq War, Iraqi warplanes dropped canisters of poison gas on Kurdish civilians killing 5,000 and injuring thousands more. Amnesty International also accused Iraqi security services of routinely torturing the children of dissidents and other opponents of the regime. Before the bodies of Kurdish children were released, families had to pay an "execution tax" to cover the expense of coffins, transportation, and bullets. Children were described as having fingernails extracted and as having been subject to sexual attacks and electric shock ("Iraq," 1989).

Reminiscent of the Spanish Inquisition, the theocracy of Iran in the 1980s and 1990s tortured in the name of the Lord. Continual condemnation by the United Nations and human rights organizations was ignored. Khomeini was well aware of the value of deliberate terror. The commander of the ayatollah's revolutionary guards, Mohsen Resa'i, acknowledged that torture and execution of political prisoners were part of a general policy. "Today in many sectors we act through terror," he said on November 3, 1985. "We create a solid nationwide terror which controls the counter-revolutionaries. When this terror is lifted, the counter-revolutionaries come to life and spread" (Anderson and Van Atta, 1985).

Iranian torture practices included:

- Injecting prisoners with morphine until they were heavily addicted and then bringing on the excruciating pain of withdrawal.
- The rape of female prisoners including the forcible marriage and rape of virgins by revolutionary guards on the eve of their executions.

- Prisoners have been drenched in alcohol and set afire or flogged with rubber hoses with thick steel cables.
- Blood was drained from prisoners about to be executed (ibid.) and used in plasma banks for wounded Iranian soldiers.
- In a similar practice, the organs of prisoners were routinely used as a source of "spare parts" or involuntary organ donor bank.
- The Shari'a, the Islamic legal code, was restored under the Iranian theocracy complete with its gissas (quesas) which calls for amputations for thievery, flogging for sexual transgressions, and stoning for female adultery. Exhibit 2.3 at the end of this chapter details Iran's human rights violations.

## *Slavery*

Human bondage, once approved by all major religions, still persists. Britain's Anti-Slavery International, perhaps the world's oldest human rights organization, estimated there were over 100 million people living in slavery throughout the world in 1992 (Masland *et al.,* 1992):

- In Mauritania, more than 100,000 descendants of Africans conquered by Arabs in the twelfth century still live as slaves.
- Slavery is even making a comeback in countries such as the Sudan with the Arab tribes people practicing raiding and slave-taking.
- In the Middle East, gulf sheikdoms treat their guest workers as slaves, often not paying them, keeping them locked up, and withholding their passports.
- Some labor practices are modern versions of slavery. In the Dominican Republic, poor Haitians are recruited to work the cane fields and are then kept in debt-bondage, their pay never covering the cost of their company-supplied housing and food.
- In Southeast Asia young girls, as young as twelve and thirteen, are sold or abducted into prostitution.
- Debt bondage in Latin America enslaves whole generations working for free to pay the debt of the previous generation.

The U.N. Commission on Human Rights and the General Assembly seldom discuss the continued existence of slavery in the world. Its U.N. Working Group on Contemporary Forms of Slavery is understaffed and underfunded. Publicity and economic sanctions would hold promise in pressuring regimes that tolerate such practices (Masland *et al.,* 1992). In 1994 a new abolitionist movement of sorts was begun when Amnesty International's American branch voted to add the emancipation of chattel slaves to its mandate (Jacobs and Athie, 1994).

## Patriarchal Crime

*Patriarchal crime* refers to crime that is committed against women and/or children in the name of traditional male authority and dominance. In 1980 the United Nations summed the burden of gender inequality:

> *Women, half the world's population, did two thirds of the world's work, earned one tenth of the world's income and owned one hundredth of the world's property. Fourteen years later, despite the fall of repressive regimes, a decade of high growth, the spread of market economics and the rise of female prime ministers and CEOs, women remain victims of abuse and discrimination just about everywhere (MacFarquhar, 1994, pp. 42–43).*

In the mid-nineties the following patriarchal practices were common:

- After the collapse of the former Soviet Union women were disproportionately thrown out of work.
- In China in the nineties most of the workers in the sweatshops fueling the country's meteoric economic ascent were women.
- In certain Asian countries where sons were more valued, medical technology provided new means of eliminating unwanted baby girls.
- A "global epidemic of violence" continues against women according to the U.N. (ibid.).
- Bride-burning in order to gain additional dowries from later brides is a growing practice in India. "Femicide" has become a common practice (Caputi and Russell, 1990).
- In Morocco the penalty for female adultery can be death, but not for male adultery.
- Genital mutilation of young females is a common practice in some African countries.

Females in particular tend to be victims of slavery and related human rights abuses, and this is supported by a patriarchal ideology. *Patriarchal ideology* is defined as a discourse which supports the abuse of women who violate the ideals of male power and control over women in intimate relationships (DeKeseredy and Kelly, 1993, p. 26). DeKeseredy and Kelly (Ibid.) further explain:

> *Feminist scholars argue that a substantial number of male actions, values and beliefs are microsocial expressions of broader patriarchal forces. While there is no precise definition of patriarchy, Dobash and Dobash (1979) point out that it consists of a structure and an ideology. Structurally patriarchy is an hierarchical organization of institutions and social relations that enable men to maintain more power and privilege than women. Ideologically, patriarchal relationships are legitimated to the extent of creating an acceptance of subordination, even by those subordinated.*

Patriarchal authority (pater potentes) over wife, child, and chattel still underlies family law (Millett, 1994, p. 99). Thus ideological justification for political criminality is not limited to political or religious causes, but includes preservation of a gender status quo of male superordination.

Throughout history human beings have been subject to the whims of arbitrary authority and repression. In fact, much of the celebrated history of humankind has been the ever-so-grudging victories of common people to carve out rights and freedoms from government tyrannies. Even in developed, democratic societies perceived emergencies and threats have led authorities to suspend constitutional guarantees or seek shortcuts in the name of protecting the state from danger. The fact that slavery, torture, genocide, and major human rights violations still stalk the globe calls for the need for continuing vigilance and revelation of such practices by countries and world bodies rather than a policy that tolerates business as usual in the name of economic or political harmony. In the mid-nineties China, Iran, Iraq, and Serbia should remain on the world's list of pariah nations until they are willing to honor human rights and act as civilized nations.

---

**EXHIBIT 2.2   State Department Human Rights Report on Bosnia-Herzegovina**

*Bosnia and Herzegovina*

Bosnia and Herzegovina, one of six constituent republics of the former Yugoslavia, became a sovereign state in April 1992 when 63 percent of its voters endorsed independence in a free and fair referendum. Pan-Serbian nationalists loyal to Serbian Democratic Party (SDS) leader Radovan Karadzic boycotted the referendum, and former Yugoslav National Army units which had organized themselves into a Bosnian Serb armed militia (BSA) declared their support for Karadzic. Backed by the Serbian authorities in Belgrade, the BSA began a brutal campaign of terror—in which acts of genocide took place—to establish an ethnically pure state linking Serb-occupied territory in Croatia with Serbia/Montenegro to form "greater Serbia." Human rights abuses in Bosnia occurred in an environment of war,

occupation, a struggle for territory and power, the breakdown of a multiethnic system, and efforts to force the duly elected Bosnian Government to accept an ethnic division of the State. The Bosnian Government is Muslim-dominated but continues to support a multiethnic society, and elected officials are drawn proportionally from all national groups.

Bosnia's population consisted of 4.4 million people before the war, 44 percent of whom were Muslim, 31 percent Serb, 17 percent Croat, and 8 percent other nationalities. By October 1993, some 200,000 Bosnians were said to have died as a result of the conflict; over 800,000 became refugees outside Bosnia; and another 1.2 million were displaced within the nation.

*Continued*

---

Source: U.S. State Department. Country Reports on Human Rights Practices for 1993. Washington, D.C.: Government Printing Office, 1994, pp. 806–814.

**EXHIBIT 2.2**  *Continued*

As BSA units swept through northern and eastern Bosnia in 1992, Karadzic declared the establishment of the "Republika Srpska" or "Serb Republic." Techniques employed by the BSA, which Serbs themselves referred to as "ethnic cleansing," included: laying siege to cities and indiscriminately shelling civilian inhabitants; "strangling" cities (i.e., withholding food deliveries and utilities so as to starve and freeze residents); executing noncombatants; establishing concentration camps where thousands of prisoners were summarily executed and tens of thousands subjected to torture and inhumane treatment; using prisoners as human shields; employing rape as a tool of war to terrorize and uproot populations; forcing large numbers of civilians to flee to other regions; razing villages to prevent the return of displaced persons; and interfering with international relief efforts, including attacks on relief personnel.

In early 1993, the BSA, supported by paramilitary forces from Serbia and Montenegro, moved to complete ethnic cleansing campaigns in eastern Bosnia. The BSA virtually destroyed the hamlet of Cerska, chasing its residents into forests and mine fields, and subjected Srebrenica, Gorazde, and Zepa to strangulation and intense shelling. International protective forces which reached the enclaves in March described conditions as the worst they had ever seen and noted that there were virtually no residents left to help.

By late spring, the BSA had consolidated most of its military and territorial gains in the east. Facing international pressure and tightened economic sanctions against Serbia/Montenegro, it scaled back assaults on the enclaves. But at midyear, the BSA renewed attacks on Sarajevo and tightened its grip on vital humanitarian supply lines, prompting a North Atlantic Treaty Organization (NATO) threat of air strikes. This led to a reduction in shelling until December, when attacks again approached July levels. Ethnic cleansing campaigns in 1993 also took place in Banja Luka and Bijeljina, and the BSA waged sporadic attacks on Tuzla, Doboj, Brcko, Olovo, Teocak, and Maglaj (this last town in conjunction with the Bosnian Croats) through December.

In April periodic skirmishing between the Bosnian government army and the militia of Mate Boban's Croatian Defense Council (HVO), the main representative of the Bosnian Croat minority, escalated into outright war. Regular Croatian army units, originally in Bosnia under a bilateral military cooperation pact, fought on the side of Boban's forces; Croatian authorities also offered material to the HVO but significantly less than that which Serbian authorities provided to the BSA.

The trigger for the surge in government-HVO fighting was Boban's insistence on the creation of a separate Bosnian Croat "Republic of Herceg-Bosna" within Bosnia and Herzegovina. Mostar was to be its capital, and government troops in the region were told to submit to HVO command. When the Government refused, the HVO blockaded Mostar, attacked it, and brutalized, confined, and raped its Muslim residents in an assault containing some of the most extreme human rights abuses in Bosnia and Herzegovina in 1993.

The HVO also engaged in vicious acts in central Bosnia. In April the HVO

**EXHIBIT 2.2**   *Continued*

killed up to 100 noncombatants in the central Bosnian hamlet of Ahmići and then razed the village. In October it massacred at least a score of Muslim civilians at Stupni Dol. The HVO and BSA engaged in localized collaboration on the battlefield in the central Bosnian enclave of Maglaj, creating conditions of extreme deprivation there.

Bosnia government forces perpetrated a number of abuses and atrocities in 1993, for the most part against the Bosnian Croats. In September government troops killed dozens of Croat civilians at Uzdol; the HVO charged that many more government massacres not yet investigated occurred in central Bosnia. As the tide in the fighting turned in favor of the Government in the fall, tens of thousands of Bosnian Croats fled or were driven from their homes, most going either to Croatia or to parts of Bosnia under HVO control. In November government forces killed two Franciscan friars in Fojnica and openly looted Bosnian Croat-owned shops in Vares.

In 1993 as in 1992, all national groups were victimized by the conflict, and all sides violated the Geneva conventions. But the BSA, with Belgrade's complicity, launched the Bosnian conflict through its aggressive ethnic cleansing campaign. Its pursuit of a policy of dispersing and destroying populations based on religious and national affiliation created a climate of prejudice and fear that ultranationalists on all sides subsequently exploited.

International efforts to stop the conflict were not successful by year's end. At best, international attention diminished the level of fighting for short periods of time. The participants to the conflict negotiated and signed numerous ceasefires but did not adhere to them. Bosnian Serb ethnic cleansing campaigns in eastern enclaves in the spring occurred even as Karadzic and Serbian President Slobodan Milosevic negotiated aspects of a settlement plan. Bosnian Croat atrocities in the spring, summer, and fall took place in spite of Boban's formal acceptance of several internationally sponsored peace initiatives. Bosnian government offensives against Bosnian Croat enclaves in central Bosnia late in the year occurred during sessions of the Geneva negotiations. Resolutions adopted by the United Nations Security Council failed to have a significant impact on the human rights situation or the war itself. U.N.-deployed peacekeepers (UNPROFOR)—some units of which were being investigated for abuses, corruption and partiality—were not equipped for peacemaking and found that there was no peace to keep.

The U.N.'s Commission of Experts, established by a Security Council resolution in October 1992 to investigate possible war crimes, continued to study abuses of human rights in Bosnia, Serbia, and Croatia. The War Crimes Tribunal was created by a subsequent resolution in February to assess the culpability of alleged perpetrators of atrocities and issue a comprehensive report on violations of human rights and humanitarian law. At year's end, all judges had been sworn in and a chief prosecutor named. Between September 1992 and June 1993, the United States Government submitted eight separate reports to the War Crimes Commission summarizing thousands of instances of

*Continued*

**EXHIBIT 2.2**    *Continued*

killings, torture, rape, interference with humanitarian deliveries, mass deportations, and other violations of humanitarian law. In addition, the United States provided the United Nations with 400 refugee reports totaling over 1,000 pages. Illustrative examples from these submissions appear in sections of the report below.

*Respect for Human Rights*

*Section 1. Respect for the Integrity of the Person, Including Freedom from:*
   a. *Political and Other Extrajudicial Killing.*—In the circumstances of the Bosnian war, targeted killings were difficult to distinguish from killings resulting from indiscriminate attacks and unpremeditated actions. (See Section 1.g. for a description of large-scale, war-related atrocities committed against civilians, including killings.) While only the pro-Karadzic Bosnian Serbs pursued ethnic cleansing as a matter of broad policy, local units of HVO soldiers and Bosnian government troops, as well as Serbian and Montenegrin paramilitaries and civilian gangs and mobs, killed many people out of nationalistic or religious hatred. The United Nations confirmed the existence of dozens of mass grave sites, as yet unexhumed. The Bosnian Government, HVO and Bosnian Serbs alleged that there were many more.

   During ethnic cleansing campaigns in the early part of 1993, the BSA targeted local civic and religious leaders with the goal of figuratively decapitating Muslim society. Among the prominent individuals assassinated for political reasons was Bosnian Deputy Prime Minister Hakija Turajlic, who was shot at point-blank range by Bosnian Serb soldiers in

January while riding in a U.N. vehicle that had been stopped—against U.N. procedures—at a roadblock.

   At least 10 international relief workers died in 1993, shot by BSA or HVO soldiers or snipers of unknown affiliation. Sixty-some UNPROFOR soldiers died in outright attacks or as a result of sniper fire, and 34 journalists were killed (10 in 1993) since the beginning of the conflict. The U.N. High Commissioner for Refugees (UNHCR) and some international relief agencies suspended operations on several occasions during 1993 because of danger to personnel.

   b. *Disappearance.*—There were no reliable figures for the numbers of missing persons, but with hundreds or thousands dead, thousands incarcerated, and over 2 million having fled their homes, many more were missing. The Bosnian Government claimed that 26,000 Bosnians were missing as of May. Two international journalists were known to be missing.

   c. *Torture and Other Cruel, Inhuman, or Degrading Treatment or Punishment.*—In spite of intense international pressure to close the prison camps discovered under BSA control in mid-1992, there were probably still scores of detention facilities for civilians, including women, children, and the elderly, in operation throughout Bosnia at the end of 1993. As many as 260 camps have been known to exist at one time or another during the conflict. In January 1993, the U.S. Government estimated that there were 135 Serb-run detention centers in Bosnia. Many of these formed part of the penal system established in BSA-held areas in mid-1992; a significant number in this network were closed by the end of 1993. Many HVO and

**EXHIBIT 2.2**  *Continued*

Muslim camps, numerous in the summer and fall of 1993, were also closed by the end of the year.

Because camps closed down and reopened depending in part on the status of negotiations and the presence of international observers, it was difficult to estimate the numbers of persons detained. The three sides defined all males between 16 and 65 as combatants, so some civilian detainees were listed as prisoners of war. In October the UNHCR reported that the HVO was holding 4,200 Muslims and Roma in registered centers, down from the summer's high of 15,000 (many of whom were Muslim soldiers formerly in the HVO.) According to the UNHCR, the government held 1,100 detainees in registered centers as of October. The BSA was believed to be holding 550 Muslims and Croats in registered camps as of October, significantly less than the number of those incarcerated in 1992. Far more were held in unregistered centers. Observers stated throughout the year that the three sides hid prisoners and criticized the HVO's refusal in mid-1993 to allow international officials to visit camps around Mostar, where numerous refugees reported conditions to be dreadful.

Camps with poor living conditions in 1993 included those in Batkovici, Kamenica, Trnopolje, and Doboj (operated by the BSA); Rodoc, Otok, and Dretelj (operated by the HVO); and Zenica and Konjic (operated by the Government). At Dretlj, perhaps the most notorious camp of 1993, the UNHCR found prisoners in conditions of "appalling brutality and degradation," with broken ribs and fingers, bruises, and heart irregularities. Amnesty International said prisoners at Dretelj were so cramped

that they could not lie down. Beatings and torture were reported at BSA camps in Manjaca, Batkovici, and Prijedor in the spring, at HVO camps in Rodoc and Jablanica in the summer, and at government camps in Visoko and Konjic, also in summer. Summary executions and deaths due to torture or neglect were attested to in 1993 and almost certainly continued through December.

Individuals detained in 1993 told of meager and sometimes poisoned or spoiled rations, malnutrition, poor or nonexistent sanitation, withholding of medical care, forced labor (performed by women as well as men) including trench-digging on the front lines and removal of corpses and the wounded, forced blood donations, overcrowding, and lack of amenities such as bedding. There were scattered reports of groups of prisoners being conscripted into enemy armies and of prisoners of one nationality being sold as conscripts from the second to the third nationality. The three sides were accused of using prisoners as human shields. In June the BSA arrested non-Serbs in Doboj and forced them to stand as a living front line in combat areas nearby.

Bosnian Muslim women in the spring and summer accused HVO and BSA soldiers of perpetrating mass rape. The UNHCR noted that HVO soldiers may have raped 100 or more women, some in gang-rape situations; many of the rapes occurred in connection with evictions from Mostar in mid-1993 and fighting near Vitez earlier in the year. Reports of rapes by Bosnian Serb civil and military police and soldiers continued, but the number of such charges was lower for

*Continued*

**EXHIBIT 2.2**  *Continued*

1993 than for 1992, when the BSA first practiced mass rape as a tool of war. Reports from Brcko, Nerici, Stolina, Skijana, and Grcica described the continuing confinement and sexual abuse of a total of at least 130 young Muslim women by the BSA. UNPROFOR troops were accused of frequenting some locations where Muslim women were held. Bosnian Croat women charged government troops with raping them in Mostar and Bugojno; the Bosnian Serbs also said government soldiers had raped Bosnian Serb women. International observers were not able to corroborate most accusations because access to victims was very limited.

d. *Arbitrary Arrest, Detention, or Exile.*—The BSA continued to round up members of the intelligentsia and target regional and local political, economic, and religious figures in an effort to destroy the social structure of other nationality groups. Sarajevo's Catholic Archbishop, Monsignor Vinko Puljic, was abducted by the BSA and held temporarily along with his UNPROFOR guards in November. Ransom was sometimes an additional motive for arbitrary arrest and detention. BSA and HVO troops abducted government bodyguards of international officials from UNPROFOR vehicles on several occasions and held UNPROFOR soldier hostage for brief periods.

In addition to the large number of civilians detained in prison camps (see Section 1.c.), some civilians were detained for prisoner exchanges. Families of military officers were abducted with regularity because they had a high exchange value. In Vitez in April, both the NVO and the government forces arrested large numbers of civilians for use in future exchanges. The residents of some entire villages were prevented from leaving municipal confines (see Section 2.d.) so they could be used in prisoner exchanges. The Serbs detained Muslims, Croats, and Roma for use as unpaid labor in combat zones (see Section 6.c.).

While the Bosnian Government did not practice exile per se, detainees released by the Government, as well as those released by the BSA and HVO, were sometimes forced over the border (see Section 1.g.). Ethnic cleansing and mass population movements before advancing troops resulted in forced dislocation that was equivalent to exile for the half of Bosnia's prewar population that at the end of the year was seeking refuge abroad or protection elsewhere within Bosnia.

e. *Denial of Fair Public Trial.*—In areas under its control, the Bosnian government attempted to maintain a functioning judicial system. International legal experts have said the March trial for war crimes of two Bosnian Serb soldiers who had confessed to mass killings and mass rape at the behest of commanding officers was fair.

Summary trials and executions of local warlords who served as irregular government army commanders took place in Sarajevo in October, during a government crackdown on rogue elements in the military. The individuals who were tried and executed had been identified as responsible for seizing UNPROFOR vehicles and controlling extensive black market activities.

Near the front lines and in BSA and HVO-controlled areas, military authorities who held power did not guarantee the legal rights of non-Serbs and non-Croats, respectively.

**EXHIBIT 2.2** *Continued*

f. *Arbitrary Interference with Privacy, Family, Home, or Correspondence.*—Virtually all officials of the three sides (and international observers as well) assumed they were subjected to systematic surveillance. Most were unwilling to use telephones or the mail system, to the extent that they functioned, for any but the most routine business. Citizens who were interrogated reported that their questioners did not conceal the practice of surveillance.

g. *Use of Excessive Force and Violations of Humanitarian Law in Internal Conflicts.*—Violations of humanitarian law and international conventions on the treatment of civilians in time of war were widespread and egregious. Many human rights violations committed by the BSA occurred as part of specific policies to expel Muslims and Croats from areas the Serbs desired for themselves. The HVO engaged in localized efforts to drive Muslims away from territories they sought to occupy. Other abuses took place on a more haphazard basis. Paramilitaries, vigilantes, "weekend warriors," criminal gangs reporting to local warlords, and civilian mobs were responsible for numerous instances of crimes against civilians. Atrocities detailed in this section include indiscriminate attacks against civilians; forced population movements; interference with the delivery of humanitarian relief, including attacks on international relief workers; interference with utilities and infrastructure; and forced conscriptions. Mistreatment of prisoners of war resembled mistreatment of civilian detainees and is handled in Section 1.c. Use of prisoners as human shields is also treated in Section 1.c. (See the Country Report on Serbia/Montenegro for information on Bosnian Serb paramilitaries who crossed the border into Serbia to attack Sandzak Muslims.)

The BSA's relentless military assault on the eastern enclaves in early 1993, its periodic attacks on Sarajevo, and ethnic cleansing campaigns in Banja Luka, Bijeljina, and towns in north-central Bosnia throughout the year resulted in tens of thousands of civilians deaths. U.N. observers reported that mass killings of civilians and attacks on refugees trying to flee Srebrenica, Gorazde, and Zepa were commonplace. UNPROFOR claimed the BSA was attacking and seizing one or two Muslim villages a day in the eastern region throughout March. In April and May, concern over conditions in besieged enclaves prompted the passage of U.N. resolutions that declared Srebrenica and subsequently Gorazde, Zepa, Sarajevo, Tuzla, and Bihac "safe areas" where security and relief deliveries were to have been guaranteed. Heavy BSA attacks on the safe areas continued through June, and more sporadic attacks occurred during the rest of the year. By the summer, most of Gorazde and surrounding hamlets had been leveled. Many villages outside Srebrenica were completely destroyed, as were some villages in the vicinity of Zepa.

In Banja Luka, the BSA killed and mutilated Muslim and Croat civilians as part of ethnic cleansing campaigns throughout the year. When a group of Muslims under attack sought protection in a local mosque in February, the BSA attacked the mosque. BSA advances also destroyed much of Maglaj and Doboj and many smaller communities near Brcko. Several civilians in Maglaj were killed

*Continued*

**EXHIBIT 2.2** *Continued*

while attempting to retrieve airdropped parcels, their only source of food in the latter half of the year. BSA killings of individuals in central Bosnia, as in the eastern enclaves and Banja Luka, sometimes involved mutilations.

Sarajevo was under heavy BSA pressure throughout the year. Thirty civilians, including a leading physician delivering baby food, were killed in the first 10 days of December. In November, 9 children were killed and 20 injured by a BSA shell that fell on a school. As in the eastern enclaves, the BSA deliberately aimed shells at hospitals, mosques, markets, cemeteries, and residential areas.

HVO attacks, particularly on Muslims, increased dramatically in 1993. The HVO slaughtered approximately 100 Muslims in the central Bosnian village of Ahmici in April. Masked Croats killed Muslim civilians in Vitez in house-to-house fighting later that month. In September, the United Nations said HVO shelling killed 10 to 15 Muslims a day in Mostar. The HVO in the spring also reportedly shot two Serb women who were part of a small contingent of Serb inhabitants of Mostar forced out of the city and told to walk to BSA-held positions. In October between 25 and 50 Muslim villagers, including women and children, were killed by the HVO at Stupni Dol, near Vares; the remainder of the town's population was taken captive and the village entirely destroyed. The HVO shelled UNHCR officials attempting to gain access to Stupni Dol for 3 days before finally letting medical examiners through. Later in the month, the Bosnian Government claimed the discovery of a mass grave in Tasovcici containing the bodies of alleged victims of HVO attacks in Stolac and Capljina.

Government troops also targeted civilians in 1993, particularly Bosnian Croats. Thirty Bosnian Croat civilians were massacred at Uzdo in September. Survivors of the attack said they were used as human shields. Government soldiers murdered two Franciscan friars in Fojnica in November. The HVO charged the Government with killing more than 100 other Bosnian Croat civilians between April and October in a variety of central Bosnian locations including Trusina, Doljani, Bugojno, Jakovice, Kiseljak, and Kopijari. Witnesses described torture preceding the killings and mutilation afterward. The United Nations is investigating the charges. Government soldiers killed a score of Bosnian Serb civilians in the village of Skelani, in the Srebrenica pocket, in January, and shot several Bosnian Serbs in Sarajevo, including two elderly people being evacuated.

The Bosnian conflict has brutally uprooted millions of civilians. The residents of Cerska and the populations of several villages in its vicinity were driven out of their homes as part of the BSA's ethnic cleansing campaigns in eastern Bosnia in early 1993. The BSA then plundered and burned or shelled virtually all houses. Large segments of the populations of other eastern enclaves also fled the BSA in the spring, some across mined territory. Many refugees from the BSA went to Tuzla (behind the front lines,) the population of which increased four-fold in the spring. World Health Organization (WHO) officials in the city termed conditions "desperate" because the limited infrastructure could not handle the huge refugee population.

Bosnian Serbs pursuing cleansing operations in southern Herzegovina

**EXHIBIT 2.2** *Continued*

ordered residents of Trebinje and Bileca to leave the district in January, killed several who did not comply, and bombed mosques. Over 1,000 Muslims fled to Montenegro. In an effort to frighten non-Serbs into leaving Banja Luka, BSA soldiers cut phone lines, beat residents, sealed off and bombed non-Serb shops, seized non-Serb apartments, fire-bombed mosques, threatened citizens with rape, and warned non-Serbs via the local television station they would have to pay heavy fines for remaining. (As noted above, they also killed and mutilated non-Serb residents of Banja Luka.) Some non-Serbs in Jijeljina were reportedly forced to give up house keys and property deeds before being driven to front lines and ordered to walk across them. In August a group of Muslims from Bijeljina was driven through Serbia proper to the Hungarian border, where they were dumped. Cleansing operations in central Bosnia continued. Of 43,000 Muslims recorded as living in Doboj in the 1991 census, only 1,000 remained in November 1993, according to the United Nations.

HVO troops worked most actively around Mostar to force non-Croats to move out. In May the HVO rounded up thousands of Muslims and imprisoned them temporarily in the heliodrome stadium while simultaneously running thousands more out of town. When several made their way back, they found former Muslim areas empty and buildings shot full of holes. In June the HVO burned the personal papers, including apartment leases, of Muslims who had not so far been detained or chased out and forced them across a bridge under a hail of gunfire to a section of east Mostar where they were ghettoized. By the end of June, international relief agencies said the HVO had destroyed virtually all Muslim property in Mostar. In July a number of the ghettoized Muslims in Mostar were boarded onto buses and dumped in Croatia against their will. In September the UNHCR described signs of malnutrition and physical abuse among the 14,000 Muslims who had escaped Mostar and surrounding towns and made it to Jablancia, behind the front lines in central Bosnia.

The HVO chased Muslims out of several central Bosnian locations in early 1993, including an Italian-run refugee camp whose staff and inhabitants were forced to flee; local HVO commanders said they planned to expel more Muslims from the region to make room for Bosnian Croats who were homeless as a result of government-HVO fighting. At midyear, the HVO began evicting Muslims from Stolac, Capljina, and Livno, forcing as many as 20,000 across the front lines. Before the evictions began, local HVO officials disconnected Muslims' telephones, requisitioned their cars, and made radio broadcasts saying their security could not be guaranteed.

Tens of thousands of Bosnian Croat refugees fled Konjic, Travnik, Novi Travnik, and Vitez in fear of advancing government troops in the spring. In September government forces used death threats and extortion to pressure Bosnian Croats to leave Zenica; a month later government soldiers rounded up 1,000 Bosnian Croat refugees trying to flee Konjic, robbed them, beat them, and fired shots at them. In November the UNHCR described the situation around Vares as

*Continued*

---

**EXHIBIT 2.2**  *Continued*

"chaotic," with gunmen terrorizing 15,000 mostly Bosnian Croat civilians who had fled their homes in fear of attack. Boban claimed 150,000 to 190,000 Bosnian Croats had been displaced by fighting in central Bosnia or driven out by the Government as of late fall.

All parties to the conflict interfered with humanitarian assistance, but abuses by the BSA were most widespread in 1993. In February BSA troops issued orders formally sealing off Bihac, Zepa, Gorazde, and Srebrenica from relief deliveries, which in any case had not occurred for many months. In Zepa, Cerska, Srebrenica, Konjevic Polje, Kamenica, and Gorazde, deaths due to a combination of severe malnutrition, exposure, and wounds that could not be treated for lack of medicine occurred in the winter and spring. WHO doctors said 20 to 30 people died of untreated wounds, lack of food, and exposure every day in Srebrenica during the month of March. When observers reached Zepa at the end of January, they found the population eating bread made of straw. After seizing 14 villages near Cerska in March, the BSA blocked international evacuation of the wounded, resulting in more deaths. The BSA then shelled UNPROFOR troops attempting to carry a field hospital into Srebrenica and threatened to fire on German relief planes if Germany participated in the relief effort. The WHO reported that tuberculosis and hepatitis were increasing sharply among the refugee population of Tuzla as the "pharmaceutical situation collapsed." In April the BSA blocked convoys bound for Gorazde, where starvation was reportedly imminent, as the ICRC announced from Zagreb it was considering withdrawing from Bosnia because of BSA

harassment. In June BSA positions shelled a UNHCR convoy near Maglaj, killing three relief workers.

Throughout the remainder of the year, more relief workers were killed, more citizens died of deprivation, and more vitally import medical evacuations failed to take place both inside and outside the United Nations' safe zones due to BSA threats and harassment. U.N. Secretary General Boutros Boutros-Ghali, on a trip to the safe areas shortly after they were declared, described conditions brought about by longterm BSA denial of relief as "appalling."

The HVO began closing roads leading to Muslim areas of central Bosnia to all commercial traffic in February. In April the HVO seized and briefly held several international relief workers near Kiseljak, claiming they had sided with the Government. In May the HVO began blocking all relief convoys bound for Mostar; as a result, almost none reached the city until late August. Participants in an HVO attack on a U.N. convoy in central Bosnia in mid-1993 said they were acting under orders to threaten European Community (EC) and U.N. officials. In July the HVO began charging tolls termed "extortionate" by relief workers. In August the UNHCR temporarily suspended relief deliveries to central Bosnia because its convoys were being harassed by the HVO. International relief agencies reported that the HVO had targeted its workers for harassment and abuse, bound and gagged UNHCR employees in Mostar, and fired a grenade (which did not explode) at an ICRC truck. In November an HVO commander accused of leading the attack on Stupni Dol ordered all U.N. relief workers to depart Kiseljak.

**EXHIBIT 2.2** *Continued*

Later in the month, a combination of malnutrition and exposure brought about by HVO interference with relief resulted in several deaths in Mostar.

In February the Bosnian Government responded to the BSA's order to seal off the eastern enclaves and Bihac from relief by refusing relief deliveries to Sarajevo. Frustrated at the politicization of humanitarian assistance, the UNHCR temporarily suspended aid to many parts of Bosnia. In March local officials in Srebrenica detained UNPROFOR General Phillipe Morillon as a shield against further BSA shelling. (Morillon subsequently elected to remain as a gesture of solidarity with the people of the enclave.) In Sarajevo the Government refused the delivery of fuel bound for Bosnian Serb hospitals. In Mostar local government officials detained the first convoy to arrive in the city in 3 months and a UNPROFOR contingent as well, apparently in the hope that keeping them in Mostar would prevent the HVO from renewing its attacks on the city. In the fall, government soldiers attacked a UNHCR convoy near Novi Travnik and killed the driver; they subsequently shot and wounded a U.N. driver in Kakanj after his convoy refused to hand over fuel. In December government soldiers attacked a Croatian convoy attempting to deliver relief to Bosnian Croats in Nova Bila.

At the end of 1993, UNPROFOR forces were under investigation for showing favoritism in the provision of humanitarian assistance. At year's end, the United Nations was investigating reports that some UNPROFOR units attempted to influence the outcome of the conflict through preferential deliveries of aid.

The BSA interfered with utilities and infrastructure to a much greater extent than the HVO or Government. The WHO, terming the situation in Sarajevo "desperate" in January, said several elderly residents of nursing homes had frozen to death due to Bosnian Serb diversions of natural gas to the capital. The BSA cut the water supply to Srebrenica in April and prevented U.N. workers from repairing it. In July a U.S. Office of Foreign Disaster Assistance relief team visiting Sarajevo reported that most houses lacked electricity and gas; water was generally unpotable, and dysentery was spreading. The UNHCR noted in July that Gorazde's water supply was contaminated with human waste as a result of BSA interference. In October, 10 days after the announcement that the BSA had achieved its aims and ended the siege of Sarajevo, heavy shelling resumed, and gas supplies were reduced. The WHO reported an increase in burns as residents used more "do-it-yourself" heating contraptions in an effort to keep warm. In November the UNHCR said some patients had died in hospitals that remained unheated due to the BSA cutoff of gas, and cold had made some patients too weak to withstand operations. As of the end of the year, Sarajevo was under the heaviest mortar fire since before NATO's August warning, and water, electricity, and gas flows remained sporadic and at barely usable levels.

The HVO prevented international relief workers from supplying water pumps and water-purifying equipment to Mostar in the summer. In November the HVO destroyed Mostar's 400-year-old UNESCO-protected Ottoman Foot Bridge, which supplied the Muslim ghetto in the

*Continued*

**EXHIBIT 2.2**  *Continued*

eastern sector with water. A Belgrade architect noted that the bridge had "linked cultures and people" and remarked that, "with a loss like this, people lose their place in time." No instances of government interference with utilities and infrastructure have come to light, but government forces near Mostar in August did threaten to release the floodgates on the Neretva River to drive the HVO out of the area.

The three sides practiced forced conscriptions to a limited degree in 1993. In some BSA-held areas, those who refused the draft were dismissed from work and detained. Some families of men who refused conscription were also dismissed. In April the BSA forced evacuation flights from Srebrenica to divert to BSA-held Zvornik, where evacuees were taken prisoner and threatened with conscription. The HVO segregated Bosnian Croat males from among displaced persons on the run near Stolac and Capljina and forced them to enlist in the HVO in October. There was no right to conscientious objection under Bosnian law; Serbs and Croats who refused the draft in Vanovici were arrested by local officials, conscripted into the government army, and taken to the front lines in the spring. Also in the spring, the Government prevented draft-age men from leaving Zepa and Sarajevo.

*Section 2. Respect for Civil Liberties, Including:*

a. *Freedom of Speech and Press.*— Bosnian Serb refugees complained of living in a virtual police state under Karadzic's SDS. They suffered harassment, dismissal, and incarceration at the hands of BSA soldiers and pro-Karadzic local officials for taking a public stance in support of the Bosnian government or for opposing the ideology of the SDS. A BSA

military court sentenced a Bosnian Serb worker to a prison term this summer for trying to broker cease-fire talks between the Government and BSA. A Bosnian Croat family living near the BSA detention facility in Trnopolje was shot because they "looked at the camp" too frequently, and officials feared they might talk about it. In 1993 as well as 1992, numerous Bosnian Serbs were killed by BSA soldiers for speaking up in defense of Bosnian Muslim neighbors.

Freedom of speech and debate was protected as a matter of principle in Bosnian schools, but due to security concerns educational institutions were open only sporadically, sometimes in unusual settings such as underground bunkers. In a move that denied freedom of thought and expression to all Bosnians, the BSA fire-bombed the national library in Sarajevo, destroying major collections of cultural importance to all nationalities.

Before the war, the principal Bosnian media—Sarajevo radio and television, the Sarajevo daily Oslobodjenje, the independent television station Yutel— were widely regarded as accurate and balanced. Olsobodjenje, with a multiethnic staff, has maintained standards of objectivity and accuracy that won international prizes and acclaim even under the difficult circumstances of the war. The newspaper endorsed the notion of a pluralistic Bosnia and supported democratic and progressive elements in the Government. Editorials freely criticized government policies and officials. Sarajevo also had a tabloid press that the Government tolerated, but authorities detained several reporters from Tanjug, the Belgrade-based news service, and denied visas to Radio Zagreb personnel.

**EXHIBIT 2.2**   *Continued*

The single television station operating in Sarajevo in 1993, funded by the Government, took a pro-government line. The Government also ran a radio station and allowed an independent station to broadcast. The government news agency, BH Press, emphasized reports of attacks against Muslims and downplayed reports of atrocities committed by government forces.

The SDS news agency SRNA, headquartered in Pale, provided biased and distorted reporting. Both SRNA and Tanjug, the Serbian news service, carried unsubstantiated reports of crimes against Serbs in order to reinforce ethnic Serb solidarity, promote ethnic hatred, and instigate violence. A pro-Karadzic television station that broadcast from Banja Luka transmitted reports directly from Serbia and received financial support from Belgrade Television. As noted in Section 1.g., in February it advised Muslims and Croats to leave Banja Luka or pay fines for remaining.

The HVO's newly established news agency, HABENA, reported Bosnian Croat casualty figures far in excess of those attested to by international relief organizations. Radio Zagreb regularly issued distorted reports. For example, in November it reported that Swedish peacekeepers detained by the HVO had been helping Muslims when in fact they were attempting to escort Bosnian Croat civilian refugees near Vares to safety.

b. *Freedom of Peaceful Assembly and Association.*—The right of peaceful assembly and association could not be observed in the conditions of war and violence. In areas not under he control of the Government, assemblies of persons whose nationality and religion were not

the same as those in power were regarded with suspicion and in some cases participants were subjected to harassment and attack. Even in government-controlled areas, large gatherings such as queues often attracted snipers.

c. *Freedom of Religion.*—Religious tolerance has been a tradition of the diverse Bosnian population for 500 years. Serbian Orthodox Bosnian Serbs, Roman Catholic Bosnian Croats, and Muslim Bosnians are largely indistinguishable in terms of language and physical appearance. But the war and ongoing atrocities radicalized many, and religion became one of the justifications for fighting. Citizens living in government-controlled areas enjoyed the greatest freedom of religion in 1993, as the Government remained committed to pluralism and included representatives of all religious groups.

In connection with ethnic cleansing campaigns, BSA troops systematically destroyed religious institutions and made cultural monuments specific targets. In areas under BSA control, virtually all mosques and Roman Catholic churches have been bombed, shelled, burned, or bulldozed, and statuary has been defaced. The BSA destroyed the last of Trebinje's mosques in April, after expelling the majority of the town's Muslims. Banja Luka's historic 16th century mosques were also demolished, as were all the mosques in Bijeljina.

The HVO destroyed mosques as well, including four in Stolac and one in Pocitelj this summer. The HVO charged the BSA and the Government with the destruction of 66 churches in the course of the conflict. All told, hundreds of mosques and

*Continued*

**EXHIBIT 2.2**  *Continued*

churches have been demolished, including several of unique architectural and cultural significance, since the war began.

Mixed marriages accounted for 20 to 30 percent of unions before the war began; citizens in mixed marriages faced difficult choices as the war expanded. In some cases, they hid their religious backgrounds or sought shelter with those of a different faith to avoid being separated from their families. In government-held areas, where commitment to religious diversity was a matter of law, individuals in mixed marriages had an easier time than those in BSA- or HVO-controlled areas.

d. *Freedom of Movement Within the Country, Foreign Travel, Emigration, and Repatriation.*—The wartime situation, coupled with mass detention and expulsion (discussed in Sections 1.d. and 1.g above), interfered with the free movement of millions of Bosnians. The changing front lines made many others virtual hostages within broad geographic areas. Sarajevo was the most heavily populated island of "hostages" in Bosnia. The lack of safe transportation into or out of the capital put citizens and officials at risk when they attempted to travel to other parts of the country or abroad. The airport was one of the most frequently attacked targets in the city.

In some cases citizens of whole villages were given orders to remain within specified confines, or be shot or fined, in order that a pool of people to perform labor and take part in prisoner exchanges could be maintained. In some areas, the BSA established local "Commissions for Exchange" to ensure that non-Serbs wishing to leave were exchanged for Serbs who wished to return. In March the BSA put in place procedures whereby non-Serbs wishing to go to other regions were not permitted to carry valuables or travel by car; non-Serbs were also required to pay higher prices for bus tickets and exorbitant transit taxes in BSA-controlled towns they crossed.

The Government inhibited movement by citizens in part to avoid a mass exodus. During the BSA sieges against the eastern enclaves in the spring, local officials sometimes prevented UNPROFOR from leaving areas under attack. The Government prevented large numbers of Bosnian Croats from leaving Bugojno and Banovici during the summer, using the civilians in prisoner exchanges and as forced labor. Local authorities announced in September that Zenica's 23,000 Bosnian Croats could not leave the city. (Earlier in the month, government soldiers had pressured them to depart against their will.) In Sarajevo the city's Secretariat of Evacuations often refused Bosnian Serbs permission to leave or delayed their departure for many months.

*Section 3. Respect for Political Rights: The Right of Citizens to Change Their Government*

The duly elected Bosnian Government did not have the means to protect its territory, to defend its sovereignty, or to guarantee its citizens' rights. Nearly 80 percent of the country was under the military control of various separatists supported by Serbia or Croatia. In this environment, the Bosnian Government's goal of establishing a secular, pluralistic, democratic society in an undivided land had little chance of success. Bosnia's only election, which occurred in April 1992, created a bicameral National Assembly with 240 seats, of which 99

**EXHIBIT 2.2** *Continued*

were filled by Muslims, 84 by Bosnian Serbs, 50 by Bosnian Croats, and 7 by others, in proportion to the composition of the population of the country at the time. There were no elections scheduled for 1993.

*Section 4. Governmental Attitude Regarding International and Nongovernmental Investigation of Alleged Violations of Human Rights*

The Bosnian Government, the BSA, and the HVO all agreed in principle to allow international observers access to territory under their control so alleged human rights abuses could be investigated. In practice, political and military authorities imposed obstacles and made it difficult for international officials to carry out investigations.

All sides in the war viewed the work of international organizations through the prism of their political interests. All sides downplayed their own culpability for atrocities. Both the BSA and HVO denied responsibility for human rights abuses that international investigators assigned to them, claiming for example that the Government was killing its own civilians in the hope of blaming the other side for atrocities. No side has cooperated fully on the issue of examination of prisoners.

*Section 5. Discrimination Based on Race, Sex, Religion, Disability, Language, or Social Status*

*Women.*—In addition to being subjected to rape (Section 1.c.), women suffered other sorts of physical abuse in 1993. Muslim women in Mostar reported they were strip-searched (and in some cases raped) by male HVO soldiers before being evicted from the city. Before the war, discrimination against women was not officially practiced, although there were few women in prominent positions.

*Children.*—The United Nations Children's Fund (UNICEF) reported in June that 1,400 children had been killed and 12,800 wounded since the beginning of the conflict; 91 percent had witnessed shooting in the course of the conflict, 72 percent had had their homes shelled, 41 percent had witnessed a person being injured or killed, and 81 percent thought they could have been killed during 1993. Many lived on a diet of bread, rice, and pasta, when those goods were available, and had not eaten fresh fruit or vegetables since early 1992. The result was widespread anemia and other wasting conditions in children who did not suffer more serious injuries or illnesses. Children witnessed atrocities, including murder and rape committed against their parents and neighbors. Tens of thousands were orphaned, and tens of thousands more lived in refugee centers. Assessing the psychological effects of war trauma on children in Sarajevo, Bihac and Banja Luka, UNICEF found that virtually all suffered from nightmares and inappropriately apathetic or aggressive behavior as a result of exposure to the conflict.

*National/Racial/Ethnic Minorities.*— Extreme nationalism precipitated the war to cleanse non-Serbs from parts of Bosnia. Other micronationalist ideologies developed in the context of violent separatism, and at the end of 1993 national identity was a critical factor in whether one would keep a job or lose it, remain at home or be driven out, or all too often live or die. Throughout Bosnia, violence, fear, and the collapsing social structure eroded

*Continued*

**EXHIBIT 2.2** *Continued*

support for pluralism. No group was more victimized than Bosnia's Muslims.

*People with Disabilities.*—The pervasiveness of the war, the destruction of the economy, and the Government's reduced means limited assistance to the disabled, including those disabled by the war. An example of disregard for the needs of the disabled occurred as the HVO withdrew from Fojnica: troops evacuated the doctors from a hospital for mentally impaired children, but left the patients behind.

*Section 6. Worker Rights*

a. *The Right of Association.*—Legally, all workers were free to form or join unions of their own choosing without prior authorization. Before the outbreak of the war, this right was generally respected. Bosnian workers had independent trade unions, while journalists, teachers, and others organized independent professional associations to address labor issues. The bulk of Bosnian workers were probably members of the semi-official Council of Independent Trade Unions of Bosnia and Herzegovina (CITUBH), although new trade unions were also organized. The right to strike was recognized but not exercised in connection with work-related grievances in 1993.

b. *The Right to Organize and Bargain Collectively.*—Bosnian law formally guaranteed this right, but the fighting among the three sides interrupted Bosnia's economic transition from state domination to a market-oriented system. As a consequence, the management of state-owned enterprises had not adopted collective bargaining as a practice prior to the war.

c. *Prohibition of Forced or Compulsory Labor.*—Forced labor was legally prohibited and did not occur before the outbreak of the war. In some villages, however, citizens found themselves under virtual "house arrest" so surrounding forces would have a convenient labor pool. As with civilians placed in detention centers, villagers under house arrest were sometimes forced to erect shelters or fill sandbags in dangerous conditions near the front lines. Although the BSA was the main user of forced labor, government troops also occasionally surrounded villagers and forced them to work. Bugojno was surrounded for most of the summer, and in May government troops surrounded the residents of Banovici and sent some of them to the front lines to dig trenches. As the trenches were completed, the troops advanced.

d. *Minimum Age for Employment of Children.*—The minimum age for employment was 16, although children in agricultural communities sometimes assisted their families with farm work before they reached that age. As in 1992, there were occasional reports in 1993 that children were employed for military functions such as reconnaissance and running messages.

e. *Acceptable Conditions of Work.*—In principle, minimum wages were guaranteed; with the economy in total disarray, however, workers had no assurance they would be paid for work performed. Dismissals because of ethnicity or political affiliation occurred throughout Bosnia. The prewar 42-hour workweek, with a 24-hour rest period, was formally still in effect, and sick leave and other benefits were generous. But in the context of the war, benefits counted for little. Regulations on occupational health and safety were adequate but not enforced.

## EXHIBIT 2.3    Human Rights Violations in Iran

### *Iran\**

Iran is an Islamic republic under the leadership of Ayatollah Ali Khamenei. The formal system of government, based on a Constitution approved in 1980 by popular referendum and revised in July 1989, features a Parliament and a President elected from among multiple candidates by universal suffrage. However, all candidates must meet highly restrictive religious and political criteria imposed by the Council of Guardians, and as a result the choice offered to voters is narrow. The Government, dominated by a political elite composed of Shi'a Muslim clerics and of laymen allied with these clerics, attempts to impose its views of political and socioreligious orthodoxy. However, there remain significant factional differences on important economic and political issues.

The Government continues to reinforce its hold on power through arrests, summary trials and executions, and other forms of intimidation carried out by an extensive internal security system. The Revolutionary Guards and security forces operating under the Ministry of Intelligence and Security and the Interior Ministry are known to make political arrests and commit other human rights abuses.

Iran has a mixed economy. Although Islam guarantees the right to private ownership, the Government has nationalized the banks and owns several basic industries, including the petroleum and utilities sectors. Oil exports are the primary source of foreign exchange. The disruptions of the revolution, the destruction from the Iran-Iraq war, and government mismanagement have caused serious economic deterioration. However, inflation has apparently been reduced from previous years, although it is thought to be still over 20 percent; about 30 percent of the work force is unemployed, and widespread corruption and black-market activities continue.

There was no evidence of significant improvement in Iran's record as a major abuser of human rights. As in the past, the Government went to considerable lengths to conceal its abuses and continued to obstruct the activities of international human rights monitors. It is thus difficult to know precisely the details and numbers of such abuses. Similarly, domestic elements that might monitor and report on the Government's practices are ruthlessly suppressed. Abuses continued to include denial of citizens' right to change their government; summary executions; widespread torture; arbitrary detentions; lack of fair trials; repression of the freedoms of speech, press, assembly, and association; systematic repression of the Baha'i religious community; and severe restrictions on women's and worker rights. The Government has not allowed Reynaldo Galindo-Pohl, the U.N. Special Representative on Human Rights, to revisit Iran since 1991 and did not implement the measures he recommended in his 1993 report.

*Continued*

Source: U.S. State Department. Country Reports on Human Rights Practices for 1993. Washington, D.C.: Government Printing Office, 1994, pp. 1176–1183.
*Because of the absence of a United States Mission in Iran, this report draws heavily on unofficial sources.

**EXHIBIT 2.3**    *Continued*

*Respect for Human Rights*

*Section 1. Respect for the Integrity of the Person, Including Freedom from:*

a. *Political and Other Extrajudicial Killing.*—Given the lack of basic procedural safeguards in political trials, most of the executions ordered each year in such cases amount to summary executions. Furthermore, the Government has repeatedly indicated in public statements that it equates active political opposition to Iran's Islamic revolution with terrorism.

The Iranian press stopped reporting most executions in 1992, making it difficult to determine the number of people killed for political reasons in 1993, but it appears executions continue at their previous rate of several hundred a year. In September the U.N. Special Representative reported obtaining a copy of an Iranian government document showing that Iranian media had eliminated most coverage of executions in order to preempt the Special Representative's criticism. Reports from exiles and human rights monitoring groups indicate many of those executed for alleged criminal offenses are in fact political dissidents.

For example, Amnesty International (AI) reported the execution during 1993 of Mohsen Mohammadi Sabet, who had been held incommunicado in Rasht prison since September or October 1992. The Government has refused to reply to AI's requests for information regarding the precise charges brought against Sabet. According to AI, the legal proceedings in Sabet's case failed to meet minimum international standards of fairness and impartiality.

In addition, the Government continued to carry out political assassinations of its opponents residing abroad. On January 24, Turkish journalist Ugur Mumcu was killed in Ankara by a car bomb; an Iranian-backed Turkish group was believed responsible. On March 16, Naghdi Mohammed Hussein, a leader of the opposition Mojahedin-e-Khalq, was assassinated in Rome. (Naghdi's name was among those on a list of 32 Iranian oppositionists found in the possession of one of the suspects in the 1992 assassinations of Kurds in Berlin.) On March 18, three Iranian Baluchi insurgency leaders were murdered in Karachi. In June another Mojahedin-e-Khalq activist, Mohammed Hassan Arbab, was killed in Karachi along with a bystander; another bystander, a child, was seriously injured. In October an assailant wounded William Nygaard, the Norwegian translator of Salman Rushdie's book "The Satanic Verses." Investigators have not yet determined the motive for the assault.

The French Government's investigation into the assassination in August 1991 of former Prime Minister Shahpour Bakhtiar and his assistant continued; two suspects, Iranian government officials, were under arrest awaiting trial. In the case of the murder in Berlin of four Iranian Kurdish dissidents in 1992, a German prosecutor announced in May that Kazem Darabi, who is in a German prison awaiting trial for the killings, is an agent of the Iranian intelligence service.

b. *Disappearance.*—No reliable information is available on the number of disappearances in 1993. Many families of executed political prisoners reportedly have not been informed officially of their relatives' deaths. In 1993 the Government again responded to many of the U.N. Special Representative's requests for information on specific prisoners by denying that it had any judicial record of them.

**EXHIBIT 2.3**  *Continued*

c. *Torture and Other Cruel, Inhuman, or Degrading Treatment or Punishment.*—There continued to be credible reports of the torture and ill-treatment of detainees. Common methods of torture are said to include suspension for long periods in contorted positions, burning with cigarettes, and, most frequently, severe and repeated beatings with cables or other instruments on the back and on the soles of the feet. Prisoners are frequently held in solitary confinement or denied adequate rations or medical care as a way of forcing them to confess.

The U.N. Special Representative reported in 1993 that the Government has taken no measures to establish legal or procedural safeguards against the torture of prisoners. There were no reports of law enforcement personnel being held accountable for torture or other abuses. In 1992 the Government expelled workers of the International Committee of the Red Cross (ICRC) who had been visiting detainees. The Government has still not permitted the ICRC to resume this activity in Iran. Information on prison conditions in 1993 was not available. However, prisoner protests against poor prison conditions in the past reportedly prompted beatings, denial of medical care, and, in some cases, execution.

d. *Arbitrary Arrest, Detention, or Exile.*—Arbitrary arrest and detention have been common in the past, but it is not known how many cases there were in 1993. It is known that some persons were arrested on trumped-up criminal charges when their actual "offenses" were political. The lack of fair trials and other procedural safeguards encourage such practices.

Baha'is continued to face arbitrary arrest and detention. The Government

continued its practice of detaining a small but relatively steady number of Baha'is at any one time.

No judicial determination of the legality of detention exists in Iranian law, and there is reportedly no legal time limit on incommunicado detention. Suspects are held for questioning at local Revolutionary Guard offices or in jails.

e. *Denial of Fair Public Trial.*—There are essentially two different court systems. The civil courts deal with criminal offenses, and the revolutionary courts, established in 1979, try "political" offenses as well as cases involving narcotics trafficking and "crimes against God."

In January the Special Representative reported that trials in Iran continue to fall far short of internationally accepted standards. Trials by revolutionary courts, especially, cannot be considered fair or public. Some trials are conducted in secret. If the trial is staged publicly, it is generally because the prisoner has already been forced to confess to a crime. Persons tried by the revolutionary courts (including in drug trafficking cases) enjoy virtually no procedural or substantive safeguards. The accused are often indicted under broad and all-encompassing charges such as "moral corruption," "antirevolutionary behavior," and "siding with global arrogance." Trials lasting 5 minutes or less are common.

The right to a defense counsel is theoretically provided for in Iranian law and in the Constitution, but in the revolutionary courts defendants are not known to have access to a lawyer; moreover, they are not able to call witnesses on their behalf or to appeal. Courts have failed to

*Continued*

**EXHIBIT 2.3**  *Continued*

investigate allegations by defendants that they were subjected to torture during pre-trial detention. Some persons have been imprisoned beyond the limit of their sentence and even executed after the formal expiration of their prison time.

There was again no evidence in 1993 of any judicial reform that would bring Iranian courts into compliance with international standards; the Special Representative noted in his January 1993 report that a new law on legal representation—which provides that any Muslim is eligible to represent the accused in court—does not in fact provide for qualified legal counsel.

The judicial system is further weakened by the fact that revolutionary courts may consider that revolutionary courts may consider cases formally under the jurisdiction of the civil and criminal courts. Assignment of cases to regular rather than revolutionary courts is haphazard and apparently occurs mainly when arrests are made by regular police. Revolutionary courts may also overturn the decisions of the civilian courts. The review authority of the Supreme Court is limited.

For common criminal offenses, many elements of the prerevolutionary judicial system survive, and the accused often have the right to a public trial with benefit of lawyers of their own choosing. Even this judiciary is not fully independent, however. Many of the former judges were retired after the revolution, and new judges were selected. One criterion for new judges is grounding in Islamic law; political acceptability is a requirement for any government position. According to the New York-based Lawyers Committee for Human Rights, the 1982 Law on the Qualifications for the Appointment of Judges discriminates on the grounds of religion, sex, and political opinion, while at the same time permitting the appointment of judges and prosecutors who have no legal training or experience. Some judges reportedly prefer to base their judgments on the guidance of religious scholars rather than on the law.

Because the Government continues to block the activities of international human rights observers, no reliable estimate is available on the number of political prisoners, but knowledgeable sources estimate them in the thousands.

f. *Arbitrary Interference with Privacy, Family, Home, or Correspondence.*—The Government rejects the Western distinction between a public sphere which the State may control and a sphere of private life (religion, culture, thought, and private behavior) which the State may not properly control. Before 1982, authorities entered homes and offices, wiretapped telephones, and opened mail. These activities are reportedly less common now.

Special Revolutionary Guard units and security forces check on social activities. Women whose clothing does not completely cover the hair and all of the body except hands and face, or who wear makeup, are subject to arrest (see also Section 5). Crackdowns often result in widespread harassment of women in the streets. Men have also periodically been required to dress "modestly." During the spring and summer of 1993, both official and self-appointed enforcers campaigned against insufficiently modest dress and even sunglasses. For example, the commander of the law enforcement forces in Tehran stated that 802 men and women were detained from June 16 through 23 for various dress code violations in Tehran.

**EXHIBIT 2.3** *Continued*

*Section 2. Respect for Civil Liberties, Including:*

a. *Freedom of Speech and Press.*— According to the Constitution, "publications and the press may express ideas freely, except when they are contrary to Islamic principles, or are detrimental to public rights." In practice, most publications are controlled by the Government; independent publishers run the risk not only of press shutdowns, pressure from the Government, newsprint monopoly, and confiscation of publications and equipment, but of arrest and summary punishment if they are overly critical of the Government. The editor and two employees of the magazine Farad were jailed in 1992 for publishing a cartoon which the authorities deemed insulting to the late Ayatollah Khomeini. In October after the cartoonist, Manoucher Karimzadeh, completed his sentence, the Supreme Court ruled that his punishment had been insufficient and sentenced him to an additional 10 years' imprisonment.

In August Revolutionary Guards detained the publisher of the radical daily Salam, Musavi Kho'iniha, as well as the newspaper's chief editor, 'Abbas 'Abdi. The detentions were apparently in retaliation for criticism of the judicial authorities. Both men were freed on bail after the newspaper printed a retraction of its criticism. In September authorities detained Mehdi Nasiri editor of the Tehran daily Keyhan, after the newspaper printed criticism of Ayatollah Mohammad Ali Yazdi, chief of the judiciary. Nasiri was released on bail after several days in detention but still faces a trial before a special "press jury" on charges of slander. In October Colonel Nasrullah Tavakoli, a retired army officer, was arrested and placed in incommunicado detention, apparently for writing a series of open letters critical of the current Government.

All books must be submitted to the Ministry of Islamic Culture and Guidance for review before they may be published. Publishers, authors, and printers also engage in substantial self-censorship before submitting books to the Ministry in an effort to avoid the substantial penalties, including economic losses, incurred when books are rejected. Iranian authorities have interpreted broadly their authority to censor on religious grounds, including official acceptance of the February 1989 religious decree condemning British author Salman Rushdie to death for his book "The Satanic Verses." On each anniversary of the decree since 1992 , a group of exiled Iranian writers has signed a public condemnation of the decree; the Iranian Government has responded by banning the writings of the authors signing the condemnation. By mid-1993, the Government had banned the works of 162 such signatories.

Newspapers, which are usually associated with various government factions, reflect a variety of viewpoints. Generally, newspapers can and do criticize government policies and officials both in their reporting and editorials. They are forbidden, however, to criticize the concept of the Islamic republic or to promote ethnic minority rights. Nevertheless, some independent publishers out of favor with the Government are published without reprisal. Foreign Books, newspapers, and magazines may be imported only after they have been reviewed by the Ministry of Islamic Culture and Guidance.

*Continued*

**EXHIBIT 2.3** *Continued*

All broadcasting facilities are government owned, and the content of their broadcasting reflects the political and socioreligious ideology of the Government.

Although restrictions on academic freedom have been eased somewhat, course content is still monitored and there is little genuine critical discussion on issues. Informers are said to be common on campus and in the classroom. Admission to universities is politicized; all applicants must pass "character tests" in which officials review applicants' background and ideology with the students' hometown religious authorities and neighborhood groups. This process serves to exclude from universities and the professions those who are critical of the Government's revolutionary ideology. To achieve tenure, professors reportedly must cooperate with government security agencies over a period of years.

b. *Freedom of Peaceful Assembly and Association.*—The Constitution permits unarmed assemblies and marches "provided they do not violate the principles of Islam." In practice, the only ones permitted are those sponsored by the Government, such as Friday prayers and parades and demonstrations on official occasions. According to opposition sources, a student protest in March at Beheshti high school in west Tehran was crushed by antiriot police units who arrested approximately 80 students.

The Constitution also allows the formation of political parties, groups, and professional associations, as well as Islamic and some minority religious associations, provided they do not violate the principles of "freedom, sovereignty, (and) national unity" or question Islam or the Islamic Republic. In practice, most independent organizations have either been banned, co-opted by the Government, or are moribund.

The authorities continued to harass the Freedom Movement, founded in 1961 and declared illegal in 1991, tapping its telephones, opening its mail, and subjecting its members to intimidation. While the Freedom Movement participated in the first parliamentary election after the revolution, it has been prevented from doing so in all subsequent elections.

c. *Freedom of Religion.*—The state religion is Islam, and religion is almost inseparable from government in Iran. The President and many other top officials are mullahs (Islamic clergymen), as are the Speaker of the Parliament and many of the parliamentary deputies.

Approximately 90 percent of Iranians are Shi'a Muslims. Aside from slightly over 1 percent who are non-Muslims (Baha'is, Christians, Zoroastrians, and Jews), the rest are Sunni Muslims. The Sunnis are mostly Kurds, Arabs, Turkomans, Baluch, and other ethnic minorities whose political influence is very limited. The Constitution declares that "the official religion of Iran is Islam and the sect followed is Ja'fari Shi'ism," but it also states that "other Islamic denominations shall enjoy complete respect."

The small Christian, Jewish, and Zoroastrian (the pre-Islamic religion of Iran) populations are concentrated mainly in urban areas. The Constitution recognizes their religions, and they elect representatives to seats reserved for them in the Parliament. They are permitted to practice their religions, to instruct their children, and—although with a great deal of disruptive interference—to maintain schools.

**EXHIBIT 2.3**  *Continued*

Nevertheless, official harassment is commonplace. In June the U.N. Committee on Economic, Social, and Cultural Rights observed that the U.N. Special Representative's report "confirm(ed) the broad consensus that there has been practically no progress in ensuring greater respect and protection for the rights of the non-Muslim religious communities" in Iran.

Mehdi Debadj, a Christian convert from Islam arrested in 1983, was held in prison until December 1993, when Christian missionary groups reported that a court in Sari sentenced him to death for apostasy. Following international appeals on his behalf, Debadj was released in January 1994. According to the Government, his case is still "under investigation."

The Government continues to discriminate against the Baha'i community, Iran's largest non-Muslim minority (300,000 to 350,000 members). The Baha'i religion is considered a "misguided sect" by the authorities. It is not officially recognized, and Baha'is may not teach their faith.

In 1993 Tehran municipal authorities built a cultural center on the site of a Baha'i cemetery. Immediately after the 1978–1979 revolution, the cemetery's markers were removed (some reportedly were auctioned off), and the site was turned into a park. The new construction in 1993 involved excavations that reportedly desecrated Baha'i graves. The U.S. and other governments condemned the desecration and called on Iran to halt the project. There is no indication, however, that the Iranian authorities stopped the construction.

The treatment of Baha'is varies somewhat, depending on the jurisdiction; in other places, Baha'is were still able to bury their dead in Baha'i cemeteries.

d. *Freedom of Movement Within the Country, Foreign Travel, Emigration, and Repatriation.*—Iranians may travel to any part of Iran, although there have been restriction on travel to Kurdish areas at times of heavy fighting. Persons may change their place of residence without obtaining permission. According to the Government, approximately 3 million refugees, primarily Afghans but also Kurdish and Shi'a refugees displaced from Iraq in the aftermath of the Gulf war, remained in Iran in mid-1993.

Males of draft age are not issued exit permits except for approved courses of study, and Iranians who are suspect politically, such as some retired military officers and high-level public officials under the former regime, are not able to leave the country. Some Iranians, particularly those whose skills are in short supply and who were educated at government expense, have had to post bonds to obtain exit permits. There was no evidence that this situation improved in 1993.

Iranian Jews are permitted to obtain passports and to travel (including to Israel), but they are normally denied the multiple-exit permits given to most Iranians and must make a new application (with another fee) for each planned trip. Permission is not normally granted for all members of a Jewish family to travel outside Iran at the same time.

The Government actively encourages the many thousands of skilled Iranians living abroad to return to help rebuild the country. Of those who have returned in recent years, a number have been able to pursue, through the Iranian judicial system, the restoration of their properties.

*Continued*

**EXHIBIT 2.3**  *Continued*

However, many exiles complain that formal legal guarantees of their safety have not yet been provided, and, as a result, many remain reluctant to return.

There are some categories of persons who may be in danger if they return to Iran. Some of those with close ties to the former regime, draft evaders, and those who departed the country illegally face possible arrest upon their return. Members of or sympathizers with the People's Mojahedin Organization of Iran or the Communist Tudeh Party, both opposition groups banned by the Government, are subject to imprisonment and torture or even execution should they return. In his 1993 report, the Special Representative recounted several cases of exiles and Baha'is who were harassed after returning to Iran. Nevertheless, immediate relatives of persons wanted by the Government are often able to live in Iran, travel abroad, and return without undue difficulty.

Iranian passports have always been stamped "not valid for emigration," but the Government does not make a clear distinction between legal residence in another country and emigration. According to the regulations, Iranians with a legal residence outside Iran may be issued passports and advance exit permits by the Iranian embassy, consulate, or interests section in their country of residence. The Government does not recognize dual nationality and considers Iranian-born U.S. citizens to be Iranians unless they formally renounce their Iranian citizenship in accordance with Iranian law. There have been many instances in which Iranian authorities have confiscated the passports of dual nationals.

The Government of Iran and the United Nations High Commissioner for Refugees (UNHCR) estimate there were approximately 2.1 million Afghan refugees in Iran in mid-1993. The majority of these refugees have been integrated into Iranian life. The remainder live either seminomadic lives or reside in government settlements in central and eastern Iran. The Government provided assistance to those refugees. The UNHCR is supervising the repatriation of Afghan refugees to Afghanistan.

*Section 3. Respect for Political Rights: The Right of Citizens to Change Their Government*

Iranian citizens do not enjoy the right to change their government peacefully. Iran is ruled by a group of religious leaders (mullahs) and their lay associates who share a belief in the legitimacy of a theocratic state based on Ayatollah Khomeini's interpretation of Shi'a Islam.

The revolutionary Government has held elections at fairly regular intervals for president, Parliament deputies, members of the Assembly of Experts (responsible for choosing the Revolutionary Leader's successor), and members of local government councils. Presidential elections were held in June, resulting in the reelection of Hojjat ol-Eslam Ali Akbar Hashemi-Rafsamjani. Voting is by universal suffrage of everyone age 15 and older and is by secret ballot. All candidates must be approved by the Council of Guardians, however, and only those meeting the Council's vaguely described political and religious criteria may run. In practice, only supporters of the theocratic state are accepted, and even clerics are often disqualified if their positions vary from the official line.

A few political parties have been licensed following the Ministry of Interior's announcement in December 1988 that political parties would be allowed to

**EXHIBIT 2.3**   *Continued*

form, provided they met the Government's religious and political criteria.

The Constitution provides for an independent Parliament, which exists to a large degree in practice. While Parliament deputies are typically allied with various powerful political and religious officials, they may speak and vote independently and may shift from one faction to another. Vigorous parliamentary debates—normally covered extensively in the press—cover a wide variety of issues. Harsh criticism of government officials is often heard in these debates, and, in some cases, laws proposed by the executive branch have been voted down.

The Constitution provides for a Council of Guardians composed of 12 members: 6 clerics unilaterally appointed by the Leader, and 6 lay members well grounded in Islamic law who are nominated by the head of the judiciary, subject to the Parliament's approval. The Council of Guardians must certify all bills passed by the Parliament as being in accordance with Islamic law and the Constitution. If bills fail to be certified, they are sent back to the Parliament for revision. The Council of Guardians can and does reject important bills and portions of bills passed by the Parliament. The Council for the Discernment of Expediency, a body created in 1988, resolves those legislative issues on which the Parliament and Council of Guardians disagree. Approximately 4 percent of Parliament members are women.

*Section 4. Governmental Attitude Regarding International and Nongovernmental Investigation of Alleged Violations of Human Rights*

Iranian organizations that attempt to speak out on human rights, such as the Freedom Movement and the Association for the Protection of Liberties and Human Rights, face severe harassment by the Government. In the past, the Government generally has been uncooperative with foreign human rights groups, whether government sponsored or independent, regarding their activities as interference in the country's internal affairs.

The U.N. Special Representative has not been able to visit Iran since his third visit in 1991; by the end of 1993, the Iranian Government had not replied to his repeated requests to restrict the Special Representative's mandate.

*Section 5. Discrimination Based on Race, Sex, Religion, Language, or Social Status*

*Women.*—The discrimination that women have traditionally faced in Iranian society has increased since the revolution. Ultraconservative dress, entirely hiding the hair and all of the body except the face and hands, is a requirement for all women, regardless of their religion, national origin, or citizenship. Women have been harassed, detained, or physically attacked if they appeared in public in clothing that official or self-appointed guardians of public morality deemed insufficiently modest. Enforcement of these rules has varied considerably since Ayatollah Khomeini's death in 1989; there was a widespread surge in enforcement during 1993 (see Section 1.f). According to press reports, a teenaged girl was accidentally shot in Tehran in late August after being stopped on the street by a police conscript for breaking the Islamic dress code.

Although violence against women is known to occur, little is known about its extent. Abuse within the family is considered a private matter in this conservative

*Continued*

**EXHIBIT 2.3** *Continued*

society and is seldom discussed publicly. There are no official statistics on the subject. In the past, there have been credible reports of the torture and execution of women detainees.

Under legislation passed in 1983, women have the right to divorce their husbands, and regulations promulgated in 1984 substantially broadened the number of grounds for which a woman may seek divorce. A husband may obtain a divorce without stating a reason or going to court. In December 1992 the Council for the Discernment of Expediency reversed itself and ratified a bill already passed by the Parliament which added somewhat to a divorced woman's right to financial support from her ex-husband. It is not clear yet whether this adjustment has had any impact in practice.

*Children.*—Iranian law includes provisions that prohibit the use of child labor in industry (see section 6.d) No information was available on the enforcement of these statutes.

*Religious Minorities.*—The Christian, Jewish, Zoroastrian, and Baha'i minorities suffer varying degrees of officially sanctioned discrimination in a number of areas, particularly with respect to employment, education, public accommodations, and property ownership. In 1993 non-Muslim owners of restaurants were required to post a distinctive notice in the windows of their establishments.

Muslims who have converted to Christianity are similarly discriminated against. University applicants are required to pass an examination in Islamic theology. This has the effect of limiting most religious minorities' access to higher education, although all students must receive instruction on Islam regardless of their religion. Applicants for public sector

employment are similarly screened for adherence to standards of Islamic orthodoxy, with much the same effect. Religious minorities have also suffered discrimination in the legal system, receiving lower awards in injury and death lawsuits and suffering heavier punishments than those imposed on Muslims. Although Sunnis have encountered religious discrimination on the local level, the Government has tried to reduce Shi'a-Sunni antagonism.

The Government has stated that it will protect the "social and legal rights" of Baha'is as "normal citizens," but in practice there is widespread persecution and discrimination in many areas of public life. Baha'i marriages are not recognized, and Baha'si are forbidden to participate in social welfare organizations.

In 1993 the Special Representative reported obtaining reliable information on an internal Iranian government directive setting out policy on the Baha'is. In the directive, dated February 1992, the Supreme Revolutionary Council instructed government agencies to block the progress and development of the Baha'i community; expel from the universities students identified as Baha'is; seek to cut the Baha'is' links outside Iran; restrict employment for those who identify themselves as Baha'is; and deny Baha'is "positions of influence," including in the education sector. The Government claims the policy directive is a forgery; it appears, however, to reflect accurately current government practice.

The Government continued to return some of the property of individual Baha'is that it had previously confiscated, although the amount represents a small fraction of the total seized. Property of

**EXHIBIT 2.3** *Continued*

the community, such as places of worship remains confiscated. Most Baha'is are now able to obtain food ration booklets. Baha'i children are now permitted to attend grade school and high school but are generally not permitted to attend college or be employed on college faculties. A small number of Baha'is were permitted to leave the country. While some Baha'is have been issued passports, the majority of such applications are denied.

Some Baha'is continue to be denied public sector (and often private sector) employment on account of their religion; in a number of cases, ration cards have been denied on the same grounds. Thousands of Baha'is dismissed from government jobs in the early 1980's receive no unemployment benefits and have been required to repay the Government for salaries or pensions received from the first day of employment. Those unable to do so face prison sentences.

d. *People with Disabilities.*—There is no information available on government policy with respect to people with disabilities.

*Section 6. Worker Rights*

a. *The Right of Association.*—Article 131 of the Labor Code grants workers and employers alike the right to form and join their own organizations. In practice, however, there are no real labor unions in Iran. A national organization known as the Workers' House, founded in 1982 as the labor wing of the now defunct Islamic Republican Party, is the only authorized national labor organization with nominal claims to represent all Iranian workers. It works closely with the workplace Islamic councils that exist in many Iranian enterprises. The Workers' House is largely a conduit of government influence and

control, not a trade union founded by workers to represent their interests.

The officially sanctioned Islamic labor councils also function as instruments of government influence and not as bodies created and controlled by workers to advance their own interests, although the councils have frequently been able to block layoffs or the firing of workers.

A network of guild unions operates on a regional basis. These guild unions issue vocational licenses, fund financial cooperatives to assist members, and help workers to find jobs. The guild unions operate with the backing of the Government.

According to opposition sources, there were several protests and strikes during the spring, including a strike involving thousands of workers at a tractor factory in Tabariz, a walkout to protest nonpayment of salaries at a government sugar factory in western Iran, and strikes in textile factories in northern Iran and near Tehran. In the past the Government has not tolerated any strike deemed to be at odds with its economic and labor policies.

b. *The Right to Organize and Bargain Collectively.*—The right of workers to organize independently and bargain collectively cannot be documented. It is not known whether labor legislation and practice in the export processing zones differ in any significant respect from the law and practice in the rest of the country. No information is available on mechanisms used to set wages.

c. *Prohibition of Forced or Compulsory Labor.*—Section 273 of the Iranian Penal code provides that any person who does not have definite means of subsistence and who, through laziness or negligence,

*Continued*

**EXHIBIT 2.3**  *Continued*

does not look for work may be obliged by the Government to take suitable employment. This provision has been frequently criticized by the International Labor Organization (ILO) as contravening ILO Convention 29 on forced labor.

d. *Minumum Age for Employment of Children.*—Iranian labor law, which exempts agriculture, domestic service, family businesses, and, to some extent, other small businesses, forbids employment of minors under 15 years of age (compulsory education extends through age 11) and places special restrictions on the employment of minors under 18. In addition, women and minors may not be used for hard labor or, in general, for night work. Information on the extent to which these regulations are enforced by the Labor Inspection Department of the Ministry of Labor and Social Affairs and the local authorities is not available.

e. *Acceptable Conditions of Work.*— The Labor Code empowers the Supreme Labor Council to set minimum wage levels each year determined by industrial sector and region. It is not known if minimum wage levels are in fact issued annually or if the Labor Ministry's inspectors enforce their application. The Labor Code stipulates that the minimum wage should be sufficient to meet the living expenses of a family and should take into account the announced rate of inflation. Information on the share of the working population covered by the minimum wage legislation or the share of the work force receiving a decent wage is not available.

Labor law establishes a 6-day work-week of 48 hours maximum (except for overtime at premium rates), with 1 day of rest (normally Friday) per week as well as at least 12 days per year of leave with pay and a number of paid public holidays.

According to the Labor Code, a Supreme Safety Council, chaired by the Labor Minister or his representative, is responsible for promoting workplace safety and health and issuing occupational safety and health regulations and codes of practice. The Council has reportedly issued 28 safety directives. The Supreme Safety Council is also supposed to oversee the activities of the safety committees that have reportedly been established in about 3,000 enterprises employing more than 10 persons. It is not known how well the Labor Ministry's inspectors enforce the safety and health legislation and regulations nor whether industrial accident rates are compiled and show positive trends (Iran does not furnish this data to the ILO for publication in its Year Book of Labor Statistics).

Given the large segments of the economy exempted from the labor law, the State's still unresolved administrative disorganization resulting from the revolution, the effects of the war with Iraq, and the general lack of effective labor unions, it is unclear to what extent the provisions of Iran's labor law affect most of the labor force.

The ILO has long been concerned with official discrimination in employment against adherents of the Baha'i religion.

# 3

# Crime by Government: The Reagan-Bush Era

> *The President, Vice President and all civil officers of the United States shall be removed from office on impeachment for, and conviction of, treason, bribery, or other high crimes and misdemeanors.*
> —*UNITED STATES CONSTITUTION ARTICLE II, SECTION 4*

The terms "high crimes" and "misdemeanors" were first used against the Earl of Suffolk in 1386 for misappropriation of funds. The term for lesser crimes at the time was "trespass." High crimes and misdemeanors referred to political crimes against the state whereas misdemeanors involved criminal sanctions for private wrongs (Pincus and Lardner, 1994).

## Crimes of the Reagan Era

> *"Plausible deniability," "October Surprise," "The Savings and Loan Scandal," "Corruption in the Environmental Protection Agency," the "Iran-Contra Affair," the "Pentagon Procurement Scandal," "Wedtech," "Influence Peddling at the Department of Housing and Urban Development."*

Both alleged and actual crime and wrongdoing during the Reagan administration far exceeded those of previous presidential administrations including those of Nixon, Harding, Grant, and Buchanan. The interconnections of some of these events during the Reagan era with yet other events such as the Bank of Commerce and Credit

International (BCCI) collapse and past CIA programs in Central America might, to borrow Winston Churchill's phrase in describing Russia, represent "a riddle wrapped in a mystery inside an enigma."

The period from revelation to denouement of most of these events is so protracted that perspective on the stories tends to be lost. In discussing the lengthy investigation of the collapse of the savings and loans of the eighties, a dull-technical topic, O'Rourke (1989, p. 43) notes that the story was:

> *an awful example of what's replaced democracy in modern America—dictatorship by tedium . . . This allows the boring government officials to do anything they want, because anytime regular people try to figure out what gives, the regular people get hopelessly bored and confused, as though they'd fallen a month behind in their high school algebra class.*

## Crime in Earlier Presidential Administrations

In order to gain some perspective on crimes of the Reagan era, a brief description of wrongdoing during previous presidential administrations is instructive (Hagan and Simon, 1993). Nathan Miller in *The Founding Finaglers* (1976) and in *Stealing From America* (1992) describes corruption in various administrations which includes activities such as ordinary bribery, conflict of interest, till-tapping, improper and illegal use of government authority for financial gain or political advantage. Such illicit activity goes back to the earliest colonies and to George Washington's administration in Alexander Hamilton's treasury office where members of his staff financially benefitted from inside knowledge (Miller, 1976, p. 100). In this review of past scandals, presidents themselves may not always be directly involved in wrongdoing; but, as James Madison suggested in the First Congress, a president is "responsible for the conduct of the person he has nominated and appointed" (Johnson, 1991, p. 184). Because merchants and thieves share the same god—Mercury—little surprise is engendered by noting that many early fortunes were made through swindles, often due to connections with crooked politicians (Myers, 1936).

The Reagan years have been described as a new "gilded age," the original term being derived from Mark Twain's novel by the same name which was a satirical, political commentary on the corrupt post-Civil War period in which the accumulation of material wealth was glorified.

In this writer's estimation the top five presidential eras for crime, corruption, and scandal were those of Ronald Reagan, Richard Nixon, Ulysses Grant, Warren Harding, and James Buchanan. The seriousness of wrongdoing is not necessarily reflected by the ordering, however.

Shelly Ross in *Fall From Grace: Sex, Scandal and Corruption in American Politics from 1702 to the Present* (1988, p. 235) points out: "If it's a sex scandal, you're more likely to find a Democrat involved; if it's a financial scandal, you're more likely to find a Republican." In referring to Congress as well as to the presidency, Rosenbaum (1994) claims that Democratic corruption tends to involve graft whereas

Republican corruption is more likely to involve abuses of the power of government. While the former is an example of occupational and/or corporate crime, the latter tend to be examples of political crime.

## The Nixon Era

On September 8, 1974, President Gerald Ford granted former President Richard Nixon an unconditional pardon for all federal crimes he had "committed or taken part in" while in the office of president. Due to the Watergate scandal and other misconduct associated with it, Nixon had become the first American president to resign in disgrace rather than face the certainty of impeachment.

Perhaps no one event evokes the visage of political corruption and deceit as does Watergate. This involved the discovery of the illegal break-in of the offices of the Democratic National Committee located in the Watergate complex in Washington, D.C., by agents in the employ of Richard Nixon. Among the offenses by and charges against Nixon and associates were burglary, illegal surveillance, attempted bribery of a judge (Ellsberg Case), selling ambassadorships in return for illegal campaign donations, maintenance of an illegal "slush fund," destruction of evidence, plans of "dirty tricks" in political campaigns, the president and attorney general requesting IRS audits on political opponents, use of the CIA and FBI to halt the investigation, perjury, withholding information, altering evidence, and deliberate lying to the American public by the nation's top officeholder (Simon and Eitzen, 1993).

## The Reagan Era

At the very least the Reagan era matched, if not surpassed, the foregoing political administrations with respect to graft and corruption. Between 1980 and 1988 over 200 Reaganites came under either ethical or criminal investigation, the greatest number of scandals in any administration in American history (Ross, 1988, p. 1). It is difficult to determine whether public or private corruption was greater during the "Roaring Eighties." Perhaps giving vent to some testiness regarding which sector contains the most corruption was an editorial appearing in the *Wall Street Journal* (the nation's business newspaper) attacking a headline in the *Washington Post* (the nation's political newspaper) ("Editorial," 1991, p. A18):

### The Geography of Lying

*It is hard not to be drawn into the* Washington Post*'s front-page story yesterday, headlined: "For Wall Street Pros, Lying Comes Easily." And the sub-headline: "Deep-Seated Practice of Deception Is Complicating Scandal Probes." It was fascinating, and we will be looking for a front-page feature later this week discussing a related phenomenon under the headline: "For Washington Pros, Lying Comes Easily: Deep-Seated Practice of Deception Is Complicating BCCI Keating Probes."*

Although the presidential administration of Ronald Reagan was not directly involved or primarily responsible for either the collapse of the nation's savings and loans or the insider trading scandal on Wall Street, the deregulatory, laissez-faire, antigovernment philosophy fostered by Reaganites provided an atmosphere that would particularly present itself in the public sector.

### October Surprise

A pattern may have been established even before Ronald Reagan was elected with charges, in what has come to be called "Debategate," that Reagan secretly "obtained" a looseleaf notebook containing his opponent Jimmy Carter's debate strategy. In addition on April 15, 1991, former Carter National Security Council aide Gary Sick charged in an Op-Ed article in the *New York Times* that in 1980 the Reagan-Bush campaign had secretly arranged a deal with the Iranians to delay the release of fifty-two American hostages in return for a later arms deal. Delaying their release until after the election would prevent President Jimmy Carter from pulling an "October Surprise" and winning reelection (Kenworthy, 1991). If such charges, which were never proven, were true, this would be tantamount to treason. Although the charges remain dubious, the fact that serious observers and the American public gave any ear at all to the charges was an illustration of the suspicion, doubt, and critical view that had emerged regarding the Reagan presidency since Ronald Reagan left office (Hosenball, 1991, pp. 24–25).

In May 1992 the FBI made available to the congressional committee investigating October Surprise long-missing surveillance tapes of the late Cyrus Hashemi, an Iranian arms merchant who was believed to have had close contacts with the late William Casey, former CIA director and former Reagan-Bush campaign director. The FBI investigation of Hashemi's secret arms purchases for Iran was slowed down when the Reagan administration took office; and the Justice Department was believed to have purposely botched their prosecutions of Hashemi and another conspirator, Cyrus Davari, by alerting them through their defense attorneys, including former Attorney General Elliot Richardson, not to return to this country. Hashemi subsequently died in London in 1986 of a "rare and virulent form of leukemia" (Unger, 1992). The head of the congressional task force, Lee Hamilton, announced in July 1992 that the task force cleared George Bush who had been alleged to have flown to Paris for secret meetings with Iranian representatives ("Panel Clears Bush," 1992).

### The Iran-Contra Conspiracy

*"I don't recall . . ."*

—statement made 187 times under oath
by then-President Ronald Reagan
during the Iran-Contra investigation

*"Ronald Reagan knew everything . . ."*

—statement made by Lt. Col. Oliver North
under oath during the Iran-Contra trial

On November 4, 1986, the Lebanese magazine, *Al Shiraa,* revealed the existence of a secret American arms sale to Iran. This would begin one of the longest (over 5 years) and most expensive probes in the nation's history, over $30 million ("North Freed," 1991, p. A16). Money obtained in the sale of arms for hostages was utilized secretly to fund the Contras, rebels opposing the Marxist Sandinista regime in Nicaragua (Report of the Congressional Committee, 1987). At the conclusion of the televised Senate Iran-Contra hearings, Senate chairman for the hearings Daniel Inouye (D-Hawaii) said in his closing statement:

> *The story has now been told. Speaking for myself, I see it as a chilling story, a story of deceit and duplicity and the arrogant disregard of the rule of law. It is a story of withholding vital information from the American people, from the Congress, from the secretary of state, from the secretary of defense, and according to Admiral (John M.) Poindexter, from the president himself.*

Tom Blanton, deputy director of the National Security Archive indicates:

> *Watergate was the great tragedy. The high and mighty were brought low, and so on; it was Shakespeare. Iran-Contra is like Samuel Beckett: Everyone keeps wandering on and off the stage, but you don't know what to make of it (Williams, 1991, p. 11).*

One observer called Iran-Contra an MTV version of Watergate. Details of the story certainly contained high drama. The same day that the arms-for-hostages story broke in Lebanon, an American hostage was released. In addition an even more bizarre tale appeared describing former Reagan National Security Advisor Robert C. (Bud) McFarlane having travelled to Teheran the previous spring bearing arms and gifts to the Ayatollah Khomeini, including a chocolate cake with a confectionery key to symbolize a new relationship and, of all things, a bible autographed by Ronald Reagan (Johnson, 1991, p. 296). McFarlane later unsuccessfully attempted suicide in part due to the failure of this mission.

It is difficult to present succinctly the tangled web of the privatization of foreign policy that the Iran-Contra affair represented. Williams (1991, p. 12) describes the plot:

> *Popular president sells arms to archenemy hostage-taker Iran, violating not one but two U.S. policies (against arming Iran and dealing for hostages), marking up the price of the arms and sending the profit to the Nicaraguan contras in violation of a third policy, the congressional Boland Amendments forbidding contra aid.*
>
> *From there, it was all denouement, a tangled skein of money and guns, middlemen and bank accounts, dates and times and findings and channels. Polls began to show that as the narrative fragmented, the American people, initially outraged, ceased to follow it.*

The televised Iran-Contra hearings and subsequent coverage (which was not televised) of the trial of Lt. Col. Oliver North, a National Security Council staffer, at first fascinated the American public. Along with former National Security Adviser John Poindexter, North and others were charged with conspiracy to divert Iranian arms sales profits to the Nicaraguan Contras. Among the charges filed by the grand jury was that North and others had "deceitfully and without legal authorization" organized, directed, and concealed "a program to continue funding of and logistical and other support for military and paramilitary operations in Nicaragua by the Contras" at a time in which U.S. law forbade such activity (Leeden, 1988, p. 248). As Theodore Draper, author of *A Very Thin Line: The Iran-Contra Affair* (1991, p. 580), puts it:

> *The Iran-Contra affairs . . . were made possible by an interpretation of the Constitution which Poindexter and North thought gave them a license to carry on their secret operations in the name of the president, in defiance of the law and without the knowledge of any other branch of government . . . Somehow the highly dubious theory of a presidential monopoly of foreign policy had filtered down to them and given them a license to act as if they could substitute themselves for the entire government.*

The indictment also charged that North and retired Air Force General Richard Secord had conspired to divert millions from the sale of U.S. arms to "Enterprise." Enterprise, a secret organization created to privatize foreign policy, conducted an arms-for-hostages deal with Iran and diverted nearly $4 million in profits to the Contras. Draper (1991) estimated that the Contras may actually have received only about 20 percent of the millions raised (Bliven, 1991, p. 114). Both of these activities represented policy disputes between the executive branch and Congress, with Oliver North, having lied to Congress and shredded evidence, the designated scapegoat. Was a lieutenant colonel in the U.S. Marines seriously to be held solely responsible for criminal acts, or were higher up individuals, including former CIA Chief William Casey (head of Enterprise) who died during the hearings, and/or President Reagan, to be allowed to conduct foreign policy in defiance of Congress (Hagan, 1993, pp. 417–418)?

North (1991) was willing to "take the rap" until it became clear that he faced criminal charges without protection from higher-ups. North's boss, General Secord, described how President Reagan was able to truthfully deny knowledge of these activities. Reagan would employ "plausible deniability," that is, by giving general policy guidelines and letting the details without his specific knowledge be carried out by others (ibid.). He could then believably lie about having no knowledge of the particulars of operations.

North and Poindexter were convicted in 1989 of various charges including altering and destroying evidence and obstructing Congress, but these charges were overturned in 1990 and 1991 on the grounds that Independent Counsel Lawrence Walsh had utilized immunized testimony to Congress to subsequently prosecute them. In these investigations, the central conspiracy charges were dropped in order to avoid disclosing official secrets. Hersh (1993, p. 47) alleges that senior members of the Iran-Contra Committee "agreed from the outset that specific evidence of a Presidential 'act of commission' would be necessary before Reagan himself would become a target. No amount of Presidential negligence or nonfeasance, they decided, would justify a potential impeachment proceeding that could be dangerous for the nation." Unbelievably, the committee also believed that the president "did not have the mental ability to fully understand what happened" (ibid., p. 64). Hersh concludes that the committee purposely chose not to pursue many leads. As part of the investigation President Ronald Reagan reluctantly agreed to testify (answer prescreened questions) wherein he claimed he "could not remember" or "could not recall" 187 times (Ross, 1988, p. 279).

The Iran-Contra saga continued with the federal grand jury in September 1991 indicting a CIA official (Clair George, former director of operations) for lying to Congress; and in October 1991 Elliott Abrams, the State Department's top officer in Central America in the mid-1980s, admitted that he also lied to Congress about Contra arms. Abrams pleaded guilty.

In June 1992 special prosecutor Lawrence Walsh indicted former Secretary of Defense Caspar Weinberger in order to attempt to prove a conspiracy to cover up Reagan's involvement. Although the Iran-Contra grand jury expired in May 1992, Walsh could go to any sitting grand jury to seek indictments; however July 31, 1992, was the end of the statute of limitations for new indictments ("Iran-Contra," 1992). The charges included Weinberger lying to Congress and obstructing justice based on entries in his diaries. Weinberger made his diaries available to the Library of Congress in 1988 and even wrote a letter asking the library to show the materials to the special prosecutor ("Walsh's Hostage," 1992), although another source claims he stipulated only that he could approve their availability (Cohn, 1992). The trial was scheduled for November 1992. While Walsh claimed that former President Reagan was not the object of his inquiry, the full drama of the Iran-Contra affair obviously had not been played out. President George Bush's role in the final chapter of Iran-Contra will be discussed shortly.

The constitutional questions raised by Iran-Contra were more than a partisan policy dispute. Bandow (1991, p. A19) notes:

> *the diversion scheme was a direct assault on our system of constitutional liberty. A small group of men apparently bypassed the president [perhaps], lied to Congress, and used part of the proceeds of the sale of weapons paid for by taxpayers to implement their own foreign policy. That these people were well-meaning doesn't matter: the Constitution places the power of the purse in Congress, not with a handful of executive appointees. It is for the voters, not the CIA director and a Marine Corps detailee to the NSC, to decide that Congress is 'on the other side.'*

Many of the examples of graft and corruption particularly in the EPA, HUD, and Wedtech affairs were symptomatic of a general lack of concern with conflict of interests or ethical rules characteristic of the Reagan years. This existed in both the public and private sectors. Of particular note were antigovernment officials appointed to public office and then cashing in and personally profiting from these positions. Despite the antigovernment, bureaucracy bashing that is a favorite target of political rhetoric, Meier (1987, p. 129) points out the general rule: "A careful examination of examples of incompetence and unresponsiveness by the bureaucracy would reveal that political appointees rather than career civil servants were responsible." Many of these activities represented classic corruption, occupational and corporate crime, in which either the individual or his organization personally benefitted by criminal activity which took place as part of a legitimate occupation. Ideological considerations were behind the political crime of Iran-Contra in which the president and/or his charges took it upon themselves for perceived patriotic reasons to violate laws or policy guidelines. Johnson (1991, pp. 370–371) notes the congeniality of the president was not the issue:

> *The hand that steals the Constitution comes in a velvet glove as dangerous as that which appears in a mailed fist. . . . People did not understand the implications of disrespect for law that took root inside the White House. In the Reagan White House, laws were something to be evaded rather than faithfully executed. . . . Don't worry about process and procedure. Don't worry about laws. Just get the job done. In the ethical wasteland of the eighties that was the bottom line.*

Many of these cases had allegations of interconnections with other operations which will most likely never be unraveled. Some S&L collapses are described as being related to the largest international bank collapse, BCCI (the Bank of Credit and Commerce International); and both of these may have been used to launder Iran-Contra funds, drug trafficking funds, and CIA monies. Despite growing concern that ex-government officials were selling influence and national sovereignty to the Japanese and other foreign powers upon leaving office (Choate, 1990), ex-President Reagan shortly upon leaving the presidency cashed in by receiving $2 million for making two appearances and speeches in Japan. Although not illegal, the lack of sensitivity or concern with appearances in accepting such a fee was perhaps a metaphor of the Reagan era.

## Crimes of the Bush Era

In 1988 George Bush was elected the forty-first president of the United States after serving 8 years as vice president under Ronald Reagan. Bush had a distinguished public service career which included ambassador to China, U.S. delegate to the United Nations, and director of the Central Intelligence Agency. He also inherited some of the protracted scandals of the Reagan era which had included the savings and loan crisis, corruption in the Environmental Protection Agency, the Iran-Contra conspiracy, the Pentagon procurement scandal, Wedtech, and the HUD scandal.

Following the record-breaking Reagan era and being only half as long in duration, the Bush era hardly rivalled its predecessor in wrongdoing; however, it had more than its share of elite deviance including some continuing scandals inherited from the Reagan administration. Among the scandals of the Bush era to be discussed are the Brett Kimberlin case, the Inslaw affair, the Iran-Contra conspiracy, Iraqgate, and the Clinton passport break-in.

## The Brett Kimberlin Case

The Brett Kimberlin case involved Vice President Dan Quayle and the allegation that Brett Kimberlin, while serving time as a federal prisoner for drug offenses, was on two separate occasions placed in detention and incommunicado from the media in order to silence him. Kimberlin claimed that in the early seventies he frequently sold marijuana to Quayle, who was then a law student (Singer, 1992, p. A17).

During the 1988 presidential campaign, Kimberlin was invited twice by reporters to discuss these charges. In both instances before he could speak he was put into detention by order of J. Michael Quinlan, then-director of the Federal Bureau of Prisons. This was unprecedented—"never before had a bureau director isolated an individual inmate" (ibid.). Kimberlin claimed he was a "political prisoner," that his civil rights had been violated as were his First Amendment rights, and that he was a victim of false imprisonment.

A report issued by Senator Carl Levin (D-Michigan), chairperson of the Subcommittee on Oversight of Government Management, concluded that Kimberlin was silenced for political reasons. According to one source, the DEA had informed the Bush campaign that it had a file on Quayle alleging cocaine use (ibid.).

## Inslaw

The Institute for Law and Social Research (Inslaw) was a private consulting organization founded by Bill and Nancy Hamilton in 1973. The Inslaw case charges that the U.S. Department of Justice, beginning during the Reagan administration, stole proprietary software from the Hamiltons and tried to force their small company out of business in order to pirate its software and sell it for the benefit of Reagan cronies (McGrory, 1991; Fricker and Pizzo, 1992).

The events of Inslaw read like an unbelievable plot in a Robert Ludlum novel. Investigative journalists Mary Fricker and Stephen Pizzo (1992, p. 35), who studied the case, describe it:

> *The biggest problem we had with the story was that there are two levels:*
> *one, a business-contract dispute involving verifiable facts, and the second,*

*a through-the-looking-glass world of spies, mobsters, and so on. . . . Is the Inslaw flap an ugly contract divorce? Or did someone in Ed Meese's Department of Justice force the small software company out of business and keep its technology for the benefit of Reagan Administration insiders?*

In its defense the Department of Justice (DOJ) claims Inslaw failed to meet its contractual obligations and lost its contract to computerize the Justice Department worth over $100 million.

Two court cases have ruled in favor of the Hamiltons and against DOJ. The software they had developed that was the subject of dispute was PROMIS (Prosecutor's Management Information System), which enabled the computerization of law enforcement and criminal justice system files. When the government claimed that Inslaw was not fulfilling its part of the contract and demanded a good faith security deposit (the use of Inslaw's proprietary version of PROMIS until the contract was ironed out), the Hamiltons reluctantly agreed. Despite this, 3 months later the government cancelled the bulk of their contract (ibid.).

Then began the Part Two spy plot portion of the story. The DOJ's disingenuous scheme attempted to force federal bankruptcy officials to force Inslaw into liquidation and break their pledge and secretly expand their use of the Hamiltons' software without paying royalties. When a bankruptcy judge in 1988 ruled in favor of the Hamiltons, he was punished by not being reappointed. This decision against DOJ ordering the government to pay $7 million to the Hamiltons was upheld in federal district court but later overturned by the U.S. Supreme Court. The latter reversed on a jurisdictional technicality, feeling that the case should not have been heard in bankruptcy court.

The Hamilton's defense attorney, Elliot Richardson, discovered that Inslaw's lucrative contracts and software had been planned to be passed on to then-Attorney General Meese's friends. Both Meese and his successors in the Bush administration, Richard Thornburgh and William Barr, were uncooperative with Senate and House judiciary committee Inslaw investigations. By now this pattern of stonewalling may have taken on a *raison d'etat,* national security angle since apparently the Inslaw contract had been given to one Dr. Earl Brian, a Reagan associate. PROMIS had by now been installed at the CIA as well as sold to foreign intelligence agencies including Canada, Iraq, Libya, and Korea (ibid., p. 34). Now the Hamiltons found themselves in a bizarre world of secret contract agents and foreign intelligence. Fricker and Pizzo conclude their investigation by noting (1992, pp. 35–36):

*Inslaw's allegations raised serious questions about corruption and lawlessness with the Department of Justice, and the canning of federal bankruptcy Judge Bason [who had ruled in favor of the Hamiltons] had sent the judiciary a chilling message. . . . So long as the administration [Bush's] refuses even to consider the appointment of an independent special prosecutor, no credible answers to the mysteries swirling around the*

*Inslaw matter will emerge. Instead, the case is likely to join the growing list of events, such as the Iran-Contra scandal and the JFK assassination, that feed a heightened sense of public cynicism toward those who govern us.*

Further intrigue was added to the Inslaw case when, in 1990, freelance writer Danny Casolaro mysteriously "committed suicide" while hot on the trail of what he described as an outlaw intelligence operation behind Inslaw (ibid., pp. 34–35).

## The Iran-Contra Conspiracy—Operation Polecat

George Bush's involvement in the Iran-Contra conspiracy is a continuation of a cover-up and protracted investigation of events that largely took place during the Reagan presidency and Bush's vice presidency. At the State Department the Iran operation was described as Operation Polecat because they thought it stunk so much (Pincus and Lardner, 1993, p. 8). Among those convicted in the investigation were CIA spy chief Clair George, former White House National Security Advisor Robert McFarlane, former Assistant Secretary of State Elliot Abrams, and former CIA officers Alan Fiers, Jr., and Duane Clarridge. The convictions of Lt. Col. Oliver North, who had been a national security staffer, and former National Security Advisor John Poindexter were overturned on the grounds that independent counsel Lawrence Walsh had utilized previously immunized testimony to Congress to subsequently prosecute them. Also convicted in the scandal were retired Air Force General Richard Secord, his business partner Albert Hakim, and former CIA official Thomas G. Cline.

George Bush at first lied and claimed that he had been "out of the loop" and unaware of Iran-Contra activities. Even though as vice president Bush headed the Vice President's Task Force on Terrorism which urged that it was futile to make deals with hostage takers, he later admitted that he was aware of the hostage deal, but did not admit to knowledge of diversion of funds to the Contras. Ironically, by violating their own rules and dealing for hostages, the Reagan-Bush team proved their own point. Such secret operations released three hostages but encouraged the taking of more.

The entire cover-up, lying to Congress, and hiding of evidence had been intended to protect Ronald Reagan from possible impeachment. In June 1992 Special Prosecutor Walsh indicted former Secretary of Defense Caspar Weinberger in order to attempt to prove a conspiracy to cover up Reagan's involvement. The charges included Weinberger lying to Congress and obstructing justice based on entries in his diary.

Finally came the "Christmas Eve massacre" (December 1992), in which lame-duck President George Bush issued pardons to most of those convicted or under investigation claiming that they "did not profit or seek to profit from the conduct," that they were acting in what they believed to have been the national interest, and that the Iran-Contra investigation represented an unnecessary "criminalization of policy differences." Bush did not pardon Secord, Hakim, and Cline, whose motivations appeared to be more of a mercenary nature.

The pardons left special prosecutor Lawrence Walsh little choice but to close down the probe; however, his final report did give him the final word (Walsh, 1994). According to the executive summary of the Iran-Contra report: "President Bush was the first president to grant a pardon on the eve of a trial [Caspar Weinberger's]" (ibid.).

By diminishing the affair as a "criminalization of policy differences," Bush never condemned what the conspirators had done. Drawing a parallel with Watergate, Carl Bernstein (1993, p. 3B), coauthor of *All The President's Men,* points out:

> *Thus, the disparate cover-ups of the whole Reagan-Bush era began as untruthful responses to disparate secret policies, and then became almost a continuum of illegality, a state of mind in which political exposure and fear of defeat were met with conspiracies to hide the truth from the people and their representatives and, eventually, the law. Watergate was only the beginning.*

The message sent by George Bush in issuing the pardons was that government officials are free to violate the law whenever they believe their behavior is for the good of the country and even if it is in violation of the Constitution. One is reminded of Samuel Johnson, who once stated: "Patriotism is the last refuge of a scoundrel."

The final report on Iran-Contra held little that was new or unexpected. It reiterated that the sale of arms to Iran violated the Arms Export Control Act and that the support for the Contras violated the Boland Amendment. These policies were fully reviewed and developed at the highest levels of the Reagan administration, and the Iran operations were carried out with the knowledge of Reagan and Bush. The special prosecutor also concluded that large volumes of relevant documents were systematically and willfully withheld from the investigation and that Reagan administration officials deliberately deceived Congress and the public about the level and extent of official knowledge of and support for these operations (Walsh, 1994).

## Iraqgate—The Banca Lavoro Affair

In the Iraqgate or the Banca Nazionale del Lavoro (BNL) affair it is alleged that the Bush administration helped provide financing and arms to Sadaam Hussein in an effort to win him over and then covered up the policy after he invaded Kuwait. Banca Nazionale del Lavoro is an Italian bank, which through the Atlanta branch was used by Iraq to finance its arms buildup. Billions in loans to Hussein to finance his military were guaranteed by the U.S. Department of Agriculture in a labyrinth of deceit. All of this began when George Bush first took office and after the Iran-Iraq War. Ironically, Bush and his Secretary of State James Baker had secretly built up the armed forces of the same Sadaam Hussein that the United States would go to war with in Operation Desert Storm.

Under the guise of promoting grain sales, James Baker discovered a means to secretly finance Iraq's military at a time in which Congress would not approve such subsidies (Safire, 1993, p. A13). Prosecutors accused Christopher Drogoul, BNL's Atlanta branch manager, of hatching the plot. The Justice Department indicted Drogoul and assumed that the money was lent without the approval of the bank's Rome headquarters and thus the bank was defrauded. It is alleged that the Bush administration had been less than candid in explaining its involvement (Sciolino, 1992). Drogoul maintained that the loans were made with the tacit approval of the Bush administration and Rome headquarters. As late as 1990, after Iraq had used poison gas against the Kurds (a rebel ethnic group seeking independence), it was Congress and not the administration that wanted to impose sanctions. As late as 6 days before the Kuwait invasion, the administration had opposed Congress' attempt to cancel agricultural subsidy credits to Iraq (Gejdenson, 1992). The CIA was apparently well aware as was the Rome BNL headquarters of the fraud, but the Bush administration was certainly uninterested in any such findings prior to the Kuwait invasion. Former Attorney General Barr refused to appoint an independent counsel to investigate the Banca Lavoro case. Friedman (1993, p. 237) notes that "no attorney general of the United States had ever turned down a request from Congress to appoint a special prosecutor. William Barr became the first to do just that." He chose instead to pick his own private investigator, retired New Jersey Republican Judge Frederick Lacey. All told the Reagan and Bush administrations provided Iraq's Hussein with over $5 billion in loan guarantees, helping to broker him into a major military power and, of course, invader of Kuwait. Waas and Under (1992, p. 83) succinctly drew the parallels between Iran-Contra and Iraqgate:

*And, of course, there is the evidence that Bush secretly played an important role in a covert mission designed by William Casey to maximize Iraq's military power in the first place, and to escalate the Iran-Iraq War as part of an elaborate strategy to facilitate the arms-for-hostage deal. Coming, as it did, at a point at which the two clandestine initiatives to Iran and Iraq converged, the Casey-Bush mission embodied all that is most dangerous about secret foreign policy: hidden from the American people, and almost certainly in defiance of federal laws, the covert initiatives not only led to the taking of more American hostages and to the development by Iraq of weapons of mass destruction, but contributed to an escalation of the Iran-Iraq War, which cost tens of thousands of lives. Ultimately, the policies propelled the United States itself into war.*

Columnist William Safire (1993) of the *New York Times* claimed that the Clinton administration had been unusually silent regarding investigating Iraqgate due to a secret quid pro quo with George Bush in which the former president agreed not to criticize the new president during the first year of his term.

Both the Iran-Contra and Banca Lavoro scandals are related to the largest financial collapse in international banking, the BCCI affair. Passas (1992) told us that while the full interrelationships are not known, BCCI served as a clearinghouse for secret operations, money laundering, drug money, and terrorist financing. BCCI has been heavily involved with arms merchants through letters of credit and financing (Brewton, 1992; Truell and Gurwin, 1992).

## The Truth Commission

In March 1993 the U.N. Commission on the Truth concerning the crimes committed against civilians in El Salvador's 12-year civil war released its official report. Among its conclusions, the majority of the political murders in that nation's civil war occurred at the very least with the reluctant agreement and financial support of the Reagan and Bush administrations. Over 80,000 people, one in seventy Salvadorans and mostly unarmed civilians, were murdered in the war. The Reagan administration had long protected its cohorts in the Salvadoran military. In 1981 when the U.S.-trained Atlacatl Battalion massacred 800 civilians in the village of El Mozote, Reagan officials denied it took place and attacked the reporters from the *New York Times* and the *Washington Post* who first reported it. The Bush administration itself would not cooperate with the Truth Commission when the Pentagon refused to supply names and phone numbers of former U.S. military advisors (Rosenberg, 1993, p. 23). Mark Danner (1993, p. 132), in a feature article in the *New Yorker* entitled "The Truth of El Mozote," noted that "El Mozote could not have been a guerrilla graveyard, as some had claimed, especially since all but twelve of the one hundred and forty-three remains identified turned out to be those of children under twelve years of age. . . ." (Lewis, 1993). Despite official denials by the Reagan and Bush Administrations there was little doubt that the massacre and others had taken place. Questions have been raised also regarding the Bush administration's handling of evidence in the slaying of six Jesuit priests in El Salvador in 1989.

Since the release of the report in March 1993, the Clinton administration and more specifically Secretary of State Warren Christopher appointed a panel to investigate charges that members of the State Department misled Congress about the El Salvador atrocities throughout the eighties (Krauss, 1993a). In November 1993 over 12,000 documents were released by the State Department, Defense Department, and Central Intelligence Agency at the request of Congress. These materials demonstrated that the Reagan and Bush administrations had been advised by intelligence reports that the Salvadoran military was dominated by those involved in death squad activities. The CIA described one leader, Roberto d'Aubuisson, as a drug trafficker, arms smuggler, and plotter in the assassination of Archbishop Oscar Romero (Krauss, 1993b).

## Related Deviance

Other wrongdoing by officials during the Bush administration included the Passport Cases. During the presidential reelection campaign of 1992 (more specifically, September 30 and October 1) rival Democratic candidate Bill Clinton's passport files were searched in an attempt by Republicans to attack his anti-Vietnam War activities while he was a student at Oxford University in England. Also searched were his mother's records as well as those of Independent candidate H. Ross Perot. Before leaving office Bush dismissed Assistant Secretary Elizabeth Tamposi, who was the most apparent official responsible for the search. A special prosecutor was appointed by Attorney General Barr in part to investigate whether the Bush White House instigated the illegal search.

### The Bush Boys

During the presidential campaign George Bush took umbrage at what he viewed as unfair political attacks on his sons; however, the three Bush boys all made private fortunes by trading on their father's position and being involved in a number of questionable business transactions (Pizzo, 1992a and 1992b). Bush has three sons—John Ellis ("Jeb"), George W., Jr. ("Junior"), and Neil.

John Ellis Bush ("Jeb") of Miami, Florida, had received considerable financial support from Miami's right-wing Cuban community. Along with business partners he defaulted on a shared $4.6 million loan from Broward S&L, which later collapsed. Later, federal regulators reduced the estimated amount owed by this group to $500,000, stiffing taxpayers for the remaining $4 million (Pizzo, 1992a, p. 30). One of his business partners, Camilo Padreda, had previously been accused and indicted for looting Jefferson S&L (McAllen, Texas). Another partner of Padreda's, Hernandez Cartaya, has been associated with CIA operatives and contractors who had systematically misused ("looted") at least twenty-six S&Ls as part of Iran-Contra operations (Brewton, 1992). In 1989 Padreda pleaded guilty to defrauding HUD of millions of dollars during the 1980s.

While working for Miguel Recarey, Jeb's employer facilitated the largest health maintenance organization Medicare fraud in U.S. history involving overcharges, false invoicing, and outright embezzlement. Recarey was convicted and has since fled the country. This same medical business is also believed to have been tied into Iran-Contra operations. A Health and Human Services (HHS) agent, who was continually blocked in his investigation by Washington, claims Recarey and his hospital were treating wounded Contras from Nicaragua "and part of the $30 million a month was given by the government to treat Medicare patients was used to set up field hospitals for the Contras" (ibid., p. 32). Recarey could have been a CIA "cutout" or asset having the equivalent of a "Get Out of Jail Free" card. Another of Jeb's business associates had a $2 million mansion in the Bahamas transferred to him by Charles Keating shortly before Keating filed for bankruptcy (ibid., p. 33). Some of the federal inaction against S&L thieves may be related to secret CIA money laundering operations. In examining the disastrous policy of deregulating S&Ls Brewton (1992, p. 393) states: "Reagan-Bush deregulation opened a Pandora's box and George couldn't close it, and didn't want to considering all his friends, offspring and political backers who were happily getting richer."

George W. Bush, Jr. ("Junior"), was accused of being involved in an insider trading scandal, while Neil Bush received the most attention in the media for his involvement on the board of directors of Silverado Savings and Loan in Denver and its subsequent collapse.

Unlike Ronald Reagan, George Bush did not appear to attempt to cash in or directly benefit financially immediately upon leaving the presidency. Hersh (1993), however, claims that two of his sons as well as his closest former advisers, who accompanied Bush on a post-Persian Gulf War trip to a grateful Kuwait, were cashing in on that nation's gratitude for America's leading the military victory.

The Reagan and Bush administrations almost made a national sport out of secret policies, noncooperation with congressional oversight, shredding information, and stonewalling the judiciary and Congress. Prior to departing from office Bush wanted to purge all White House electronic files, arguing that these were private internal communications and not records as such. In the wake of Watergate, a federal law holds that a former president's records belong to the people. While hard disk drives were packed up for their trip to the National Archives, critics charge that some materials may have purposely been lost. Archivist of the United States Don W. Wilson apparently signed an 11:30 P.M. (literally eleventh hour) memorandum of agreement giving Bush full legal control over the computerized records of his presidency as well as of other derivative information. The *Washington Post* described this deal as "A Departing President's Midnight Raid on History" (Lardner, 1993). The deal looked particularly questionable when it was later announced that Wilson would receive a $129,000 a year job as executive director of the George Bush Center for Presidential Studies at Texas A&M University.

## Discussion

The Bush administration, while having its share of traditional graft and corruption, did not come close to the record number of occupational criminals who cashed in during the Reagan era. Rivalling Reagan, however, were cover-ups of political crimes. Participants in the Iran-Contra conspiracy had received full pardons, since Bush viewed them as not personally benefitting or as having acted in the national interest, a classic description or rationalization of political criminals. These are ones who commit their crimes either for or against the government for ideological reasons. Brendan Sullivan, general counsel to Oliver North, radically objected to a line of questioning by Senate Committee Chair Daniel Inouye (D-Hawaii) during the Iran-Contra hearings when Inouye drew parallels between North's defense and those claimed by Nazi war criminals at Nuremberg, who also claimed that they were just following orders.

In pardoning Iran-Contra conspirators, Bush was really practicing the doctrine of "sovereign immunity" in which authorities of the state view themselves as above the law. Kelman and Hamilton (1988) refer to this as "crimes of obedience." The government political criminal is motivated not by self-interest, but by a commitment to a particular belief system, feeling that he or she is defending the status quo or pre-serving the existing system (Hagan, 1994, p. 426). This ideological motivation is distinct from the desire to preserve personal power (occupational crime). The latter was better illustrated by Watergate. For political crimes government officials or their agents have historically sought justification in the "doctrine of *raison d'etat* (reason of state)," which is usually attributed to Italian political philosopher Niccolo Machiavelli (1469–1527). This doctrine holds that some violations of the common law are necessary for the end of public utility (Friedrich, 1972, pp. 21–22). In cases of crime committed in the act of political policing, labels of "official secrets," "national security," and "reasons of state" shroud many incidents and evidence (Turk, 1982). In the Iran-Contra case the conspirators even invented a new word for lying: "plausible deniability," or being able to claim believably that you did not know about something. Reagan would avoid knowing the detailed means of policy making and thus could believably lie that he was not aware of various incidents.

## C. Wright Mills and the Higher Immorality

The crimes of the Bush era were an outcome of a number of structural and ideological trends that emerged with Franklin Roosevelt's presidency, accelerated during the Nixon and Ford years, and came to full fruition in the Reagan-Bush period. These structural and ideological trends include (Hagan and Simon, 1993, p. 25):

1. The centralization of fiscal and monetary powers within the executive branch. Arthur Schlesinger described this as the growth of "the imperial presidency" (1973).
2. The creation (in 1947) of the National Security State and, within it, a "secret government" (Moyers, 1988; and Simon and Eitzen, 1993).
3. The constant interchange of personnel between the various factions representing the American power elite (Mills, 1956; Dye and Ziegler, 1990; and Dye, 1986). This is especially the case with corporate executives, politicians from the nonfederal level, military officers, and members of the "secret government" including organized crime figures. Many serve in government just long enough to make contacts, peddle influence, and then cash in on these networks.
4. This interchange of elites brought new personnel to the federal government as well as a set of ethics from nouveau riche business elite based on a combination of social Darwinism, laissez-faire capitalism, and supply-side economics.

These trends resulted in an intensification of what C. Wright Mills termed "the higher immorality" (Mills, 1956, Chapter 13). The higher immorality refers to illegal or unethical practices among upper levels of the nation's corporate, political, and military elite. The structural basis of the higher immorality finds that institutionalized forms of corruption often involve interrelated scandals. Events in one major scandal are often linked to events in one or more additional scandals. Some of the same players in one scandal are involved in one or another additional debacle. Many of the actors involved in Iran Contra-Inslaw and Iraqgate were also involved in the S&L scandal, the BCCI collapse, drug trafficking, money laundering, and a vast network of "off-the-shelf" covert activities.

Fundamental changes have taken place in American democracy in the postmodern era (Hagan and Simon, 1993). Key trends have been increasing centralization of power, wealth, and information in American government and big business. Policy making in Washington is increasingly controlled by corporate-financed polling organizations, lobbying organizations, public relations firms, and think tanks of which 51 senators and 146 house members are either founders or officers (Greider, 1992). These organizations, along with those established in the National Security Act of 1947, have created power centers that have bypassed the checks and balances set up in the Constitution. Institutionalized structures of power and corrupt practices in the Reagan-Bush era are merely one more step in an environment of opportunity that could threaten the very structure of democracy. These trends will be explored more thoroughly in Chapter 8.

*4*

## Crime against Government: Protest and Dissent

*Violence has formed a seamless web with some of the noblest and constructive chapters of American history: the birth of the nation (Revolutionary violence), the occupation of the land (Indian wars), the stabilization of the frontier (vigilante violence), the elevation of the farmer and laborer (agrarian and labor violence), and the preservation of law and order (police violence). The patriot, the humanitarian, the nationalist, the pioneer, the landholder, the farmer, and the laborer (and the capitalist) have used violence as a means to a higher end.*
—*RICHARD BROWN (1969, pp. 69–70) IN REPORT TO THE VIOLENCE COMMISSION*

*The Founding Fathers were political offenders all.*
—*NICHOLAS KITTRIE AND ELDON D. WEDLOCK, JR., THE TREE OF LIBERTY, 1986, p. XI*

### Protest and Dissent

Political crime, particularly in America, has been an intimate part of the dynamic social change characteristic of the country. Figure 4.1 illustrates the fact that activities by political criminals against government are often mirror images of crimes by

| Crime by Government | | | Crime against Government | | |
| --- | --- | --- | --- | --- | --- |
| Genocide | Human rights | Illegal surveillance | Protest | Revolution | Terrorism |
| Terrorism | violations | | Dissent | Social movements | Assassination |
| | | | Civil disobedience | | Treason |

**FIGURE 4.1    The Continuum of Political Crime**

government. As we move from the center to the polar extremes of the continuum, the activities become more violent and radical/reactionary.

Crimes against the government vary from illegal protests, demonstrations, and strikes to treason, sabotage, assassination, and terrorism. Throughout history social movements that seek change are viewed as threatening or subversive to the existing society. The American Revolution, the labor movement, the anti-Vietnam War movement, and the struggle for civil rights serve as examples. Demonstrators for civil rights and other causes have purposely violated laws and been arrested for disorderly conduct, breach of peace, parading without a permit, trespassing, loitering, and the like. They have been arrested for refusing to pay income taxes that may be used for military purposes, for picketing military bases, for student protests, or for refusing to register for military draft. Many student activists of the sixties viewed their universities as involved in the military, industrial, and racial status quo (Skolnick, 1969, p. xxi).

While dissent and protest activities against the government are usually perceived as "radical" (leftist) in attempting to bring about change in the existing order, they may also represent "reactionary" (rightist) activities which attempt to preserve the existing order, institutions, or organizational schemes that are no longer acceptable. Neo-Nazi groups, skinheads, the Ku Klux Klan, militia groups, and the like serve as examples.

Groups express dissent and civil disobedience by means of activities including employing sit-ins, boycotts, and Freedom Rides (to desegregate facilities) in order to challenge unjust laws. They consciously violate certain laws to call public attention to their cause and to force change in the law. Dr. Martin Luther King, Jr., a Protestant minister, a civil rights leader, and director of the Southern Christian Leadership Conference, was criticized by other clergy for neglecting God's work and becoming too radically involved in disruptive activities.

## Letter from Birmingham Jail

The Nuremberg principle or precedent supports the view that, if one is faced with the choice of either obeying unjust laws or following one's moral conscience, the latter holds precedence; to blindly follow orders when they violate human rights and dignity is unacceptable. King's (1963) "Letter from Birmingham Jail" describes his view that immoral laws must be disobeyed:

*My Dear Fellow Clergymen:*

*While confined here in the Birmingham city jail I came across your recent statement calling my present activities "unwise and untimely . . ." I am in Birmingham because injustice exists here. . . . Anyone who lives inside the United States can never be considered an outsider anywhere within its bounds. You deplore the demonstrations. . . . But your statement, I am sorry to say, fails to express a similar concern for the conditions that brought about the demonstrations. . . . Birmingham is probably the most thoroughly segregated city in the United States. Its ugly record of police brutality is widely known. There have been more unsolved bombings of Negro homes and churches in Birmingham than in any other city in the nation. . . . The purpose of our direct action program is to create a situation so crisis-packed that it will inevitably open the door to negotiation. . . . We know through painful experience that freedom is never voluntarily given by the oppressor; it must be demanded by the oppressed. One may well ask, "How can you advocate breaking some laws and obeying others?" The answer lies in the fact that there are two types of laws: just and unjust. I agree with St. Augustine that "an unjust law is no law at all. . . ." [An] individual who breaks a law that conscience tells him is unjust and who willingly accepts the penalty of imprisonment in order to arouse the conscience of the community over its injustice is in reality expressing the highest respect for the law. . . ."*

Martin Luther King, Jr., and his organization, the Southern Christian Leadership Conference, advocated civil disobedience, nonviolent, passive resistance similar to that used by Mahatma Gandhi in overcoming British rule in India. Gandhi's philosophy of passive resistance argued that violence on the part of those enforcing unjust laws must be met with nonviolence in order to appeal to the public's sense of justice. Scenes on television of segregationists and police attacking peaceful demonstrators began to win and galvanize the support of the American public for the demonstrators. Freedom Rides in which civil rights workers rode buses in a test of new civil rights laws ordering desegregation of interstate public transportation was also greeted with violence. Civil rights demonstrators also had to test the enforcement of the new laws in states that resisted such changes. This time, however, federal law enforcement personnel and the National Guard were employed to assist the civil rights workers who were now obeying the law, but violating long-standing segregationist laws in the face of often violent resistance. King's strategy had won the day, not to mention the Nobel Peace Prize. Incarcerated members of the Irish Republican Army in Northern Ireland also borrowed a tactic from Gandhi, the "hunger strike." Members of "H block" starved themselves to death in order to demonstrate their dedication to their cause and win a united Ireland.

In 1989, prior to the abolishment of apartheid in South Africa, hundreds of jailed political prisoners followed the same dietary regime as the IRA had in 1981, drinking only water. The detainees demanded their release or that they be formally charged in court. They had been detained as security risks to the state. In 1994 American protester Randall Robinson went on a hunger strike in opposition to U.S. policy toward Haiti. After a 27-day fast, the Clinton administration gave in and changed its policy (Koppel, 1994).

The indomitable spirit and dedication of political offenders in support of their cause against all odds are often awe inspiring. One of the most famous dissidents before the collapse of the former Soviet Union was Natan (Anatoly) Sharansky, who was described as a "refusenik," one who refused to give in to authorities in his struggle for human rights. In his book *Fear No Evil* (Sharansky, 1988, p. 1) Sharansky describes his experiences beginning the evening of March 15, 1977, when he was abducted by the KGB outside an apartment on Gorky Street in Moscow and taken to Lefortovo Prison and charged with espionage and treason—crimes punishable by death. He then spent the next 9 years in prison and labor camps, over 400 days in punishment cells, and more than 200 days on hunger strikes. During months of interrogation and isolation his captors tried everything to make him confess to crimes that he had never committed. They wanted to use him to discredit movements that helped Jews emigrate to Israel and for human rights dissidents. Sharansky was eventually freed and permitted to emigrate to Israel.

## Political Whistleblowers

Information usually is classified as secret to protect national security, but also in some instances to misinform the public and cover up questionable activities. It was to protest the latter that Daniel Ellsberg, an employee of the Rand Corporation (a private think tank and research organization), turned over secret government documents—the Pentagon Papers—to the press (Gravel, 1971). He felt that the government's deceit regarding U.S. involvement in the Vietnam War outweighed his duty to keep government secrets. In a more controversial case, former CIA agent Philip Agee (1975) wrote personal memoirs of his CIA activities in South America. He ideologically disagreed with many covert policies the CIA had been carrying out in that region. Agee's revelations threatened the lives of agents and operatives.

In 1995 U.S. Captain Lawrence Rockwood was court-martialled and charged with violating orders and leaving his post in order to investigate human rights violations in Haiti's prisons. Rockwood felt that the investigation and elimination of brutality superseded his military orders. In 1995 U.S. Representative Robert Torricelli broke his secrecy oath as a member of the House Intelligence Committee in order to reveal that a paid CIA informer in the Guatemalan army was involved in two murders. One was an American citizen murdered in 1990 and the other the Guatemalan husband of an American citizen who was murdered in 1992. Torricelli felt that such secrecy oaths do not extend to protecting criminal acts.

## Social Movements

*Social movements* are relatively organized groups that contain a distinctive ideology and advocate social change. Most such groups use noninstitutionalized and sometimes societally disapproved means of obtaining their objectives. Besides advocating a distinctive ideology, social movements possess specific goals and tactics as well as unique leadership. Many social movements are fragile and depend on charismatic leadership. *Charisma* refers to a personal magic of leadership, the ability to inspire a following. George Washington, Martin Luther King, Jr., Carrie Nation, Jim Jones, and Adolph Hitler were all charismatic leaders albeit some were evil ones. Most social movements are initially viewed as threatening to the status quo by the existing society but often emerge due to the need for societal change and the inability of existing institutions to adapt to such needs. Once successful, the former social movement becomes institutionalized and part of the now changed social order. Illegal protests, demonstrations, and strikes are often associated with social movements that advocate change in the status quo. Members and supporters are usually deeply committed to altering the existing society. The civil rights battle against racism, the feminist struggle against sexism, the labor and agrarian movements for fair wages, the antiwar movement against the escalation of the Vietnam conflict, the antinuclear, environmental, and the pro-life or pro-choice movements are all examples. While intent on altering the status quo and at times resorting to violence, sabotage, and other destructive behavior, most such groups do not resort to treason, assassination, or terrorism. Frequently, political criminals have done nothing more than exist and suffer attack because of race, gender, ethnicity, or nationality. Expulsion, exile, curfews, confiscations, confinement, restrictions on travel, and controls over associations may all be used to subordinate, enslave, or subject to second-class citizenship subjugated groups.

Although they may take on a number of different forms, four main types of social movements can be identified (Poponoe, 1995, pp. 488–492):

Reform movements
Transformatory movements
Resistance movements
Expressive movements

*Reform movements* attempt partial change in society. Examples are supporters of the Equal Rights Amendment, the pro-life or pro-choice movements, or the

---

**EXHIBIT 4.1    Wounded Knee and the American
Indian Movement**

On December 29, 1890, roughly 200 unarmed men, women, and children were massacred at Wounded Knee, South Dakota, by the U.S. Seventh Cavalry (Wrone and Nelson, Jr., 1973, pp. 433–438). In 1968 the American Indian Movement (AIM) was founded in Minnesota and led by Dennis Banks and Clyde Bellencourt. Begun to protest police practices, the group quickly expanded to a national mission involving social and cultural protest. Part of their new policy agenda was a call for reorganization of the Bureau of Indian Affairs and that the federal government honor past Indian treaties. The latter was a tall order given the history of "forked tongues" and broken promises characteristic of federal policy toward Native Americans.

On February 27, 1973, roughly 200 armed AIM militants seized the village of Wounded Knee on the Oglala Sioux Pine Ridge reservation. They demanded U.S. Senate investigations of Indian affairs. During a shootout two Indians were killed and several injured on both sides. The siege ended with the promise of negotiations which were later simply referred to Congress. Another incident at Wounded Knee took place in 1975 and involved another shootout in which two FBI agents were killed and four AIM members were charged with murder.

---

disabled rights movement. Others include elements of the environmental movement, MADD (Mothers Against Drunk Drivers), the victim's rights movement, as well as the antipornography movement.

*Transformatory* (revolutionary) *movements* advocate overthrow of the existing society. Examples are the American, French, Russian, or Iranian revolutions in which the existing state was viewed as irredeemable. *Resistance movements* attempt to prevent change or reverse changes that have been accomplished. Backlash against civil rights or affirmative action by a "forgotten majority" is one example; Operation Rescue (pro-life militancy) representing organized mass demonstration against liberalized abortion laws and the *Roe* v. *Wade* Supreme Court decision serves as another.

*Expressive social movements* provide redemptive or personal improvement goals for its members through a new identity and weltanschauung (world view). Religious cults, the New Age movement, even Dead Heads (followers of the rock group Grateful Dead) possess some of these qualities. Exhibit 4.1 describes a transformatory or revolutionary social movement.

While citizens living in developed democracies take for granted a free press and freedom of speech, throughout much of the world in authoritarian and theocratic regimes such ideas are subversive and practitioners of such thoughts are perceived as subversives or traitors. Salman Rushdie, who at the time of this writing was in hiding due to death threats from Iran's leaders, came to the defense of Bangladeshi author Taslima Nasrin, who also faced charges from her government for allegedly criticizing the Koran. Rushdie (1994) notes that not enough people are convinced of the oppression of women under Islam while the mullahs in many countries continue to support the sexual mutilation of women. When Islamists come to power, women are driven out of the workforce.

In analyzing black militancy, student riots, and antiwar demonstrations of the sixties, the Skolnick Report to the National Commission on the Causes and Prevention of Violence (Skolnick, 1969, pp. xix–xx) concludes:

> . . . *serious analysis of the connections between protest and violence cannot focus solely on the character or culture of those who protest the current state of the American political social order. Rather, our research finds that mass protest is an essentially political phenomenon engaged in by normal people; that demonstrations are increasingly being employed by a variety of groups, ranging from students and blacks to middle-class professionals, public employees, and policemen; that violence, when it occurs, is usually not planned, but arises out of an interaction between protesters and responding authorities; that violence has frequently accompanied the efforts of deprived groups to achieve status in American society; and that recommendations concerning the prevention of violence which do not address the issue of fundamental social and political change are fated to be largely irrelevant and frequently self-defeating.*

In July 1994 Philip Berrigan was sentenced to federal prison ("As His Backers Protest," 1994) for vandalizing an Air Force bomber. Berrigan and associates broke onto an Air Force base and used hammers to batter an F-15E jet. Berrigan, an ex-Catholic priest and longtime peace activist, claimed to have been arrested at least six times a year for his civil disobedience, which began in the sixties. Exhibit 4.2 details some of the activist groups of the sixties.

Conscientious objectors, those who refuse to serve in the military because it violates their personal, religious, or moral principles, are also political offenders. In the eighties and nineties groups such as the sanctuary movement, pro-life and pro-choice groups on the abortion issue, and antinuclear movements participated in the various forms of civil disobedience and protest activities. The sanctuary movement consisted of church and lay workers who ran an underground railroad to assist political refugees (often illegal immigrants) from being deported to their Central American homelands where they faced political repression and often death. The U.S. government viewed such groups as in violation of immigration laws and as economic rather than political refugees, and felt that the government had a right and responsibility to control the nation's borders (Crittenden, 1988; Tomsho, 1987).

## EXHIBIT 4.2    A Who's Who of Activist Groups of the Sixties

The following Who's Who is an attempt to describe in general terms the political groups whose names appear at least once in this chronology. The criterion for inclusion is that a group or individual was involved in a specific incident of terroristic or quasi-terroristic violence. An effort was made to distinguish between groups that were leftwing or rightwing in political orientation.

### *Groups of Leftwing Political Orientation*

**1. Black Muslims**—Primarily a religious and commercial organization, its believers differed from the orthodox Muslims in that only blacks were allowed to become members. Leader Elijah Muhammad's teachings, that all white men were devils and that blacks would rise up against them and establish a separate state, were carried to their extreme with the random killing of 14 whites in San Francisco by the Muslim Zebra murderers. With the exception of the Zebra killings, the violence associated with the Black Muslims has involved shoot-outs with police and assassinations within the sect. With the death of Elijah Muhammad, more internal violence was feared, but Wallace D. Muhammad's succession as Supreme Minister was peaceful. Secular affairs (at least $46 million in assets) are run by a six-man committee, with Wallace's brother Hubert, and Muhammad Ali as members. In June of 1975, Wallace B. Muhammad announced that white people would be allowed to join the Black Muslims. *Muhammad Speaks,* the Black Muslim newspaper, has stopped demanding a separate black state. Thus the sect's potential for violence seems on the decline.

**2. Student Nonviolent Coordinating Committee (SNCC)**—Founded in the early 1960's, this small, multiracial group was primarily involved in voter registration in the South. In 1966, it was a staunch verbal advocate of Black power—but by 1970 it had declined, with its leader H. Rap Brown still in prison, and its other major spokesman, Stokely Carmichael, traveling around the world promoting Pan-Africanism.

**3. Revolutionary Action Movement (RAM)**—Organized in 1963, this group advocated militant self-defense for blacks. In June 1967, police in New York City and Philadelphia rounded up 16 members and seized rifles, carbines, and shotguns. Two were charged with plotting to assassinate black moderates. Four more were later arrested in Philadelphia on charges of conspiring to foment a riot by poisoning the water supply. By 1968, the group had declined.

**4. Republic of New Africa (RNA)**—Founded in April 1968 with a few of its members formerly in RAM, this group had similar separatist goals. In August 1970, after a police raid on the residence of their leader, Imari, 11 members were charged with murder, assault, and waging war against the State of Mississippi.

**5. Black Panther Party (BPP)**—Founded in 1966 by Huey Newton and

Source: National Advisory Committee on Criminal Justice Standards and Goals. Report of the Task Force on Disorders and Terrorism. Washington, D.C.: Government Printing Office, 1976, pp. 517–521.

**EXHIBIT 4.2**   *Continued*

Bobby Seale in Oakland, Calif., its membership swelled to several thousand with chapters in major U.S. cities. Their papers urged blacks to arm themselves for self-defense and liberation. On April 2, 1969, in a New York bomb plot case, 21 Black Panthers were indicted on charges of plotting to set off bombs in five midtown department stores. All were acquitted. On July 4, 1969, Stokely Carmichael, prime minister of the Black Panther Party, called a meeting to form a National Committee to Combat Fascism. The House Internal Security Committee stated on August 23, 1971, that the Black Panthers posed a danger to policemen but were "totally incapable of over throwing the government." On January 30, 1972, Huey Newton said the party had abandoned the pick-up-the-gun approach. The violence associated with the Black Panthers has come out of confrontations with police, factional clashes within the party, and feuds with the rival black power group, the U.S. Cultural Organization (US). (The enmity between the BPP and US was allegedly encouraged by the FBI.) No longer instituting armed patrols in Oakland, the few hundred still active operate a shoe distribution program, an exterminating service, and health clinics.

**6. U.S. Cultural Organization (US)**—Based in Southern California, this black power group, led by Ron Karenga, competed with the Black Panthers to represent the radical Black community. Its members have been traced to at least two shoot-outs with the Black Panthers, in which three Panthers were killed.

**7. Black Liberation Army (BLA)**—Founded in 1971 as an offshoot of the Eldridge Cleaver faction of the Black Panthers, these more militant members have allegedly been responsible for several police killings in New York and San Francisco, and armed robberies to fund the organization. In New York, numerous attempts have been made by BLA members to escape from prison With the November 15, 1973, killing in New York City of Twymon Meyers, police believe that most BLA members have been either imprisoned or killed in shoot-outs with the police.

**8. Fuerzas Armadas de Liberación Nacional Puertorriquena (FALN)**—Although the main ideology of this group is the belief that Puerto Rico should be independent from the United States, many of its communiques concern themselves with exploitation by bankers and stockbrokers (yanqui imperialists) of the working classes. The FALN introduced themselves in October 16, 1974, with the bombing of five banks in New York City. The bombings seem to occur in groups, with New York City as the central location. The FALN does not seem overly concerned with the preservation of life: they are responsible for booby-trapping an explosion for a police officer and the bombing of a crowded restaurant in New York City. The FALN is suspected of causing 27 bombings in New Jersey, New York City, Chicago, Philadelphia, and Washington, D. C., resulting in 4 deaths and 57 injuries.

**9. Jewish Defense League (JDL)**—Founded in 1968 to protest Soviet treatment of the Jews, its leaders were a lawyer named Bert Zweibon and an orthodox rabbi named Meir Kahane. Members were trained in karate and the use of weapons to defend themselves

*Continued*

**EXHIBIT 4.2**    *Continued*

against anti-semitism, their motto being "Never Again." During JDL's first 3 years they harassed Russians, Arabs, and Black Panthers with demonstrations and relatively harmless activities, such as letting loose mice and toads. Targets of their sabotage and bombings have been the offices of Soviet airlines (Aeroflot) and the trade agency (Amtorg). Their first reported bombing took place at Aeroflot and Intourist offices on November 25, 1970. One person died as a result of the bombing of agent Sol Hurok's office, an event that is widely attributed to JDL, though this was never proven. Early in 1976, a group calling itself the Jewish Armed Resistance began claiming bombings in New York City directed at targets similar to those of the JDL. Though the JDL acts as a conduit for the Jewish Armed Resistance's communiques, it disclaims any connection.

**10. American Indian Movement (AIM)**—This group of young, militant Indians has sought better treatment of American Indians through dramatic occupations. AIM first gained national prominence with its Trail of Broken Treaties to Washington, D.C., and the nonviolent occupation of the Bureau of Indian Affairs (BIA) building. AIM leaders Russell Means and Dennis Banks negotiated with a Presidential commission set up in response to the occupation of Wounded Knee in 1973. The violence attributed to AIM is associated with shoot-outs with Federal marshals or FBI agents or infighting with the more traditional tribal leaders at the Pine Ridge Reservation in South Dakota.

**11. Students for a Democratic Society (SDS)**—Founded in 1959, this loosely knit student organization did not emerge as a political force until Tom Hayden's and Al Haber's Port Huron Statement at the 1962 convention. The statement called for an alliance of blacks, students, peace groups, and liberal organizations to influence the Democratic Party. The first anti-Vietnam War march was organized by SDS in the spring of 1965, which resulted in a sudden growth of membership. In April and May 1968, black and white SDS convention in Chicago, a serious dispute arose when the Maoist Progressive Party attacked the Black Panthers as being more nationalist then revolutionary. The factions that developed around this issue led to SDS's disintegration. One of the more militant factions was the Revolutionary Youth Movement I, most members of which became Weathermen. The "Weatherman Paper," sponsored by Bernadine Dohrn, Jeff Jones, Bill Ayers, Mark Rudd, et al., was delivered at this convention and called for guerrilla tactics to bring about the destruction of U.S. imperialism.

**12. Weather Underground Organization (WU)** (Changed from the original **Weathermen** because of its sexist connotations)—In 1969, the Weather Underground concentrated on recruiting high school students for their mass action in Chicago, by picketing high schools and rushing into classes screaming "jailbreak." Disappointed with the poor showing by radicals at their October 8–11, 1969, Chicago Days of Rage, and angered by the killing of two Black Panthers in a police raid, the decision was made to turn the Weather Underground into an elite, paramilitary organization to carry out urban guerrilla warfare; thus it became the grandperson of American revolutionary organizations. On May 25, 1970, the

**EXHIBIT 4.2** *Continued*

New York Times received the first communique from the Weather Underground, stating that the group would go underground and that "within the next 14 days we will attack a symbol or institution of American justice." With hardly a day to spare, the New York police building was bombed on June 9.

The only fatalities associated with the Weather Underground (buildings are typically bombed late at night and the bombing is preceded by a warning call) occurred on March 6, 1970, when three Weatherpeople were killed in a New York City townhouse after a series of explosions. Police investigations revealed the townhouse was being used as a bomb factory with the bombs manufactured being of the kind used to kill or maim people rather than destroy property. Some of the more spectacular incidents credited to the group include the bombing of the Capitol on March 1, 1971, the bombing of the Pentagon on May 19, 1974, and the freeing of Timothy Leary from a San Luis Obispo prison on September 13, 1970. The Weather Underground's bombing activities lessened considerably in 1972 (there was only the Pentagon bombing) and 1973 (there were only two bombings), but picked up again with four evenly spaced bombings in 1974. In July 1974, copies of their statement of revolutionary ideology and interpretation of American History, "Prairie Fire," were distributed in the San Francisco Bay Area and in Boston. The authors claim credit for 19 bombings in the United States since 1969. In terms of predicting future strategies of Weather Underground activity, the document asserts that "legal and clandestine struggle are both necessary; . . . peaceful methods and violent methods . . ." will be used.

**13. Sam Melville**—Arrested in the act of bombing U.S. Army trucks, he admitted to a number of 1969 bombings in the New York City area; the United Fruit Co. pier, the Marine Midland Bank, and simultaneous bombings of the General Motors building, the R.C.A. building, and a chase Manhattan Bank. A former plumbing hardware designer, this 33-year-old revolutionary typically positioned his bombs so as to wreak the maximum amount of destruction. He was killed in the 1971 uprising at the Attica Correctional Facility.

**14. Symbionese Liberation Army (SLA)**—Formed out of associations between prison-reform-minded white radicals and members of a prison group called the Black Cultural Association at the California Medical Facility at Vacaville, the SLA emerged with the November 7, 1973, incomprehensible killing of Oakland school superintendent Marcus Foster. Their next act was to kidnap newspaper heiress Patricia Hearst on February 4, 1974. As the terms for her release, they demanded that $2 million in food be given to the poor of the Bay Area. When that food giveaway broke down into chaos, another distribution date was arranged; though it went much more smoothly, Patricia Hearst was not released. Through the taped communiques sent to radio stations, Patricia Hearst appeared to be progressively more alienated from her parents until she eventually declared her new revolutionary identity as Tanya and took part in the April 15th robbery of the Hibernia Bank. On May 18, 1974, six SLA members died in a gun battle and ensuing fire in a suburb of Los Angeles, with Emily

*Continued*

**EXHIBIT 4.2**  *Continued*

and Bill Harris and Patricia Hearst viewing the entire incident in a nearby motel. Aside from a suspected role in a Sacramento bank robbery, the SLA concentrated on anonymity until Patricia Hearst and the Harrises were recaptured in San Francisco on September 18, 1975.

It is suspected the remnants of the SLA have joined with the New World Liberation Front (NWLF). On February 12, 1976, San Simeon, the Hearst mansion, was bombed. The NWLF claimed credit for the bombing, and James Kilgore (former fellow painter of Stephen Soliah, in whose apartment Patty Hearst was arrested, and also suspected in an SLA bank robbery in Sacramento) was identified as being on the tour that day at San Simeon.

**15. New World Liberation Front (NWLF)**—Based in the San Francisco Bay area, this leftist group has adopted techniques similar to those of the Weather Underground—bombing accompanied by warnings and communiques. The NWLF has developed the communique into an art form, to the point of having designated above-ground spokesmen. NWLF espouses a variety of leftist causes and directs its attacks primarily against major corporations or government buildings. In 1970, the NWLF published the late Brazilian revolutionary Carlos Marighells's *Minimanual of the Urban Guerrilla.* Their first recorded entry into violent action was the August 5, 1974, unsuccessful bombing of an insurance agency in Burlingame. In 1974, the NWLF claimed eight bombings; the majority of the targets were linked to International Telephone and Telegraph, which the NWLF claimed "drained the life of poor people" and

"must . . . admit complicity in Chile's murderous coup." In 1975, 22 bombings were attributed to the group, many of them directed against utility towers belonging to Pacific Gas and Electric (PG&E). Their demands have ranged from better health care at the San Bruno jail to free utilities for retired people. The most active revolutionary group in the United States today, it is believed by some that the NWLF acts as an umbrella for other terrorist groups in California, such as the Chicano Liberation Front, the Red Guerrilla Family, and the remnants of the SLA.

**16. Red Guerrilla Family (RGF)**—This Bay-Area-based group emerged on March 27, 1975, with the bombing of the FBI office in Berkeley. Though less active than the NWLF, the bombings claimed by the Red Guerrilla Family have been more powerful. The similarities between the two groups (on two occasions they have bombed on the same day; their targets are similar) has led to speculation that either the Red Guerrilla Family is another name adopted by the NWLF members to make revolutionary groups appear to be more numerous, or the two groups are working in cooperation with each other.

**17. Chicano Liberation Front (CLF)**—Another group with possible ties to the NWLF, this group was formed in the barrios section of Los Angeles in response to the deaths of Chicanos in an antiwar rally. Its targets have included banks, government offices, and supermarkets. Although it was very active in the early 1970's, the group declined after receiving a great deal of criticism for the killing of a Chicano employee in one of its bombings. It too is suspected of having joined with the NWLF.

**EXHIBIT 4.2** *Continued*

**18. Emiliano Zapata Unit (EZP)**—Yet another San Francisco-based group, it appeared in October 14, 1975 with the unsuccessful bombing of a PG&E Tower in Belmont, Calif. In October, a number of Safeway stores were bombed in the Bay Area. The Emiliano Zapata Unit claimed one of those bombings (in Oakland) on October 31. Three more bombings were claimed by the EZP until on February 17, 1976, while making an arrest for an attack on a home in Marin County, the police traced the suspects to a group called the New Dawn Collective. The New Dawn Collective had described itself as an overground voice for revolutionary groups. From that arrest, agents and local police were able to raid a house in Richmond, Calif., on February 21, seizing 130 pounds of explosives and arresting six persons. Documents in the house linked the suspects with the Emiliano Zapata Unit.

## Groups of Rightwing Orientation

**1. Ku Klux Klan (KKK)**—After a lull during World War II, the KKK returned to intimidating blacks, Jews, and Catholics through burning crosses, bombings, beatings, murders, and lynchings. The incidents occurred in waves, in 1945, 1948, and in 1950. The KKK responded to the civil rights movement with a new wave of such incidents in the early 1960's. FBI infiltration had undermined the secret organization, but it is still active in areas where racial integration is a major issue. A recent event for which KKK members were convicted was the bombing of school buses in Pontiac, Mich., on August 30, 1971.

**2. Minutemen**—A paramilitary, rightwing organization, their primary activity was harassing leftwing organizations, building up weapons arsenals, and threatening liberals with their insignia, the cross hairs of a rifle scope. Police arrested 19 members as they reportedly prepared to sabotage three leftwing camps in New York State on October 30, 1966. On October 18, 1971, charges against the 19 were dropped due to a court decision that held that the original search warrants were defective. Some members were alleged to have participated in at least one bank robbery to fund the organization. Strongest in the 1960's, the group declined by the end of the decade following the conviction of their leader, Robert DuPugh, for a Federal firearms violation.

**3. Legion of Justice**—Between 1969 and 1971, this Chicago-based group reportedly beat and gassed anti-Vietnam War demonstrators, and sabotaged theaters housing communist performers. Considerable controversy exists as to whether or not they were assisted in their efforts by law enforcement authorities.

**4. Breakthrough**—Opposed to communism, socialism, and most leftwing causes, this Detroit-based group is represented by its ubiquitous chairman, Donald Fobsinger, who has been arrested on numerous occasions for disturbing the peace at leftwing rallies. A mayoral candidate, Mr. Fobsinger was convicted for assaulting a priest at an antiwar rally in 1973.

**5. Secret Army Organization (SAO)**—Based in San Diego and Arizona this small group concerned itself primarily

*Continued*

**EXHIBIT 4.2** *Continued*

with harassing student radicals, to the point of shooting at them in one incident. One of its members, recruited by an FBI informer, was responsible for the bombing of an erotic theater. The SAO is noteworthy in that it represents the difficulties faced by the FBI in maintaining the credibility of its informers without allowing them to become agents provocateurs. Lawsuits have been brought against the FBI and governmental officials concerning the FBI's role in funding and directing the organization.

**6. Cuban Action Commandos—** This Los Angeles-based group is believed to have been responsible for numerous bombings of consulates of countries deemed friendly to Castro's Cuba. Active in the late 1960's, many of its members were imprisoned. Particularly active in 1975, this group also directs its attacks against leftwing bookstores.

**7. Other Anti-Castro Groups—** Most of these groups are social and fraternal organizations for Cuban exiles, who hope to return to a Cuba without Castro. Over 1,000 such groups have been formed in Miami alone, but approximately 20 are now still active. Few of the groups are actually violent, but their proliferation and ties with the Cuban community make those that are violent difficult to apprehend. Bombing targets are usually government agencies or firms doing business with Cuba. With hatred of Castro as the only unifying ideology, these groups are transient and have overlapping memberships. These groups often use fictitious names for the purpose of fundraising, and use another name for terrorist activities.

**8. National Socialist Liberation Front (NSLF)—**Led by the late Joseph Tommasi, this group broke off from the insufficiently violent fascist National Socialist White People's Party to pursue more violent tactics. Tommasi was shot and killed by a regular Nazi in the summer of 1975. The NSLF is suspected of having been responsible for four bombings against leftwing groups in the Los Angeles area in 1975. With the death of Tommasi, its activities have declined.

**9. Peace and Freedom Fighters—** This Hungarian-exile group is based in Los Angeles. Police officials suspect the group has aligned itself with the Cuban Action commandos and the National Socialist Liberation Front in actions against leftist organizations.

**10. Posse Comitatus—**Founded in Portland, Oreg., in 1968 in the home of Mike Beach, this vigilante group believes that the American Constitution has been subverted and that its members are justified in taking the law into their own hands. In their applications for charters, they state that they want "to aid the local sheriff in the exercise of his duties." Their literature asserts that Federal income tax and all licenses (particularly those involving weapons) are unconstitutional, and that the county government is their highest authority. Though their potential for violence appears to be considerable, only one incident of violence (the accidental discharging of a gun) has been attributed to the members of the organization. The Posse has been most active in the Northwest, in States like Montana, Idaho, and California.

Pro-life (right-to-life) forces are opposed to legalized abortion, viewing it as murder, and seek a reversal of the 1973 *Roe* v. *Wade* Supreme Court decision, which permits abortion on demand. Not content with protests and civil disobedience, more extreme factions have bombed abortion clinics and assassinated abortion doctors. Opponents (pro-choicers) argue that such a decision is a personal one between a woman and her physician and not the government's decision; that one group's morality should not become public policy in opposition to the will of the majority (Paige, 1985). With over 40,000 arrests by 1991 for blocking abortion clinics, Operation Rescue, a pro-life campaign to stop abortions, may have become the largest civil disobedience campaign in U.S. history (Lawler, 1991). Abortion rights advocates and physicians' groups expressed concern that doctors and abortion clinic workers were increasingly the targets of stalking, harassment, aggressive campaigns to stop abortions, and in extreme cases death threats and murder. In 1994 two different pro-life activists were convicted of such murders, in one instance receiving the backing of a since sanctioned priest who said murdering abortion doctors was "justifiable homicide." The abortion controversy promises to continue to be both protracted and intractable, but a U.S. Supreme Court ruling in 1994 may provide a model for preserving the rights of clinic patients without impinging on the rights of peaceful abortion opponents. Protesters are asked to express their opinions peacefully, but are to be willing as any protester to pay the price of prosecution and court injunction if they trespass or otherwise infringe on the rights of others ("Law and Order," 1994).

> *[H]e [God] has anointed me; to bring good news to the poor. He has sent me, to proclaim to the captives release, and sight to the blind; to set at liberty the oppressed . . .*
>
> —Luke 4:18–19

Advocates of the liberation theology movement feel that true Christians betray the values and mission of Jesus Christ if they separate their religious belief in him from the struggle on behalf of peace and justice, which includes confronting unjust structures and bearing witness for the oppressed. Such beliefs and practices in authoritarian regimes such as El Salvador in the eighties led to the murder of Archbishop Oscar Romero as well as priests and nuns whose activities on behalf of the poor peasants were viewed as communist subversion by an authoritarian military regime. Activists and sanctuary workers vowed to defy U.S. immigration laws "be it through evasion, circumvention, ignoring, feigned compliance, or open refusal. The organization, La Resistencia, wishes to help the thousands of Central Americans seeking asylum" ("Signers Vow," 1989, p. 6).

Antinuclear forces are convinced that the nuclear industry is dangerous and preventing the development of more ecologically sane energy policies such as solar energy. Such groups have violated the law in attempts to prevent start-ups of new reactors. An antinuclear activist ran onto a stage in 1992 while former President Reagan was speaking, broke a crystal statue Reagan had received, and shoved him aside and began speaking before being arrested. "Act-uppers" are activists who wish to attract public attention and action to fight AIDS. Interrupting meetings by blowing whistles, they attempt to call attention to their cause.

Antivivisectionists are those who oppose using animals in scientific experiments in which maiming, torture, death, or other harm takes place. Such groups have protested and raided laboratories, "liberating" animals (Regan, 1982) or photographed and released to the press some of the more grisly examples. Scientific researchers who use animals claim that such experiments are necessary for discovering medical cures and treatments. Members of the Animal Liberation Front vandalized and set fire to a mink research laboratory at Michigan State University, accusing the professor who ran the lab of killing "thousands of minks in painful and scientifically worthless experiments" ("Animal-Rights," 1991). The raid destroyed 30 years of research on the disappearance of minks in the Great Lakes area.

Exhibit 4.3 presents some very strong arguments against much animal testing. In October 1981, acting on evidence provided by animal rights activist Alex Pacheco, the Maryland State Police raided the Behavioral Biology Center of Edward Taub in Silver Spring, Maryland, and charged him with seventeen counts of animal cruelty. Taub was the first and only researcher ever tried and convicted of such charges in the United States (Fraser, 1993, p. 66). He needlessly tortured his monkeys. Photographs of his laboratories showed animals living in filth and suffering from pain and neglect. His experiments involved a surgical procedure called somatosensory deafferentation, the cutting of sensory nerves.

Sometimes crimes such as kidnapping, burglary, robbery, and hostage-taking are committed for political purposes. For example, in 1991 in Philadelphia a $3.6 million jewelry heist was masterminded by three brothers to help fund a civil war in Yugoslavia ("Jewel Thieves," 1991). A group calling itself Earth First! with the motto "No Compromise in Defense of Mother Earth" was on trial in 1991 for ecoterrorism, such as damaging ski lifts, sawing through power poles, and plotting to sabotage three nuclear installations ("Jury Selection," 1991). Exhibit 4.4 provides some suggestions for nonviolent protest alternatives prepared by a national task force on disorders and terrorism.

Protest, dissent, demonstrations, civil disobedience, and the social movements that used them are part of the basic order of things in dynamic democratic societies. Part of the struggle for human rights throughout the world is an attempt to extend the civil liberties enjoyed by individuals in democratic societies to all countries. It is in the very nature of a society's reaction to these demands for social change that a society defines its values and ultimately its *raison d'etre* (reason for existence).

## EXHIBIT 4.3 Nonessential Animal Testing: Luxury through Brutality

When an issue involving "animal rights" arises, whether it be a protest against the wearing of fur or the hunting of deer or the using of animals in laboratory experiments, the debate between the animal rights advocates and those who defend such ways of using animals is invariably characterized by little more than strong emotions and one-sided rhetoric. Looking at this, one might think that issues of animal rights are so inherently controversial that they defy rational analysis and resolution.

Fortunately, this pessimistic assessment is not warranted. As long as we keep firmly in mind the obvious moral truth that avoidable suffering should not be caused unless it is **truly necessary to achieve a genuinely important purpose,** we can rationally resolve at least some of the animal rights issues which confront us today.

One such issue involves the widespread practice of testing nonessential, non-medical consumer items (principally cosmetics and household products) on animals. In such experiments, various animals (including dogs, cats, monkeys, rabbits and rodents) are either forced to ingest or inhale huge quantities of potentially toxic substances or have assorted caustic materials placed into their eyes or plastered to their skin.

Just about every cosmetic or household product on our shelves, including insecticides, antifreeze, bleaches, oven cleaners, deodorants, lipsticks and paints— just to name a few, has been tested on countless animals in these ways. These tests take anywhere from several days to a few weeks, during which time many symptoms manifest themselves, including convulsions, diarrhea, bleeding from virtually every bodily orifice, massive destruction of eye tissue and/or flesh, blindness and death. In fact, in the notorious Lethal Dose 50 Test, the tests are repeated until fifty percent of the test animals die from the dose of the test substance. In almost all cases, the suffering animals are **given no pain relief whatsoever** for fear of causing minor distortions in the test data.

According to Dr. Andrew Rowan, Assistant Dean of the Tufts University School of Medicine, such testing of cosmetics and household products causes the suffering and death of approximately 14 million animals every year. Given our basic moral obligation of compassion not to cause unnecessary suffering, is such **non-medical** testing morally justified? Is the great suffering caused to untold millions of animals **truly necessary** for achieving our consumer purposes and are these purposes **genuinely important**?

Our answer should be clear. Such suffering is obviously needless; hence such experimentation is morally indefensible. After all, painfully testing these products on animals is unnecessary for three distinct reasons, any one of which alone would be sufficient to render such experimentation unjustified. First of all, the products tested are not essential to human life or health. Hence, we do not need such luxury items in the first place. Secondly, there are already

*Continued*

Source: Thomas J. Donohue, 1992, "Nonessential Animal Testing," *Networkings*, Fall, 7: 3. Used with permission.

---

**EXHIBIT 4.3**  *Continued*

many satisfactory products of these types on the market. Thus, even if we did need some such products, we certainly do not need any more of them. Thirdly, there are alternative methods of testing these products which do not use or harm animals. So, even if we needed an endless supply of largely redundant luxury items (which we obviously do not), it still would not be justified to painfully test them on animals, since such products can be tested for safety, sold and consumed **without forcing even one defenseless animal to suffer.**

These alternative, cruelty-free methods of testing (thankfully being used by an increasing number of enlightened companies) include the use of cell, corneal and skin tissue cultures, chicken egg membranes, corneas from eye banks, synthetic products which mimic the reactions of human skin and the human eye to foreign substances and sophisticated computer and mathematical models based upon our knowledge of the properties of various substances and upon information gained from past human exposure to such substances.

Companies can also make safe new products simply by using the many ingredients and combinations of ingredients already determined to be safe by the Cosmetics, Toiletry and Fragrance Association. Thus, when these **unnecessary** products are **unnecessarily** tested on animals, the resulting pain constitutes a clear violation of our basic moral obligation of compassion not to cause unnecessary suffering.

So it simply is not the case that all animal rights issues are unresolvable quagmires of conflicting prejudices. The bottom line is that neither our desire for the latest luxury item nor the producing company's desire to maximize its profits negates our basic moral duty to be compassionate.

Knowing this, we now of course have a moral obligation to take all reasonable steps to oppose such testing and we certainly are duty-bound not to subsidize and thereby perpetuate such testing by buying products which have been tested at the expense of suffering animals. Compassion and decency demand nothing less.

---

**EXHIBIT 4.4    Nonviolent Protest Alternatives**

Mass disorders involving extraordinary violence are frequently the unintended results of demonstrations and protests by persons and groups in dissent against authority. Less frequently, they occur as a form of planned protest. Acts of individual and small-group terrorism, too, may be intended to communicate—and dramatize—particular points of view on particular political and social issues.

Because the interrelationship between extraordinary violence and dissent is real, special responsibilities for the prevention and avoidance of extraordinary violence fall to the leaders and members of dissident groups, who must strive to honor ethical and legal norms in expressing even the most extreme views, and to the private community as a whole, which must be prepared to give

Source: National Advisory Committee on Criminal Justice Standards and Goals. Report of the Task Force on Disorders and Terrorism. Washington, D.C.: Government Printing Office, pp. 362–365.

**EXHIBIT 4.4** *Continued*

attention to the views of dissidents who elect means of protest short of violence. In particular:

1. Dissidents and dissident organizations should strive to adopt effective legal means of protest (such as authorized mass marches, boycotts, and picketing) in preference to illegal ones. Where a confrontation with authority is deemed essential to protest activities, only nonviolent breaches of law (such as sit-ins and unauthorized marches) should be undertaken. Where a reverence to violence is deemed essential to protest activities, it should be symbolic, rather than actual.
2. Organizers and leaders of protest demonstrations should assume responsibility for the conduct of participants, and should attempt to avoid the development of violent mass disorder through:
   a. The exclusion from participation of groups and persons with avowed or known commitments to violent tactics;
   b. The specification of clear guidelines for participants, including rules to minimize the likelihood of counterviolence;
   c. The use of marshals recruited from within the protest organization to observe and control the conduct of participants; and
   d. The development of procedures to terminate protest activities that threaten to develop into violent disorders.
3. The general public—and the news-gathering and communications organizations that serve it—should take special care to appreciate both the political context of nonviolent protest activities and the fervency with which they are held and to do so without mistaking nonviolence for a lack of commitment on the part of dissidents.

## Commentary

It is an axiom of American constitutional law that every political or social position—short of direct, practical advocacy of insurrection—is entitled to expression. And it is a fact of American political life that the attention of the public at large is most likely to be concentrated on those minority positions that receive the most dramatic forms of expression. In practice, the right to assemble for purposes of protest has proved to be among the most valuable of the rights of political expression, second to the right of citizens to dissent.

The potential for violence is implicit in any mass protest gathering; indeed it is the existence of this potential—symbolic or actual—that gives even the most determinedly nonviolent protest gatherings an impact directly proportional to the number of participants involved. Even more important for the purposes of this Report, however, is the obvious risk of real violence that any mass assembly of seriously aggrieved persons poses; only a tiny minority of the participants in a mass protest needs to be motivated to give a violent form to their expressions of dissatisfaction before the risk of a major disorder—arising from the contagious effects of the violence of the few—becomes a reality.

*Continued*

**EXHIBIT 4.4**  *Continued*

Recognizing the nexus between legitimate or nonviolent mass protest and the potential for extraordinary violence in the form of mass disorder, this standard recommends approaches to the dilemma of dissenting organizations: how to control the likelihood of violence without deflecting the protest from its purpose.

As stressed in Goal 10.1, it is believed that, adoption by dissenting organizations of a set of standards of conduct and practice to check the violent potential of mass disorders is necessary as a matter of social responsibility. It is also believed that, as a general matter, the control that such standards can afford will be of tactical benefit to the organizations adopting them, in the context of an overall strategy for the promotion of social and political change. Obviously, however, such efforts at self-governance by dissenting organizations require official and nonofficial support—in the form of a willingness to lend attention to grievances expressed in ways that do not imply the potential for violence.

Whether mass violence has in fact been a necessary catalyst to important social or political change in America is finally a moot question. Of the essence, however, is the fact that the use of mass violence as a mode of protest has been perceived as a tactically essential last resort by numbers of groups throughout American history—those believing that their positions and grievances had been ignored or overlooked by a complacent majority and a hostile or unresponsive government. Because the recommendations of this standard are addressed to groups in this posture—or likely to be found in it—as well as to those with extreme perceptions, community attention to legitimately expressed dissident views can hardly be overstressed as a correlate of self-restraint by dissenters.

*Forms of Protest*

This standard is unusual in that it recognizes the probable inevitability of illegal protests, although it does not approve illegal protest tactics. Because the thrust of this Report is toward the problem of extraordinary violence and not toward law violations of all kinds, it is believed important that attempts be made to draw clear distinctions between those illegal protests that threaten to generate violence and those that do not. Where a dissenting group is impelled to dramatize its position through intentional lawbreaking, the social responsibilities with which this chapter is concerned can be honored—at least in part—by electing forms of protest that are nonviolent even though prohibited.

The distinction between potentially violent and nonviolent mass protests is not, of course, easily made in practice. As already noted, any protest—legal or illegal—involves some risk of violence, and the extent of that risk will depend on circumstances. Thus, for example, an illegal protest in the form of a peaceful building occupation may be unlikely to erupt into violence in most environments; where there is a known possibility that counter-demonstrators may employ physical violence to oust demonstrators, however, the same protest may be highly inflammatory. It is the responsibility of any dissenting group considering any protest demonstration to assess the risks of violence realistically and to avoid demonstrations in which those risks are high. Obviously, this responsibility is

**EXHIBIT 4.4** *Continued*

especially critical when the form of protest contemplated is an illegal one. The protest organization that elects illegal tactics has—from the philosophical stance of the proponents of civil disobedience—a privilege to expose its own members to arrest and prosecution; it has no similar privilege to expose the community to violence.

Again, it should be stressed that this standard does not recommend or condone the use of illegal protest tactics. It does, however, recognize that such tactics will be employed and that there are real distinctions to be drawn—from the standpoint of avoiding extraordinary violence—between more and less acceptable forms of illegal protest.

Perhaps the most difficult problem in distinguishing protest behavior that is responsible in regard to the avoidance of violence, from that which is irresponsible, arises in protests that involve some element of aggression. Again, this standard does not condone aggressive or destructive tactics, but it recognizes that they are—to some degree—inevitable. Although such tactics go beyond conventional civil disobedience, they are nevertheless deeply rooted in the history of American dissent. A question must still be posed, however, as to what self-imposed limits dissident groups engaging in such tactics should obey as a matter of social responsibility. The answer is not easily given, but it would appear to lie in a recognition of the special character of limited, symbolic acts of aggressive protest, that have no appreciable potential for developing into more generalized and more destructive violence. Whatever view is taken of the legal and moral justification for such acts, they are relatively more

acceptable than acts posing real risks to public safety where the avoidance of extraordinary violence is concerned.

Protests of the Vietnam era provide an illustration of the point. Those protest groups that sought to bring the war home, through loosely targeted series of attacks on persons and property, were clearly violating the principles of social responsibility that underlie this standard, even though the level of violence actually employed was generally low; the perceived unresponsiveness of government to more moderately expressed grievances does not justify, although is may partially explain, the decision of these groups to expose the community at large to risks of extraordinary violence. By contrast, those antiwar groups that engaged in carefully planned aggressive protest tactics directed against symbolic property targets—such as the destruction of selective service records—did not create a similar risk of general mass violence by their actions. Those protests, even though both were clearly illegal and arguable outside the scope of conventional civil disobedience, were not dangerous ones in terms of the limited objective with which this standard is concerned—the prevention of extraordinary violence.

### *Structure and Membership of Protest Organizations*

Up to this point, the discussion has been concerned with the dissenting group's social responsibility for the prevention of violence as a factor in selecting modes of protest. Thus this standard has adopted a simplified view of the dynamics of protest and the relationships of protest to violence

*Continued*

**EXHIBIT 4.4** *Continued*

to focus attention on the importance of leadership decisions affecting collective group action. In fact, the picture is a good deal less clear—real risks of disruption leading to mass violence are posed not only by an irresponsible leadership decision, but also by the irresponsible act of a faction (or even an individual member) of a protest organization as a whole.

It goes without saying that every person who uses protest tactics, whether legal or illegal, has the same responsibility to regulate his or her own personal conduct that the organizational leadership has to regulate the conduct of any protest group as a whole. It must also be presumed, however, that not every person who participates in a protest will honor this responsibility spontaneously. The practical issue that this standard addresses is, thus, what measures the leadership of dissenting groups and the organizers of particular protests should take to help assure that the acts of individuals will not provide an impetus toward mass violence that can be avoided.

Among the measures recommended for this purpose is the exclusion from organized protests of persons and groups of persons that the organizers believe are likely to use violent tactics. Obviously, no private citizen or citizen group can prevent others from conducting a protest action on their own terms; socially responsible dissenting groups with commitments to the avoidance of extraordinary violence can, however, deny the advantage of association with them to dissidents who are not committed to the avoidance of violence. In effect, nonviolent protest organizations can attempt to isolate, rather than to assimilate, potentially violent persons.

The difficulty of this task, and the complexity of the judgments that must be made in performing it, should not be underestimated, especially under circumstances in which a coalition of groups and individuals is organizing a large, one-time demonstration. Nevertheless, it is believed that the best understanding of the potential for violence posed by the participation in a protest activity of any dissident group or person is usually in the command of those who are closest, in political views and community status to that group or person. Organizers of nonviolent protest should—and do—recognize that unanticipated violent conduct by a minority of participants can vitiate the effectiveness of a demonstration and can expose the majority of participants to legal and even physical jeopardy. Sound tactical judgment, as well as principles of social responsibility, dictates concentrated efforts to exclude the violently disruptive participant.

In organizing particular protest activities, leaders and members of dissenting groups have further opportunities to reduce the risk of extraordinary violence. Elsewhere in this Report, the importance of official initiatives in providing planning assistance to protest groups has been stressed (Standard 4.3, Facilitating Peaceful Demonstrations, and Standard 6.7, Preventive Measures Against Mass Violence); here, it is necessary to note that whether or not local law enforcement proves helpful, organizers of protest activities should plan carefully, with an emphasis on developing techniques for maintaining discipline during the protest itself. Two such techniques are specifically recommended in this standard: the use of marshals, and the

**EXHIBIT 4.4** *Continued*

promulgation of rules and standards of conduct to govern the action of individual protest participants.

The usefulness of marshals has been demonstrated conclusively in major protests of the past decade. When properly trained, clearly identified, and linked in a communications network, any group of responsible protesters can fill this function—acting as intermediaries between protesters and police, as channels for instructions from leaders to participants, and as sources of miscellaneous advice, counsel, and information. Their presence has the effect of impressing on the public at large the nonviolent intent of a demonstration; more significantly however, it can be influential in the realization of that interest.

Preparation of guidelines for protest demonstration participants is an organizational task closely linked to the style of protest organization that emphasizes the clear location of leadership and the use of marshals to maintain communication between leadership and participants. Of the guidelines that can be established for conducting protest activities, those that have most importance for the discussion concern participant interactions with nonparticipants—including law enforcement, curious members of the community at large, and members of groups hostile to the protesting organization's cause. And the essence of the guidelines for interaction that will best promote the avoidance of extraordinary violence consists of instructions to avoid all violent exchanges with others—minor as well as major, and verbal as well as physical. In the course of a major protest demonstration, participants will have many opportunities to provoke extreme reactions in

others, as well as to react extremely to provocation. In the interests of preserving order and of promoting the smooth course of the demonstration, those opportunities must be forgone. Elsewhere in this Report (Standard 6.7, Preventive Measures Against Mass Violence, and Standard 6.8, Tactical Management of Mass Disorders in Progress) forbearance is recommended as an essential element of the official reaction to mass demonstration; restraint is no less important on the part of participants in such demonstrations.

Inevitably, however, efforts to exclude violence-prone persons from participation in protest demonstrations, and to establish and enforce guidelines for the conduct of participants, will not always be sufficient to prevent the occurrence of mass violence. Whether failures by the protest organizations to take preventive measures are at fault, or circumstances (such as violence by counter-demonstrators) over which that organization has no control, the practical problem confronting responsible protesters and their leaders is how to avoid or minimize any actual eruption of violence.

To this end, the organizers of every mass protest should include in their planning—and in the guidelines provided for participants—provisions for a rapid termination of the protest and a coordinated dispersal of the participants. Marshals and other participants with field leadership responsibilities should be made aware of the possibility that a termination of the demonstration may be required and briefed on procedures for achieving it. And wherever possible, the

*Continued*

**EXHIBIT 4.4**  *Continued*

problem of termination should be discussed between organizers and law enforcement officials in advance of a demonstration, in order to assure that police action will not interfere with private efforts to avoid impending violence, or the reverse.

*References*

1. Fortas, Abe. *Concerning Dissent and Civil Disobedience.* New York: New American Library (Signet Broadside), 1968.

2. Skolnik, Jerome H. *The Politics of Protest.* New York: Simon and Schuster, 1969.

3. Thoreau, H. D. "On the Duty of Civil Disobedience," *The Rhetoric of No.* (Fabrizio, Keres and Menmuir, eds.), New York: Holt, Rinehart and Winston, 1970.

4. U.S. National commission on the Causes and Prevention of Violence. *To Establish Justice, To Insure Domestic Tranquillity.* Washington, D.C.: Government Printing Office, 1969.

# 5

# Crime against Government: Assassins and Spies

*Traditionally, roses have been the symbolic emblem of the spying profession. Greek mythology describes an incident in which the god of love offers a rose to the god of silence as an inducement to gain the latter's silence regarding the weaknesses of the other gods. In Medieval Europe a rose was hung from the ceiling of council chambers and those in attendance pledged their silence since the gathering was sub rosa, under the rose (Morrell, 1984, p. 83).*

## Assassins

*"Sic semper tyrannis"*

—John Wilkes Booth

In May 1995 Pennsylvania Avenue in front of the White House was closed to traffic for the foreseeable future in part in response to terrorist truck bomb attacks in Oklahoma City and of the World Trade Center in New York City, as well as to suggestions by security experts in light of attacks and threats against President Bill Clinton. In September 1994 Frank Corder, a drunken, despondent, unemployed, crack cocaine user, crashed a stolen, small Cessna 150 airplane into the south facade of the White House and killed himself. Although friends were not aware of any grudge Corder may have had against President Clinton, one friend indicated that Corder had talked about his committing suicide by crashing a plane into the White House. Fortunately due to ongoing repairs to the structure, the Clintons were staying at a guest facility, Blair House, at the time of the crash. On October 25, 1995, Francisco Duran, a Colorado upholsterer, opened with semiautomatic rifle fire on the Pennsylvania Avenue side of the White House, claiming he was shooting an evil mist hanging over the White House about which aliens had told him. He was subdued by two bystanders. A jury rejected expert testimony arguing that Duran was a paranoid schizophrenic or insane. The defense described him as an anarchist. Police had discovered a map in Duran's truck with the words "Kill the prez." On April 4, 1995, Duran was convicted of attempted assassination. The bizarre actions of Corder and Duran have a long and sometimes misunderstood history in American politics.

James Clarke (1982) in *American Assassins: The Darker Side of Politics* was critical of the assumption that most assassins suffer from some mental pathology, insanity, or derangement. Claiming the assassinations literature is a pyramid of inaccurate secondary sources, Clarke states that this pathological myth about assassins is continually repeated in leading works such as those by Donovan (1952), Hastings (1965), Kirkham (1969), and the Warren Commission (1964). This observation of pathological symptoms may result from post hoc error, the false assumption that since one variable or outcome follows another in time, it must be caused by the preceding variable. Clarke believes that most of the major works on assassins fail to consider the political context of assassinations (1982, p. 7) and identifies five types of assassins (the names of these types have been provided by this writer):

1. Political assassins
2. Egocentric assassins
3. Psychopathic assassins
4. Insane assassins
5. Atypical assassins

*Political assassins* commit their acts (they believe) selflessly, for political reasons. They are primarily motivated by ideology. Some examples of such assassins and attempted assassins are John Wilkes Booth (Lincoln), Leon Czolgosz (McKinley), Oscar Collazo and Griselio Torresola (Truman), and Sirhan Sirhan (Robert Kennedy). Booth committed his crime in support of the Confederacy, Czolgosz's was in support of a class revolt, Collazo and Torresola were Puerto Rican nationalists, and Sirhan felt his act would help the Palestinian cause. Such offenders are truly political criminals. John Wilkes Booth felt that Lincoln was a tyrant and enemy of his cause, the Confederacy. After fatally shooting Lincoln in his loge at Ford's Theatre, Booth leaped to the stage, breaking his leg in the process, and in the dramatic style of his acting profession said to the audience, "Sic semper tyrannis" (may it ever be thus to tyrants—the motto of Virginia).

*Egocentric assassins* are "persons with an overwhelming and aggressive egocentric need for acceptance, recognition, and status" (Clarke, 1982, p. 7). Realizing the consequences of their acts, they do not exhibit cognitive distortion characteristic of delusion or psychoses. Some examples are Lee Harvey Oswald (John Kennedy), Samuel Byck (Nixon), Lynnette ("Squeaky") Fromme (Ford), and Sara Jane Moore (Ford). They seek attention, which they feel they have been denied, and seek to place a burden on those they feel have denied or rejected them. John Hinckley, the attempted assassin of Ronald Reagan, would fit this Type 2 description. Oswald and Byck projected their personal difficulties into political extremism, while Oswald wanted to prove himself to the Cuban government and to his wife, neither of whom took him very seriously. In February of 1974 Byck died in an attempt to hijack a jetliner, which he hoped to crash into the White House and kill Nixon. Although "Squeaky" Fromme resembled a Type 1 assassin, her devotion was to a man (Charles Manson) and not a cause (Clarke, 1982, p. 262). Moore wished to demonstrate her commitment to radicals who had rejected her when they discovered she was an FBI informant. Corder and Duran, who threatened Clinton, may fit in this category.

*Psychopathic assassins* are unable to relate to others. These emotional cripples direct their perverse rage at popular political figures. Loveless and emotionally deprived in childhood, they are resentful and morally indifferent and wish to strike back at the society they blamed for their miseries. In describing Guiseppi Zangara (Franklin Roosevelt) and Arthur Bremer (Wallace), Clarke indicates "their motives were highly personal: they wanted to end their own lives in the most outrageous display of nihilistic contempt possible for a society they hated" (p. 167). Both transferred resentment for their emotional deprivation in childhood to public figures. Bremer targeted George Wallace (a Democratic primary candidate for president) after other presidential candidates he had stalked did not lend the proper opportunity.

*Insane assassins* have documented histories of organic psychosis, a type of mental illness caused by physiological factors either environmentally or genetically induced. They often have documented histories of hereditary mental illness and exhibit severe emotional cognitive distortion of reality, such as paranoia, which might be expressed in delusions of grandeur. Psychotic assassins include Richard Lawrence (Jackson), Charles Guiteau (Garfield), and Joseph Schrank (Theodore Roosevelt). Guiteau and Lawrence both believed they had been selected by God to perform His will, while Schrank irrationally believed that he was avenging McKinley's assassination and that Theodore Roosevelt had been the culprit.

*Atypical assassins* are those who defy classification, such as Carl Weiss (Huey Long) and James Earl Ray (Martin Luther King, Jr.). Weiss was a successful physician who killed Long because he felt he was protecting the lives and political jobs of his relatives. Although racism obviously was behind the King assassination, Ray, an unsuccessful career criminal, appeared to be primarily motivated by an alleged $50,000 payment for the assassination (p. 246). Clarke indicates that because of racism in the South, Ray believed he could get away with it. The possibility of an organized conspiracy in the King assassination is the behavior of Ray, a small-time hoodlum, after the assassination. He all of a sudden became a globetrotting James Bond, complete with phony documents, and was finally captured in London.

Clarke indicates that since 1963 Type 2 and 3 assassins have strived for media attention and that restriction of such coverage could help discourage some assassination attempts. He also indicates that there is less need for additional surveillance and more of a need for the analysis of information already in the possession of organizations such as the FBI. The FBI was aware of Byck, Fromme, Hinckley, Moore, and Oswald and even covered up information after the fact regarding the Oswald and Ray cases. (This, by the way, has led to a variety of conspiracy theories with respect to the King and John Kennedy assassinations.) Additionally, fourteen of the sixteen assassins analyzed by Clarke used handguns, whose possession gun lobbyists continue to insist is an inalienable constitutional right, although this has not been supported by judicial decisions.

## The Kennedy Conspiracy

In 1991 Oliver Stone's movie *JFK* gave renewed vigor to those who are convinced that a conspiracy existed in the assassination of President John Kennedy, which took place on November 22, 1963, in Dallas, Texas, by Lee Harvey Oswald. Both those who accept Lee Oswald as the lone assassin and those that propose a conspiracy tend to at times delete contrary evidence and selectively cite supporting evidence (Blakey, 1993, p. 23). Before he could stand trial, Oswald himself was assassinated by Dallas nightclub owner Jack Ruby. The Warren Commission (1963), which was appointed to investigate the assassination, concluded that Oswald acted alone, while a 1979 House assassinations committee (Blakey and Billing, 1981) concluded that there was very likely a conspiracy involving the mafia (Simon, 1993; Summers, 1980). Other conspiracy theories suggested that Oswald was a Russian agent, a CIA double agent, a pro-Castro operative, represented anti-Castro groups, or was part of a right-wing conspiracy. Part of the problem with many such scandals is that often subsequent official investigations themselves involve coverup, which further feeds allegations of conspiracy. Although this issue of conspiracy will be examined in more depth in the last chapter, a brief presentation follows of some of the conspiracy debate.

Some of the points of contention regarding the Kennedy assassination and contrary arguments include:

- Lee Harvey Oswald was a Russian agent.
  Oswald's KGB file as well as the KGB supervisor of Oswald's case indicate that he was regarded as too unstable and untrustworthy to be considered an agent.
- A second gunman on the grassy knoll fired the fatal shot that killed JFK.
  A number of the witnesses who have come forward with this story did not do so at the time of the assassination and no "smoking gun" has been demonstrated.

- Ruby was a mafia hit man paid to silence Oswald.
  A lie detector test and circumstances do not support this including Ruby leaving his beloved pet dog outside in his car at the time of the assassination. If his killing of Oswald was premeditated, he took no action on a previous occasion and would have arranged for someone to take care of his dog.
- Oswald did not have time to fire three shots.
  Enhancement of the Zapruder film (amateur video shot at the time of the assassination) demonstrates ample time for Oswald to get off three shots.
- Two men in a green Ford pickup were spotted by motorist Julia Mercer taking a gun from a case and disappearing onto the grassy knoll.
  The truck was stalled and belonged to a construction company and had been under constant surveillance by three Dallas policemen.
- A man on the motorcade route opened and closed a black umbrella as a signal to open fire.
  Louis Witt, the umbrella man, was heckling the president with a symbol, an umbrella, similar to one Neville Chamberlain carried from his "sell out" negotiations with Hitler at Munich. He was not part of an assassination plot or a person sending a signal.

The Warren Commission (1963) was appointed by President Johnson to fix the blame in the assassination and relatively quickly concluded that Lee Harvey Oswald was the lone assassin. Despite the fact that the commission failed to pursue all leads or was unaware of some additional promising ones, many conclude that its conclusions were essentially correct (Posner, 1993), whereas others point out that the deliberate destruction of evidence by the FBI in order to cover ineptitude makes it impossible for us to ever know (Fonzi, 1993; Scott, 1993) and continues to feed suspicion and conspiracy theories.

Simon (1993) indicates that a subsequent investigation by the Church Committee, the Senate special committee on government operations, discovered shocking facts:

- The CIA's assassination attempts against Castro were not known to the Warren Commission.
- The CIA knew Castro was aware of plots against him, but the Warren Commission was never informed.
- The FBI never investigated Oswald's involvement with a Cuban exile group in New Orleans.
- J. Edgar Hoover harbored intense dislike of the Warren Commission.
- The FBI covered up details regarding Oswald's trip to Mexico.

Although this discussion barely scratches the surface of the Kennedy assassination debate, it hopefully gives the reader a taste of an issue that will continue to be controversial as well as probably insoluble.

## *Treason*

Treason is one of the earliest and most universally punished crimes by society and the only crime discussed in the Constitution of the United States. Early definitions of treason such as the Roman "crimen majestatis" (injuring the honor or majesty of the Roman people) and "hochverrat" (high treason in Germanic codes) as well as the Anglo-Saxon concepts were very broadly defined, often confusing political criticism of leaders with treason against the state. Framers of the United States Constitution wanted a very restricted definition of treason in order to prevent such broad political uses of the concept (Ploscowe, 1935)..

> *Treason against the United States shall consist only in levying war against them, or in adhering to their enemies, giving them aid and comfort. (Article III, Section 3)*

As of 1983, fewer than fifty cases have been brought to state or federal court in the United States involving violation of the law of treason. Attempts at more broad political application of the law took place primarily very early in the history of the republic with cases such as the Aaron Burr trial and the Whiskey and Fries Rebellion. While the treason law remains restrictive, Hurst (1983, p. 1561) indicates:

> *In the practice of Congress and decisions of the courts, the constitutional definition has never barred creation of other statutory offenses involving subversion of the legal order. Thus,* United States v. Rosenberg, *195 F.2d 583 (2d cir. 1952) held that the defendants were validly convicted of conspiracy to violate the federal Espionage Act, 18 U.S.C. 794 (1976) by communicating protected information to the USSR.*

Because of less restrictive definitions, all of the recent spy cases to be discussed have involved prosecution for espionage and related activities rather than prosecution under the more restricted constitutional treason definition. Although not then legally meeting the constitutional definition of treason or traitors, this discussion will utilize the concept of treason in a broader, nonlegal, sociological and popular notion as the "betrayal of one's country." This concept of traitor has been virtually synonymous with espionage which, with the exception of operations by foreign agents, generally involves treason.

Under U.S. law espionage refers specifically to a violation of U.S. Code Title 18, Chapter 37, "Espionage and Censorship," Sections 792 through 799. These are:

792—Harboring or concealing persons
793—Gathering, transmitting, or losing defense information
794—Gathering or delivering defense information to aid foreign governments
795—Photographing and sketching defense installations

796—Use of aircraft for photographing defense installations
797—Publication and sale of photographs of defense installations
798—Disclosure of classified information
799—Violation of regulations of the National Aeronautics and Space Administration

Section 794 specifically fits the concept of spies and is the only section that carries the death penalty, or heavy imprisonment including life.

## The Ames Spy Case

Following a secret 1-year investigation by the Federal Bureau of Investigation, charges of espionage were filed against Aldrich Ames on February 23, 1994. Ames, age fifty-two, was a 32-year veteran of the Central Intelligence Agency, the son of a career CIA officer, and the highest ranking CIA official ever charged with espionage (Hagan, 1995a). He had begun stealing secrets and selling them to the Russians (then Soviets) since 1985. That same year while working counterintelligence in Mexico City, he recruited Maria del Rosario Casa (a Colombian native) whom he also married and allegedly collaborated with in his spying operations (Weiner, 1994).

Aldrich Ames had been chief of the Soviet counterintelligence branch in the Soviet Eastern European division in the mid-eighties as well as CIA Rome chief from 1986 to 1989. Although one media source describes his wife Rosario as a possible Russian "swallow" who recruited him into betrayal (Thomas *et al.,* 1994), most sources describe him as a "walk-in" who offered his services for monetary reasons. While the full extent of the damage done by Ames may never be known, it is clear that he condemned many CIA assets to death. He sold out at least eleven Russian agents who were executed from 1985 to 1987, including America's highest Cold War double agent, the top officer of the Soviet military intelligence agency, GRU General Dimitri "Top Hat" or "Donald" Polyakov. Ames's perfidy was motivated not by passionate commitment to some ideology but, utilizing the typology of spies to be discussed shortly, was due primarily to mercenary reasons. Similar to spy John Walker, he also exhibited a buccaneer/sport spy orientation, an "in your face" profile—wanting to show how smart he was.

Although the CIA was suspicious of Ames as early as 1985, concern had been raised as to why it took so long for the agency to catch its most damaging mole. On a salary that never exceeded $70,000 per year he lived a lavish lifestyle and also had an alcohol problem which should have attracted attention. He paid $540,000 in cash for a home in Arlington, Virginia, and proceeded to make $100,000 in improvements. He bought two new cars including a Jaguar. He bought stock worth $165,000 and charged $455,000 on credit cards. Considering he was the highest paid known Soviet informant (estimates range from $1.5 to $2.5 million), Ames could afford it. He was also able to somehow survive two lie detector tests, one in 1986 and another in 1991, although not without difficulty. While one source indicates that the FBI suspected the Russians gave him special pills and coached him on beating the polygraphs (ibid.), another claims that in addition to special tranquilizers he had been trained to lie using biofeedback techniques. Information that Ames had flunked the initial 1991 polygraph sections on personal finance and work for the Soviets was not turned over to the FBI until 1993. Case officers were permitted to retake the polygraph test until they calmed down (Walker *et al.*, 1994). Ames begged discovery with his ineptness and lazy work habits, excessive drinking, flaunting of money, and use of safe houses for sexual trysts. He was protected by an "old boys' network" and a history of noncooperation between the CIA and the FBI. It is the duty of the latter to investigate such breaches of security. Then-CIA Director R. James Woolsey promised a major shake-up of CIA agency culture which enabled Ames to survive for so long. Ames received a life sentence for his espionage activities and, due to his cooperation, gained a reduced sentence for his wife. Aldrich Ames is just one of the latest examples of spies whose changing motivations in the post-cold war climate is illustrated in the recent history of espionage (Hagan, 1986 and 1989; Adams, 1995; Maas, 1995; Weiner, Johnston, and Lewis, 1995; Wise, 1995).

> *"In the spy-game world of trapdoors and fun-house mirrors, things are seldom what they seem" (Duffy, 1987, p. 25).*

## The Evolution of Espionage

Beginning in the sixties, the popularity of fictional accounts of espionage by writers such as LeCarre, Ludlum, and Fleming has been rivalled only by romance and gothic fiction. The very clandestine nature of code names, jargon, equipment, and operations presents a secret real world which more than rivals "cloak and dagger" fiction. Apparat, black operators, residents, cut outs, dead drops, sleepers, and safe houses provide an occupational argot some of which has its basis not entirely as an outgrowth of intelligence operations. Copeland (1974, p. 179) notes that terms such as "blown," "dead drop," and "bouquet" were inventions of OSS (Office of Strategic Services) types, many of whom were former mystery writers. The term "mole," for instance, was a creation of novelist John LeCarre. These terms and similar code names for operatives such as Intrepid, A Man Called Lucy, and the Red Orchestra all add to the intrigue, mystery, and public fascination with sub-rosa criminals, agents, and traitors stealing secrets.

Despite images of Mata Hari or James Bond and "black espionage" or "covert agents" ferreting secrets, classical forms of spying have for many years ranked below "white espionage" which uses space satellites, code breaking, and technical collection (Marchetti and Marks, 1974, p. 186; Wade, 1965). While in the United States attention focuses on covert activities of the Central Intelligence Agency, the lesser known National Security Agency dwarfs the CIA in budget, manpower, and influence (Bamford, 1982). The technological revolution in espionage has replaced the "seductive, sable coated countess travelling first class on the Orient Express" (Maclean, 1978, p. 336). However, overreliance on technical intelligence without adequate appreciation of human intelligence could spell disaster for an intelligence service (Volkman, 1985). Despite the bureaucratization of spying, the continuing activity of human covert spies can be illustrated in the 1980s, heralded in the media as "the decade of the spy," by the fact that more such cases had been tried in U.S. federal court during that period than at any time since the early post-World War II period.

Espionage, the secretive theft of information by "sub-rosa criminals" (Hagan, 1986), has been a human preoccupation since early recorded history. In the Bible, God told Moses to send men to spy out the land of Canaan, and Joshua sent two spies to Jericho. Fifth century B.C. Chinese sage Sun Tzu, in his classic book *Art of War* (1963), wrote a detailed chapter on the "Employment of Secret Agents" and even included the term "double agents." Ever since then espionage has been used by all major nations to advance or defend their national interest. Although Wise and Ross (1968) claim that until modern times espionage was restricted to wartime, Thompson and Padover in *Secret Diplomacy: Espionage and Cryptology 1500–1815* (1963), a classic on medieval diplomatic intrigue, describe the role of ambassador throughout history with these words: lie, spy, and bribe. Functions of ancient ambassadors included those of negotiator and spy. Wise and Ross (1968, p. 261) point out: "The American people have traditionally dismantled their armed forces during times of peace and until World War II the United States had no formal espionage service. The prevailing prewar attitude was expressed quaintly by Secretary of State Henry L. Stimson, who in 1929 closed the 'black chamber,' the State Department's primitive code breaking section, with the explanation: 'Gentlemen do not read each other's mail.'" Industrial espionage has never been restricted to only wartime. While the ascendance of "white spying" was previously noted, Liston (1967, p. 31) adds that: "Today the old definition of spying is as impractical as the musket. . . . (it is) no longer restricted to wartime" and is practiced against friend and foe alike. Espionage may indeed have become a substitute for war. One form of spying to be discussed involves treason, the betrayal of one's country. Despite the fact that this is one of the earliest crimes punished by society and the only crime discussed in the U.S. Constitution, it is rarely discussed in the standard criminological literature.

Despite inattention to the issue in criminology, sub-rosa crime is more costly than traditional property crime. A Pentagon report of a special interagency task force estimates that the Soviet Union alone before its collapse spent approximately $1.4 billion annually on the theft of Western technology, much available as unclassified documents (Morganthau *et al.,* 1985). This pilfering of industrial secrets rescued the Soviets from economic and technological stagnation. It enabled them to keep pace in the arms race, and without such thefts it is estimated that they would have been 15 years behind in development (*NBC,* 1985). Such activities saved them billions in research and development costs while hundreds of thousands of defense industry employees with access to secrets were targeted for bribery, blackmail, and deception. Former U.S. Secretary of Defense Caspar Weinberger claimed that, as a result of federal programs such as Operation Exodus to halt illegal technology transfers to the Soviet Bloc, the U.S. taxpayer was saved $20 to $50 billion in future defense expenditures to counter Soviet improvements at the time while the Russians had to forego a $13 billion savings in military development shortcuts. In addition, a society that fails to guard its technological secrets may soon find itself a second-rate economic power.

## The Lack of Literature on Spying

One area in which criminologists provide some coverage of spying is under the label of political crime, which can be defined as crime by or against the government which is committed for ideological purposes. As previously indicated, there is a surprising paucity of criminological literature on political crime. Sagarin (1973, p. v) indicates, "the criminologist, unlike the historian or political theorist, neglected the subject." The literature remains meager. Louis Proal's (1973) classic *Political Crime,* originally published in 1898, along with works by Garofalo, Bonger, and Ferri, were mainly concerned with crimes by government or by the "oppressed classes versus the oppressor" (Schafer, 1974, pp. 121–131). Later, criminological writers on political crime such as Turk (1982), Roebuck and Weeber (1978), Schafer (1974), and Clinard and Quinney (1974) seemed more concerned with dissent, terrorism, political policing, and particularly, abuses by government, and paid scant attention to themes such as treason and espionage.

Although there is no shortage of fictional literature on espionage, with the exception of the fields of political science (international relations) and industrial security, the social science literature, particularly criminological, has been lacking in this area. There are a variety of reasons for the lack of literature on spies in criminology. In the clandestine universe of spying it is nearly impossible to ever know all of the facts. Secret service agencies do not usually open their files and archives to researchers. Even when they do, such as through Freedom of Information Act applications, the records are usually considerably edited or censored. Researchers lack direct access to perpetrators. Industrial espionage by private organizations has also received little attention by criminologists (Ogata, 1984, p. 27). Much of the literature relies heavily on media accounts of espionage which may tend toward the dramatic rather than the typical.

The history of espionage can become confused by the duplicity of double agents, ones who pretend to work for one government but really work for another. Disinformation ("black propaganda") may be purposely seeded to mislead adversaries and impress domestic audiences (Blackstock, 1966). Questions have been raised regarding the very lax security in many spy cases such as that of Aldrich Ames. Was the Marine guard scandal in 1987 in which KGB agents were let into the U.S. embassy by Marine guards really damaging or an example of a disinformation campaign? The most sensitive areas including the "bubble" sanitized communication room had permanent, separate security guards; and why were U.S. officials talking so openly about such damage (Duffy, 1987, p. 25)? Many of the voluminous biographies and autobiographies by former agents may be of dubious validity or actual commissioned pieces by intelligence agencies for disinformation purposes. Bittman's (1981) *The Deception Game,* Wynne's (1967) *Contact on Gorky Street, The Penkovsky Papers* (Penkovsky, 1965), and Philby's *My Silent War* (1968) are all most likely such examples (Marchetti and Marks, 1974, p. 18; Bittman, 1985). Since espionage and counter espionage operations are usually not the province of local policing, the subject appears to be ignored by criminological researchers. For these reasons great care must be exercised in evaluating the espionage literature. Even given these limitations, the cost and seriousness of such activities certainly justify attention in criminology.

A previous examination of twenty-five criminology textbooks by this writer confirms the paucity of coverage of political crime and, particularly, of treason and spying (Hagan, 1986). Excluding crimes by government and intelligence agencies, the majority (15) did not discuss treason, espionage against the state, or spying, whereas nine books gave limited treatment to these topics; and only one supplementary text, Clinard and Quinney's (1974) *Criminal Behavior Systems: A Typology,* contained any detailed coverage of treason, espionage, or spying in a "political crime" chapter. The general themes explored by those covering these topics generally concentrate on political abuses by government with few discussions of non-American government abuses, such as in Marxist states. Terrorism, dissidence, political corruption, and government spying on dissenters are the predominant themes. When the subject of spies is breached, it is briefly dismissed as an example of political crime in which ideological criminals commit their acts out of conviction (Hagan, 1986).

## Typologies of Spies

Many typologies of spies deal with specific role performances or tasks such as deep cover, sleepers, double agents, agent provocateurs, and walk-ins. Bottom and Gallati (1984, p. 35), citing a typology by Edward Anderson (1977), list types based on role assignment such as setup agent, undercover agent, trespasser, listener, lookout, trash collector, pollster, financial wizard, blind advertiser, reverse engineer, and solicitor. In the fifth century B.C., Sun Tzu (1963, p. 145) identified five types of secret agents: native, inside, doubled, expendable, and living. Such typologies are not very useful in that they can include a great heterogeneity of motivations and behavior systems. Miles Copeland (1974), in *Beyond Cloak and Dagger: Inside the CIA,* discusses a very interesting typology used in the CIA's training course on espionage management which includes: the Emily, the Mickey, the Philby, the Willie, the Philip, and Miscellaneous (Copeland, 1974). Each type is illustrated by a fairly lengthy anecdotal case study. "Emily" was an attractive but shy personal assistant to the assistant secretary of state who was, according to conventional principles of agent management, slowly romanced by a foreign agent and later compromised into passing increasingly more secretive information. In order to trick the Soviets Emily, although caught, was kept in place in order to feed "disinformation." She was never prosecuted and later became a librarian in New England (Copeland, 1974, pp. 18–22).

The "Mickey" (an Irish-American heavy drinker in the example) was a "walk-in spy, one who approaches foreign agents and offers his or her services. . . . Because of special knowledge and experience [he] was able to get in touch with a foreign intelligence agency and offer his services without being spotted by counterintelligence controls" (Copeland, 1974, p. 24). Former CIA Director Allen Dulles instructed newcomers to the business of agent-handling with the legend, "It's the walk-in trade that keeps the shop open" (Ronelagh, 1986, p. 255). The "Philby" (named for British traitor Kim Philby) is "the long term agent, recruited in his youth, who at the time of his recruitment was outside his assigned target and took years working his way into it" (Copeland, 1974, p. 24). The "Willie" is one who, while working for one intelligence agency for a time, was led to believe by his "principal" that he was working for another, for example, an industrial-espionage or newspaper organization. The "Philip" refers to CIA defector Philip Agee, who publicly divulged secret information as a form of dissent or protest.

Copeland, in describing "miscellaneous" agents, indicates that a review of the operational files of any espionage branch would find fewer than half fitting the above categories; thus, most fall into the miscellaneous type. While the Copeland-CIA typology may serve useful heuristic purposes in a classroom, any classification that estimates over half of the cases in an "other" category requires refinement. Defector and former KGB Major Stanislav Levchenko was, according to one source, the first to reveal the acronym MICE for describing the motivation of spies (Kneece, 1986, p. 1): motivation, ideology, compromise, and ego. Others have expanded this acronym to SMICE, adding sex as a separate motivation. As part of a SMICE recruitment strategy, espionage services look for braggarts, skirt chasers, problem drinkers, drug abusers, those with grudges against the service or country, those vulnerable to flattery or with amoral-nihilistic views, those with money problems, as well as those with an exaggerated view of their own importance (ibid., p. 66).

## A New Typology of Spies

A "typology of spies" is proposed based on the motivation or behavior system of the actor (Hagan, 1986 and 1989). This typology was suggested in part, but greatly expands on types suggested, by Stansfield Turner (1985a and 1985b) and describes ten types of spies: mercenary, ideological, alienated/egocentric, buccaneer, professional, compromised, deceived, quasi agent, escapee, and miscellaneous, and is outlined in Figure 5.1.

*Mercenary spies* trade secrets for personal monetary reward. In addition to Aldrich Ames, Andrew Daulton Lee—the "Snowman" described in Robert Lindsey's

*MERCENARY SPY*

Aldrich Ames
Andrew Daulton Lee (the "Snowman")
William Bell

Richard Mueller
Edwin Wilson (the "Mickey")

*IDEOLOGICAL SPY*

Julius and Ethel Rosenberg
Klaus Fuchs
Allen Nunn May
Dimitri Polyakov ("Top Hat")
Guy Burgess

Donald Maclean
Kim Philby
Anthony Blunt
Oleg Penkovsky (the "Philby")
Larry Wu-Tai Chin

*ALIENATED/EGOCENTRIC SPY*

Edward Lee Howard

*BUCCANEER/SPORT SPY*

Christopher Boyce (the "Falcon")
John Walker
Sidney Reilly ("Ace of Spies")

Gordon Liddy
Jonathan Pollard

*PROFESSIONAL SPY*

Richard Sorge
Rudolf Abel

Peter Herrmann ("Der Hoffnung")

*COMPROMISED SPY*

Richard Miller
Sharon Scranage (the "Emily")

Marine guards in Moscow

*DECEIVED (FALSE FLAGS) SPY*

Edwin Wilson Recruits (the "Willie")

*QUASI AGENT*

Philip Agee (the "Philip")

*ESCAPEE SPY*

Those who defect in order to avoid
personal problems

Vitaly Yurchenko

*MISCELLANEOUS SPY*

Cases not fitting above

---

**FIGURE 5.1 A Typology of Spies**

(1979) book *The Falcon and the Snowman*—could serve as an example. Lee, a highly successful drug dealer (hence the "Snowman" title) grew up in a wealthy California suburb, an environment that emphasized ambition and material success. In 1974 at the age of twenty-two, Lee began acting as a courier for his friend Christopher Boyce (the "Falcon") by flying to Mexico City and showing up at the Soviet embassy with an offer to provide secret U.S. satellite information. Although Lee had expressed some disillusionment with American policies in the late sixties and early seventies, his principal motivation appeared to be financial. Most mercenary spies are apolitical, working for the highest bidder. They may be walk-ins, such as Andrew Daulton Lee and apparently Aldrich Ames, or they may be sought out and enticed by foreign agents or rival companies. For many, a security clearance and access to secret information are marketable commodities.

Many mercenary spies have elements in common with descriptions of other criminals such as Cressey's (1953) theory of embezzlers, in which embezzlers find themselves possessing an "nonshareable problem," or perhaps Lemert's (1953) "closure theory" of naive check forgers. Faced with a financial crisis brought on, for instance, by an alcoholic binge, gambling debts, or creditors demanding immediate payment, naive check forgers resolve their crisis by writing checks for which there are no covering funds. "Closure" refers to a reduction of other possibilities for solving the crisis. William Bell, a radar engineer for Hughes Aircraft Corporation in Los Angeles, found his personal life in turmoil. He was recently divorced, his son had died, and he had been transferred to a job with a lower salary. Faced with financial need, he sold details of classified quiet radar similar to that of the Stealth bomber, a new radar system designed for the Navy, and plans for a new sonar device for $103,000 to a Polish agent. Bell in part rationalized his behavior in that the agent approached him with the idea (*NBC*, 1985). The majority of recent cases such as that of Richard Craig Smith, Ronald Pelton, and Aldrich Ames also illustrate the primarily mercenary orientation (La Franiere and Schmidt, 1985; Kapsidelis, 1985).

Professional smugglers as well as industrialists blinded by potential profits divert legal exports and ship technological secrets to unfriendly foreign powers. In 1983 Richard Mueller diverted to the East Digital Equipment Corporation's prized VAX II/782 computer system, a system highly useful for intercontinental missile guidance (Dudney, 1985). The previously described "Mickey" type may also serve as an example of the primarily mercenary spy. Such traitors rationalize their activity and outwardly remain loyal citizens (Copeland, 1974, p. 158). Magazines such as *Soldier of Fortune* advertise for individuals willing to do commercial espionage work (Broadwell, 1984, p. 50).

The *ideological spy* (the CIA "Philby" type) is motivated by strong ideological or political beliefs. They are truly political criminals. Condemned as traitors in one country they are often heralded as heroes by the recipient nation. In March 1951 Julius and Ethel Rosenberg became the first native Americans to be executed for treason. Liston (1967, p. 183) explains: "Before the Cold War, traitor was an ugly word in any language. Men who betrayed their country to the enemy were rare and their names went down in infamy. [The name of] Benedict Arnold, who went over to the British in the American Revolutionary War, has itself become a slang term for 'traitor.'" The Rosenbergs and associates, as well as Klaus Fuchs and Allen Nunn May, gave the Russians American atomic secrets shortly after World War II at a time in which the United States had enjoyed a monopoly on atomic weaponry (Hyde, 1980). All were amateur spies and intellectual adherents to communism, beliefs bred in despair of the Depression of the 1930s and the chaos of Hitler's Europe. May (code named "Alek"), an experimental physicist and member of the British atomic team, volunteered his services to the Soviets as did Fuchs. Both at first refused payment. The Rosenbergs, when caught, claimed they were innocent, persecuted victims of capitalism. Their treachery altered the postwar balance of power.

The British intelligence service was particularly hurt by ideological spies Guy Burgess, Donald Maclean, Kim Philby, and Anthony Blunt. Recruited as Cambridge University students in the thirties, these "establishment spies" rose to the highest echelons as moles in the British security establishment (Pincher, 1984; West, 1983). Colonel Oleg Penkovsky, a high-ranking officer in the GRU, Red Army intelligence, passed secrets to the British due to his disillusionment with communism. Past defections to the East and to the West may provide possible examples such as Vitaly Yurchenko, deputy chairman of the KGB and former chief of that agency's operations directorate; Oleg Gordievsky, KGB station chief in London; West Germany's top counterespionage chief Hans Tiedge; and many others who fled to the East (Morgenthau, Willenson, and Sandza, 1985). Such cases often involved mixed motivations. Retired CIA analyst Larry Wu-Tai Chin was given intelligence training by the communist Chinese in the early 1940s before he started working for the CIA and was planted as a Chinese mole at the     of his more than 40 years of U.S. government service. The fact that recent calls for more thorough security checks is no panacea can be illustrated by the fact that Chin survived all of the reexaminations (Marcus and Pichirallo, 1985). America's top double agent during the Cold War was Soviet military intelligence chief GRU General Dimitri "Top Hat" Polyakov. Ultimately betrayed by Aldrich Ames and executed, Polyakov was credited with supplying invaluable information that prevented war between the United States and Soviet Union. He considered himself a true Russian patriot and felt he was helping to fight a corrupt system and not betraying his country on behalf of the United States. With the collapse of Soviet Communism, communist ideology among spies became less of a draw in the West than it was in the thirties. Western ideology appears to be more of an enticement to those raised in the former Eastern Bloc in the post-Cold War period. During the later period of the Cold War, many KGB defectors were products of the post-Stalin era, had enjoyed the best schools, a taste for Western life during service abroad, and were less rigid communist ideologues ("Can Moscow Trust," 1985). In a sense they were victims of embourgeoisement rather than ideology. In a bizarre twist, Yurchenko escaped from CIA supervision on November 4, 1985, and redefected to the Soviet Union. Special love interests in his case may place him in the escapee spy type to be discussed, although threats to his family may have also explained his decision to return.

The *alienated/egocentric spy* is one who betrays for personal reasons unrelated to monetary or ideological considerations. Revenge may represent one such reason. In 1985 Edward Lee Howard, an ex-CIA employee, was accused of passing secrets to the Soviets. Howard, who apparently refused a transfer to Moscow and having flunked a polygraph check, was fired from the agency. He passed information to the KGB in order to get even. Howard later slipped FBI surveillance and disappeared (Alpern, Sandza, and Kasindorf, 1985). Espionage may represent a reaction to frustration or revenge against an employing organization. If the reaction is expressed covertly, it fits the alienated/egocentric type while, if expressed overtly, for example, in the form of whistleblowing (Westin, 1981), it may fit the quasi agent type to be discussed.

The *buccaneer* or *sport spy* obtains psychological fulfillment through espionage. Turner (1985b) describes them as "swashbuckling adventurers who spy for kicks." Excitement, power, and control exceed ideological, monetary, or other considerations. Some possible examples include Christopher the "Falcon" Boyce, John Walker, Sidney "Ace of Spies" Reilly, and G. Gordon Liddy. Christopher Boyce, the "Falcon" of Lindsey's (1979, 1983) *The Falcon and the Snowman* tandem, was a product of affluent California suburbia. Described as very intelligent and intensely idealistic, Boyce was also a bored 21-year-old college dropout. Boyce's father, a retired FBI agent, used his contacts to get his son a $140 per week top security cleared job at TRW, which involved developing top secret satellite communications equipment and processing information for the CIA. Boyce, along with his cohort Andrew Daulton Lee, sold information to the Russians. Lindsey (1983), in perhaps an overly romantic picture of Boyce, indicate he told a federal marshall, "I guess I'm a pirate at heart. I guess I'm an adventurer," claiming he became a Soviet spy on a whim in a blind gesture of defiance against the CIA. Caught and convicted, Boyce escaped from prison and, although he could have hidden out in obscurity, took up bank robbery before his later capture.

John Walker, head of a family spy ring, also reflected a Walter Mitty/James Bond image of spying. He was a former naval officer who began passing secrets to the Soviets in the 1960s and continued until the mid-1980s. Also involved were his son (a sailor), his brother (a retired naval officer), and his son's friend (a former navy man). Walker apparently enjoyed planning, directing, and bringing others into his schemes including entrapping and possibly compromising others. One informant described Walker unflatteringly: "He was a wimp and he was always trying to impress everyone that he was bad" (Kneece, 1986, p. 104). Walker's James Bond fantasy included props such as a big switchblade, umbrella weapons, a crossbow for silent killing, as well as a variety of pistols. His ring's perfidy included compromising naval cryptographic codes which, among other things, cost American pilots' lives in Vietnam. His gift to the Soviets of such codes may be comparable to the Poles' 1939 Enigma gift, a stolen German code machine to the allies which enabled the breaking of Nazi codes, with which we won World War II.

Jonathan Pollard, who spied against his country, the United States, on behalf of the Israelis, was described as "a flamboyant poseur who falsely portrayed himself as a master spy for Israel, then joined the U.S. intelligence community to live out his fantasies . . . a legend in his own mind" (Satchell, Sanford, and Riley, 1987, p. 22). Pollard bragged about and posed as an Israeli spy since his college days, had alcohol and drug abuse problems, and faked credentials to enter the intelligence community. In 1994 President Bill Clinton refused to reduce Pollard's life sentence, even though critics complained Pollard's spying was on behalf of an ally Israel and provided information primarily against Iraq (Blitzer, 1989). For national security reasons the intelligence community could not fully reveal the extent of damage done by Pollard. Sidney "Ace of Spies" Reilly, although a mercenary, appeared to enjoy the manipulation of governments and people—the sport of the thing (Turner, 1985a; and Kettle, 1984). Gordon Liddy (1981), in his autobiography *Will*, appeared to relish the role of "spook" as almost a contest of will against less disciplined adversaries. Romantic images of spies in espionage fiction may encourage the spy for sport. The thrill of the chase was aptly noted by Sir Robert Baden Powell (Maclean, 1978, p. 2): "for anyone who is tired of life, the thrilling life of a spy should be the finest recuperation."

*Professional spies* might best be described as agents, careerists, occupational employees of intelligence bureaucracies. While the vast majority of professionals are "white" agents, some are covert or "black agents." Although loyal and patriotic, most agents are less ideological than amateur ideological spies. Covert professional spies such as Richard Sorge, Rudolph "Lucy" Roessler, Rudolf Abel, and Gordon Lonsdale are legends in the history of espionage. Lawrence Kessner's (1981) novel *The Spy Next Door* describes the career of a "deep cover" spy—"Der Hoffnung" (The Hope), the actual case of Peter Herrmann whose father, KGB Colonel Rudolph Herrmann, was unveiled as a Soviet covert agent by the FBI in March 1980. Raised in suburban America, Young Herrmann participated in espionage activities with his father from the age of ten. He received periodic KGB training in the Soviet Union and was carefully being groomed for a career in the U.S. security establishment. Upon graduation from Georgetown's School of International Studies, he procured a job at a computer industry lobby group when federal agents discovered and broke the Herrmann operation.

*Compromised spies* are at first reluctant traitors who gradually trade secrets sometimes willingly, for example, for romantic purposes, and sometimes unwillingly, due to blackmail or other forms of coercion. Many are recruited according to conventional principles of case management which includes spotting potential clients, evaluation, recruiting, testing, training, handling, and termination (Marchetti and Marks, 1974, pp. 245–246). Previous discussion of CIA type "Emily" would fit this category. Eastern European agents used to romance female secretaries in West Germany or threaten refugees from eastern Europe with reprisals against relatives back home if they failed to cooperate. In 1985 in the United States, FBI agent Richard Miller was in court charged with giving secrets to his lover, a female KGB agent. Similarly, a CIA clerk, Sharon Scranage, gave secrets of U.S. intelligence operations to her Ghanian lover. The most celebrated case was that of U.S. Moscow embassy marine guards, particularly Sergeant Clayton Lonetree and Corporal Arnold Bracey. The guards were allegedly victims of LeCarre's spy fiction gambit, "the honey trap." In spy tradecraft jargon the KGB employed many "swallows" or seductive female agents to trade sex for secrets.

The *deceived spy* (false flag recruit) is one who is led to believe that he or she is working for one organization when, in fact, he or she has been duped and is doing the bidding of another, after the discovery of which it may be too late to withdraw cooperation. The most striking example of false flag recruitment occurred in the late seventies on the part of agents developed by Edwin Wilson, himself a mercenary spy. Wilson, an ex-CIA employee, was indicted in 1980. He had recruited assassins, smugglers, technicians, and spies to work for Libya but led them to believe he and they were working for the CIA (Epstein, 1983; Goulden, 1984). Fired from the CIA in 1971, Wilson used the false flag approach to attract over thirty agents and weaponry experts including General Richard Secord of "Iran scam" fame; procured secret CIA cable traffic information, computer secrets regarding submarine detection and missiles used by NSA, CIA supplies and assassination equipment (exporting the latter along with experts to Libya). CIA fear of penetration by agents of foreign powers (moles) was fed by the ease with which the well-financed Wilson recruited on a moonlighting basis even some high-ranking agency officials. He entertained and most likely bribed and blackmailed members of Congress and government officials at his lavish Virginia estate. The previously discussed CIA type "Willie" would fit the classification of Wilson's recruits. Copeland (1974, p. 33) claims that, once "Willies" find out they have been duped, they are likely to continue to operate rather than face exposure. Industrial spies who believe that they are working for a rival company may very well unknowingly be working for Soviet intelligence.

The *quasi agent* is one who assists the intelligence operations of foreign powers but views himself or herself as a dissenter. Dissenters publicly divulge information. Primarily ideologically motivated, quasi agents, while disappointed with the performance of their own political system, are not necessarily ideological spies committed to a foreign system. The CIA type "Philip" is named for defector Philip Agee (1975). Agee provided Cuba and the Soviet Bloc information on CIA secret Latin American operations and agents, but did so publicly by openly publishing a book compromising not only operations, but the lives of agency and foreign operatives. Such quasi agents also serve useful propaganda purposes.

The *escapee spy* is one who defects with secret information in order to save his or her life or avoid a tight spot or other unpleasantries. Although ideological, mercenary, egoistic, or other motivations may figure in, the primary purpose is to avoid anticipated undesirable personal circumstances. Former KGB agents who had become accustomed to serving in the West sometimes preferred to defect rather than to return to Mother Russia. Agents may decide to "come over" and remain with a new lover rather than return to the family back home. The defection case of Vitaly Yurchenko, deputy chairman of the KGB, and his subsequent change of heart and return to Moscow were believed to have been related to a love affair.

A *miscellaneous spy* category is provided as a "catchall" assuming, as had Copeland in a previous typology, that many spies defy classification attempts. Although there is no way of really knowing, U.S. and British intelligence estimate that they catch only about 30 percent of agents planted in their countries.

Leroy Stone (1991) noted that, despite psychological assessments to evaluate security risks, nothing has been documented as genuine social scientific research on the motivation of spies. Using publicly available sources as well as those available under the Freedom of Information Act, he created a spy data base of 184 spies each measured on sixty-eight variables. Some of his findings challenged some of the traditional screening concerns used in vetting security risks:

- Few spies showed mental problems. "Of all the spies caught since the end of World War II, only two were not charged and released because they were believed to be insane or at least to have significant mental health problems" (ibid., p. 30).
- While spies since the 1980s have received severe sentences, since the end of World War II over one fifth never came to trial or were not convicted.
- Mercenary spies are prosecuted at a higher level than are ideologically motivated spies.
- Male spies are more heavily prosecuted and convicted than are female spies.
- Spies from the U.S. Army are more severely punished than are those from other branches or civilians.
- Most spies are of average intelligence.

## Conclusion

Although the real world of spies and their motivations may perhaps defy attempts at classification, and no single case fits purely into any single type, this typology is presented in the Weberian sense of "ideal types," abstract overgeneralizations of reality which serve heuristic purposes. Despite possible shortcomings it is hoped that the typology presented serves as a modest attempt to illustrate that not all spies are ideologically motivated or even monetarily oriented as suggested in brief discussions of the subject in criminology and particularly in textbooks in the field.

# 6

# Crime against Government: International Terrorism

## Terrorism

We are all far too familiar with the obscene tragedy and continuing demonic drama of international terrorism, an all too real horror show which with minor variations in plot, setting, and characters enjoys far too many reruns on television. It is as if the demons and monsters of gothic fiction have been unharnessed and released to torment the world. When viewed outside of its ideological motivations, international terrorism represents some of the worst examples of mass murder in history. The impunity of terrorist campaigns can be illustrated by the bombing of Pan Am 103 and poison gas attacks by a religious cult in Japan.

## Pan Am 103

In December 1988 a bomb exploded aboard Pan American Airlines Flight 103 over Lockerbie, Scotland, killing all 259 passengers and crew and 11 citizens of the town. The dead included 189 Americans. In an example of state-sponsored terrorism, two Libyan intelligence officers were charged with the act, which was believed to have been committed in cooperation with Iran possibly in retaliation for the accidental downing of an Iranian jetliner, killing all 290 on board, by the U.S.S. Vincennes. The ship had been on patrol and under battlefront conditions at the time in the Persian Gulf. In 1995 the two culprits were put on the FBI's Ten Most Wanted List and a $4 million reward was posted—the largest ever offered by the U.S. government. Charged in 1991 in both the United States and Scotland with planting the suitcase bomb aboard the airplane were Abdel Basset Ali Al Megrahi and Lamen Khalifa Fhimah. The previous largest award ever offered by the United States was $2 million for the arrest in April 1995 of Ramzi Yousef for taking part in the World Trade Center bombing in 1993. That offer secured the arrest and extradition to the United States of Yousef (whose real name is Abdul Basit Mahmud Abdul Karin).

## Poison Gas Terrorist Cult in Tokyo

On March 20, 1995, packages of sarin nerve gas were planted on five trains on three Tokyo subway lines during the morning rush hour, killing eleven people and injuring more than forty-seven hundred. Two days later Japanese police raided the offices of Aum Shinrikyo, a religious cult that mixes Hindu and Buddhist practices, which the police believed responsible for the attack. The charismatic leader of the group was Shoko Asahara, who formed the cult in 1984 around the word "Aum," a mantra that is chanted by the followers. Searching over 100 cult facilities, the police found huge stores of chemicals suitable for making sarin. On March 21, 1995, Asahara went into hiding to avoid police questioning.

A terrified Japanese public then experienced a series of related incidents. On March 30, 1995, the head of the National Police Agency, Takaji Kunimatsu, was shot and seriously wounded. Asahara predicted a major disaster for April 15, 1995; but the day passed without incident. On April 19, toxic gas was released in a Yokohama train station with 560 people hospitalized; and on April 23, 1995, Hideo Murai, Aum's chief scientist, was stabbed to death. Two days later, two dozen more were injured by a gas attack at a shopping mall also in Yokohama. The police were having difficulty finding hard evidence to link the cult with the attacks.

This chapter will concentrate on international as opposed to domestic terrorism, which will be addressed in the next chapter. Described as petty criminals who coat their venal acts with an ideological gloss, terrorists are most often discussed in the criminological literature as political criminals. Surprisingly few criminology textbooks devote much coverage to terrorism, and much of what is presented is descriptive of what will be described as the "old terrorism" of the pre-1960s variety.

Much of the literature on terrorism has been dominated by journalists. Walter Laqueur (1987, p. 8), author of the classic *The Age of Terrorism,* states: "seldom in history has so much been written about so few and so little." A critical analysis of terrorism has been hindered by justifiably emotional reactions, and any study of terrorism almost of necessity must be qualitative and less dependent on rigorous sources. Furthermore, statistics on terrorism are suspect and make international comparisons difficult.

A wide variety of definitions of terrorism exist. Federal agencies such as the Federal Bureau of Investigation, State Department, Department of Defense,

Department of Justice, as well as the Vice President's Task Force on Combatting Terrorism (1986) include in their definitions elements such as:

- Unlawful use of violence by revolutionary organizations;
- Coercion or intimidation of governments for ideological or political purposes;
- Intentional use of violence for political reasons against noncombatant targets by subnational groups or clandestine state agents;
- Use of assassination or kidnapping for political purposes.

Although innocent civilians may inadvertently be killed or injured in wartime, terrorism involves the willful and premeditated targeting of innocents (Netanyahu, 1986, p. 8).

Just as there is no consensus on an exact definition of terrorism, similarly there is no single, uniformly agreed on typology of political terrorism. Figure 6.1 outlines some of the better known attempts to develop classifications of terrorism. Excluded from this discussion is nonideological, criminal terrorism such as mercenary kidnappings, hostage-taking for money or for the purpose of escape from the law. Also excluded are psychopathic forms of terrorism such as criminal mass murders. None of these is politically motivated criminal behavior. Figure 6.1 also provides a selection of various typologies of terrorism.

The Report of the Task Force on Disorders and Terrorism (National Advisory Committee, 1976, pp. 3–6) includes in its typology of terrorism: political terrorism, nonpolitical terrorism, quasi terrorism, limited political terrorism, and official or state terrorism. *Political terrorism* involves "violent criminal behavior designed primarily to generate fear in the community for political purposes." *Nonpolitical terrorism* is undertaken for either private purposes or gain; examples include activities of organized crime, or the Manson family. *Quasi terrorism* describes "those activities incidental to the commission of crimes of violence that are similar in form and method to true terrorism but which nevertheless lack its essential ingredient." Rather than being ideologically motivated, many skyjackers and hostage-takers are interested in ransom. *Limited political terrorism* refers to "acts of terrorism which are committed for ideological or political motives, but which are not part of a concerted campaign to capture control of the state." Vendetta-type executions and acts of lone terrorists for essentially private motives serve as examples. *Official* or *state terrorism* occurs in "nations whose rule is based upon fear and oppression that reach terroristic proportions" (Simpson and Bennett, 1985). Wolf (1981) differentiates "enforcement terrorism" from "agitational terrorism," the former being used by governments to control populations.

One might add state-sponsored terrorism, in which countries support terrorism as "war on the cheap." For example, in 1990 Syria was the home base of the Popular Front for the Liberation of Palestine—General Command (PFLP—GC). Syria also controlled the Bekaa Valley, the terrorist training ground in Lebanon. Iran most likely commissioned the bombing of Pan Am 103 in retaliation for the U.S. Navy's accidental downing of an Iranian civilian airliner during a crisis in the Persian Gulf

Paul Wilkinson's (1976) types of terrorism:

1. Criminal
2. Psychotic
3. War
4. Political

    a. revolutionary
    b. subrevolutionary
    c. repressive

Frederick Hacker's (1978) types of terrorists:

1. Crusaders
2. Criminals
3. Crazies

Alex Schmid and Janny de Graaf's (1982) types of political terrorism:

1. Insurgent terrorism

    a. social revolutionary
    b. separatist, nationalist or ethnical
    c. single issue

2. State or repressive
3. Vigilante

James Poland's (1988) typology of political terrorism:

1. State or repressive
2. Liberation theology
3. Identity theology
4. Nihilist
5. Insurgent

    a. revolutionaries
    b. separatist/nationalist
    c. single issue

Peter Sederberg's (1989) types of terrorism:

1. Criminal
2. Nihilist
3. Nationalist
4. Revolutionary
5. Establishment

    a. vigilante
    b. covert official
    c. overt official
    d. genocide

**FIGURE 6.1 Typologies of Terrorism**

(Wines, 1990). Libyan agents were blamed since the trigger to the device was similar to a type of detonator used by Libyan terrorist bombers. The device was hidden in a Toshiba radio similar to those used by PFLP—GC terrorists in Germany, who most likely hired the Libyans (Mossberg, 1990). The bombing turns out to have Iranian, Syrian, and Libyan connections and probably was not the sole work of isolated terrorists. Terrorism is now viewed as a variant of a new form of warfare and armed struggle: low-intensity conflict or gray area phenomena.

## Gray Area Phenomena

With the end of the Cold War and the cessation of superpower confrontation, gray area phenomena—"threats to the stability of nation-states by nonstate actors and nongovernmental processes and organizations"—became more prevalent (Holden-Rhodes and Lupscha, 1993; Ward, 1995). Such activities include low intensity conflict, for example: terrorism, insurgency, drug trafficking, warlordism, militant fundamentalism, ethnic cleansing, civil war, transnational threats, and organized crime operations. Cooperating with each other in specific operations, nonstate actors using modern technology can wage war on nation-states. Traditional strategies on the part of such nation-states may not work as well against such nonconventional adversaries.

Although we have examined a variety of typologies of terrorism, this discussion will concentrate on international (cross-border) terrorism, oppositional terrorism (Ross, 1993) which is of greatest current concern. This is not to make light of other forms of terrorism such as state terrorism (as distinct from state-sponsored terrorism). While the latter involves states such as Libya, Iran, and Iraq sponsoring terrorist groups such as Abu Nidal's, the former involves the state itself officially terrorizing its citizens whether it be the former Soviet bloc or Third World countries such as Cambodia, Chile, Indonesia, or countries in Central America. Scores of nations use torture and terror as official government policy to subjugate and control citizens. In sheer numbers the victims of state terrorism dwarf by far the toll taken by the better publicized "media terrorists" (Herman, 1983).

During the Cold War the United States often found itself backing repressive regimes primarily because they were anticommunist. The School of the Americas (SOA) at Fort Benning, Georgia, for over 50 years has trained over 56,000 Latin American military in counterinsurgency skills. Having as graduates many of the region's most notorious dictators and human rights violators, it has been called the "school for dictators" (Rockwell, 1994). Five of the nine Salvadorans responsible for murdering a group of Catholic missionaries in 1990 were alumnae. Ten of the twelve officers charged in the infamous El Mozote massacre in El Salvador had attended SOA. Also in El Salvador, forty-eight of the sixty-nine officers cited for human rights violations by the U.N. Truth Commission had attended the school. Such state terrorists were, unfortunately, trained in the United States. Exhibit 6.1, found at the end of this chapter, reports on investigations of terrorism by the FBI.

**EXHIBIT 6.1    FBI Investigations of Terrorist Incidents**

### *Terrorist Incidents*

During 1993, the FBI recorded twelve terrorist incidents in the United States. The following is a synopsis of each act:

#### *February 26, 1993*

On February 26, 1993, at 12:18 p.m., a massive explosion occurred on the B-2 level of the parking garage at the World Trade Center (WTC) in New York City. The FBI determined that the explosion was caused by a bomb consisting of roughly 1,200 pounds of explosives. The blast resulted in a crater 150 feet in diameter and five stories high.

The attack caused enormous damage to the underground parking area of the WTC and the connecting Vista Hotel. Six levels of the parking garage were perforated by the blast, and hundreds of vehicles were demolished. The Vista Hotel, located directly above the detonation site, took much of the force of the explosion and was badly damaged.

Property damage to the WTC amounted to over half a billion dollars, and caused serious disruptions in international trading. The WTC had to be closed for one month to complete extensive structural repairs. At the time of the explosion, there were approximately 50,000 people in the WTC complex, six of whom were killed and 1,042 of whom were injured.

Due to the loss of human life, serious bodily injuries, extensive property damage, and economic loss, the bombing of the WTC is considered to be the single largest international terrorist incident ever conducted in the United States. Five conspirators have been arrested for their involvement in this plot. (This incident constitutes one incident of terrorism.)

#### *July 20, 1993*

On July 20, 1993, two members of the American Front Skinheads threw a pipe bomb through a glass window in the front door of the National Association for the Advancement of Colored People (NAACP) headquarters in Tacoma, Washington. The NAACP offices, which were unoccupied at the time, suffered minor damage to an interior wall and door. At the time of the incident, no one claimed responsibility for this bombing. (This incident constitutes one incident of terrorism.)

#### *July 22, 1993*

Shortly after midnight on July 22, 1993, three members of the American Front Skinheads dropped a bomb down the chimney of the Elite Tavern, a homosexual bar in Seattle, Washington. The detonation of this bomb caused little damage. As above, at the time of the incident, no one claimed responsibility for this bombing.

Two of the Skinheads involved in the July 20 and July 22 bombings were arrested by the Salinas, California, Police Department on July 27, 1993, for shoplifting. Three pipe bombs and several weapons were discovered during a search of their automobile. The local police notified the San Francisco FBI Office upon discovery of the pipe bombs, and the FBI proceeded to interview the two Skinheads.

*Continued*

Source: Federal Bureau of Investigation. *Terrorism in the United States,* 1993. Washington, D.C.: Government Printing Office, 1994, excerpts from pp. 2–9.

## EXHIBIT 6.1 *Continued*

During these interview, it was determined that the two Skinheads had bombed the NAACP headquarters and the Elite Tavern. It was also discovered that they had constructed six pipe bombs. One of these bombs was used at the NAACP headquarters and a second on the Elite Tavern. The Skinheads proclaimed that the bombings were intended to initiate a race war. (This incident constitutes one incident of terrorism.)

*November 27–28, 1993*

On November 27–28, 1993, nine incendiary devices were placed in four Chicago department stores. They were intended to ignite flammable material located near the devices, which would activate the store's sprinkler systems.

Five of the nine incendiary devices erupted during the evening and nighttime hours. Two other devices were discovered by store employees, one of which ignited as a store security guard attempted to open the device. The two remaining devices failed to explode and were rendered safe by bomb and arson technicians. All of the fires were extinguished by store sprinkler systems. On November 29, 1993, the Chicago Sun-Times received a communique in which individuals who claimed to be representatives of the Animal Liberation Front (ALF) took credit for these acts.

The following is a detailed synopsis of the four Chicago department store incidents:

At 7 p.m., on November 27, 1993, a Saks Fifth Avenue Department Store clerk discovered a suspicious package (a tightly wrapped paper bag secured with a paper clip) on a shelf on the seventh floor. The clerk summoned a security guard, who removed and attempted to open the bag, whereupon it erupted. The security guard extinguished the flames and called the Chicago Police Department. Later that evening, at midnight, a fire began in a Christmas tree on the sixth floor of the same department store.

Also on November 27, 1993, at 11:30 p.m. two fires were ignited on the sixth floor of Carson's Department Store in Chicago. While the fire department was on the scene for these fires, a third device erupted in another section of the store.

At 2 a.m. on November 28, 1993, a fire began on the eighth floor of Marshall Fields Department Store in Chicago. The store's sprinkler system extinguished the fire. Police searching the store subsequently discovered another concealed device approximately 35 feet from the fire. This device was rendered safe by the Chicago Police Department's Bomb and Arson Squad.

On November 28, 1993, an eighth device was found at the Neiman-Marcus Department Store in Chicago. It was concealed on the fourth floor. This device, identical to the other seven, had failed to ignite. Bomb and arson technicians rendered this device safe.

On November 29, 1993, the Chicago Sun-Times received a communique which stated that the ALF had planted nine incendiary devices in four Chicago department stores. The communique further stated that the devices were designed to start small fires which would activate the stores' sprinkler systems, causing water damage to the stores and their inventories.

The ninth device was recovered after the ALF claimed responsibility for the

**EXHIBIT 6.1** *Continued*

previous attacks. Late in the afternoon of December 2, 1993, an FBI Agent conducting interviews at the Marshall Field's Department Store was advised by an employee that a suspicious package was located on the eighth floor. The Agent recognized the package as an incendiary device, identical to those found at the other stores. This device was rendered safe by bomb and arson technicians. (These incidents constitute nine incidents of terrorism.)

### Suspected Terrorist Incidents

Two suspected terrorist incidents were recorded in 1993. Responsibility for the acts listed below cannot be attributed to a known terrorist group; however, after assessing the circumstances surrounding each of these events, they are considered suspected acts of terrorism.

#### January 17, 1993

At approximately 11:30 p.m. on January 17, 1993, a fire occurred at the Serbian National Defense Council of America (SNDCA), in Chicago, Illinois. After extinguishing the fire, arson investigators determined that a large window on the front of the building had been broken, and three Molotov cocktails had been placed inside the building.

Investigation determined that only of the devices functioned and caused the fire. The building was unoccupied at the time of the fire, and damage was limited to the first floor area near the window. Damage was estimated to be $5,000. There were no injuries as a result of this incident.

The Chicago Joint Terrorism Task Force, which is headed by the FBI, responded to the scene and initiated an investigation of this incident. The task force was advised by SNDCA employees that the office had received harassing and threatening telephone calls. Additionally, in September and December, 1992, the SNDCA office had been the target of anti-Serbian vandalism. There were no claims of responsibility for this incident.

#### January 19, 1993

During the night of January 19, 1993, a fire was set at the rear door of Ideal Mikron Typesetters, in Chicago. The fire extinguished itself and was discovered on the morning of January 20, 1993. The owner and employees of the business were not aware of any specific reason for the arson. They indicated, however, that anti-Serbian slogans had been painted on the rear wall of the building. The company is located in the same building as the SNDCA and, although the front entrances are clearly marked, the rear doors are not marked. Therefore, it is possible that the anti-Serbian slogans were intended for the SNDCA. There were no claims of responsibility for this incident, and no injuries were reported. (These incidents constitute two suspected acts of terrorism.)

### Terrorism Preventions

During the latter part of 1992, information was obtained which identified a group of International Radical Fundamentalists who were receiving paramilitary training in the United States. Although it was not known at the time, several of these individuals

*Continued*

**EXHIBIT 6.1**   *Continued*

would later be identified as associates of subjects arrested in connection with the bombing of the World Trade Center (WTC). During the subsequent WTC investigation, it was determined that these individuals were part of a network which was also planning to bomb several sites in and around the New York City area.

*June 24, 1993*

On the morning of June 24, 1993, eight subjects were arrested on conspiracy charges while constructing several bombs for use against multiple targets in New York City. The targets included the United Nations (UN) Building; 26 Federal Plaza, which houses the FBI's New York Field Office; and the Lincoln and Holland Tunnels. On June 30, 1993, a ninth subject was arrested in Philadelphia, Pennsylvania, as a part of this conspiracy.

The subjects arrested in this conspiracy were Siddig Ibrahim Siddig Ali; Clement Rodney Hampton-el; Fares Khallafalla; Amir Mohamed Abdelgani; Tarig ElHassan; Victor Alvarez; Fadil Mohmoud Abdelgani; Mohammed Saleh; and Earl Grant. Trial for those charged took place in 1994. (These preventions constitute four terrorist incidents prevented.)

*July 15, 1993*

During the course of an investigation, an FBI undercover Agent and cooperating

witness met several members of the Fourth Reich Skinheads (FRS), to include Christopher David Fisher and Carl Daniel Boese, the leaders of the group. During several meetings, these two individuals discussed plans to initiate a race war by killing Rodney King. King gained national media attention when he was shown on videotape being assaulted during his arrest on March 3, 1991, by members of the Los Angeles Police Department. King was assaulted following a high-speed chase after officers attempted to stop him for speeding. The group also mentioned plans to attack the First A.M.E. Church of Los Angeles and to mail a letter bomb to a Jewish rabbi in the Los Angeles area.

The FRS members had attempted to locate King's residence and had discussed explicit details about the attack on the First A.M.E. Church. As the investigation progressed, it was learned that the FRS members intended to commit a campaign of terror against Jewish individuals and symbolic or religious targets. They intended to use pipe bombs, Molotov cocktails, and letter bombs to carry out these attacks. Fisher and Boese were arrested on July 15, 1993, before they were able to orchestrate their intended attacks.

If these individuals had succeeded in the carrying out their plans, numerous deaths and serious injuries would have resulted. (These constitute three potential terrorist acts prevented.)

### Significant Accomplishments

*International*

A number of successful counterterrorism initiatives and countermeasures were undertaken and implemented during 1993. This segment highlights some of

the most significant law enforcement accomplishments in combatting the activities of major terrorist groups. These accomplishments include arrests, indictments, and convictions.

**EXHIBIT 6.1** *Continued*

*Iranian Terrorism*

On January 13, 1993, five members of the Mujahedin-E-Kalq (MEK), pled guilty to violations of Title 18, U.S. Code (USC) Section 112, A (Protection of Foreign Officials); and Title 18, UCS, Section 970, A and B (Protection of Property of a Foreign Government). They were sentenced on September 1, 1993, to a period of three months incarceration.

By way of background, on April 5, 1992, the Iranian Mission to the United Nations in New York City was forcibly entered by five individuals identifying themselves as members of the MEK. The attack in New York City was one of 12 nearly simultaneous attacks against Iranian diplomatic establishments conducted worldwide that day. The MEK is characterized as an Iranian oppositionist group which opposes the current Iranian regime. The five subjects were ultimately arrested and charged with the above violations.

*Iraqi-Sponsored Terrorism*

On April 14, 1993, former U.S. President George Bush made a visit to Kuwait to celebrate the Allied victory in the Persian Gulf crisis of 1991. Accompanying Bush on this trip were his wife, two sons, former U.S. Secretary of State James A. Baker III, former White House Chief of Staff John Sununu, and former U.S. Treasury Secretary Nicholas Brady.

During Bush's visit to Kuwait, authorities of the Government of Kuwait arrested 16 subjects and charged them in a conspiracy to assassinate the former President and execute other "acts of terrorism, sabotage, infiltration, and robbery." The trial of the conspirators began on June 5, 1993, but sentencing, originally scheduled

to take place in December, 1993, has been postponed several times by the State Security Court in Kuwait. The alleged perpetrators could face the death penalty if convicted.

Shortly after the Government of Kuwait reported the arrests, the U.S. Department of Justice determined that the assassination attempt was a violation of Title 18, U.S. Code, Section 2331 (Extraterritorial Terrorism Statute), over which the FBI has jurisdiction. Subsequently, the FBI sent a team of investigators on several trips to Kuwait City, Kuwait, and other countries to conduct interviews and examine the evidence against the alleged conspirators. These teams were tasked with the duty of determining whether evidence existed concerning the alleged assassination plot and, if so, establishing responsibility for the conspiracy.

On June 26, 1993, after reviewing the evidence collected by the FBI and U.S. intelligence information concerning the assassination plot, President Bill Clinton ordered two American warships to launch a total of 23 Tomahawk cruise missiles against the Iraqi Intelligence Service headquarters in Baghdad, Iraq, in retaliation for the plot.

*15 May Organization*

On March 3, 1993, a five-member Greek Court of Appeals convened to review the case of Mohammad Said Rashid, a convicted 15 May Organization terrorist. On March 11, 1993, the Court rejected Rashid's request for a retrial. However, on June 18, 1993, the Court of Appeals reduced Rashid's 18-year-sentence by three years as a result of good behavior.

*Continued*

**EXHIBIT 6.1**   *Continued*

The Court's decision rules out further appeals by Rashid.

Rashid is the 15 May Organization member responsible for the August 11, 1982, explosion aboard Pan Am Flight 830, which was en route from Tokyo, Japan, to Honolulu, Hawaii. The explosion killed a Japanese teenage and injured 15 other passengers. The flight originated in Athens, Greece.

Subsequent investigation determined that 15 May Organization terrorists, Mohammad Said Rashid, his wife Christine Pinter, and Abu Ibrahim were responsible for the bombing. The 15 May Organization, a radical Palestinian terrorist group, has been relatively inactive since 1983.

On July 14, 1987, Rashid was indicted by a federal grand jury in Washington, D.C., and charged with nine criminal violations in regard to the bombing. Rashid was ultimately arrested by Greek authorities on May 30, 1988, at the Hellenikon International Airport, Athens, Greece, for possession of a false passport. Although the U.S. Government requested the extradition of Rashid to the United States, the Greek Government declined. Instead, the Government of Greece opted to hold Rashid's trial in Greece, pursuant to provisions of the Montreal Convention.

On October 7, 1991, the trial of Rashid began in Athens, Greece. FBI Agents participated in the trial as witnesses for the prosecution. Rashid was convicted on January 8, 1992, and sentenced to 18 years' imprisonment. Rashid's attorneys subsequently appealed his conviction.

*Sikh Terrorism*

On April 25, 1993, Kulbir Singh, a prominent member of the Sikh terrorist group, the Khalistan Commando Force, was detained by the Immigration and Naturalization Service at the Los Angeles International Airport, while entering the United States on a forged passport. Singh is wanted by the Punjab Police in India for 19 offenses of murder and is currently being held without bond pending extradition.

Due to the testimony of the FBI and other U.S. Government agencies, Singh was subsequently denied a request for political asylum. The FBI, in a joint effort with the U.S. Department of State and the Government of India, is currently processing Singh's extradition to India.

*Irish Terrorism*

On July 28, 1993, two U.S. citizens, Randall L. Folgate and John Joseph Lynch, were arrested in West Palm Beach, Florida, and Ridgeland, South Carolina, respectively, on charges of supplying weapons and munitions to the Provisional Irish Republican Army (PIRA). Additionally, William Francis Kelly, who was already incarcerated on an unrelated matter, was also indicted. These individuals, and five other defendants, were indicted by a federal grand jury in Tucson, Arizona.

The indictment charges the subjects with conspiring to procure weapons and munitions, including a "Stinger" surface-to-air missile, explosive detonators for use in bombs, and .50 caliber sniper rifles for use by PIRA in Northern Ireland and elsewhere. The indictment further alleges that the defendants acquired 2,900 detonators in Tucson, Arizona, shipped them in cardboard boxes aboard a bus to New York City, and then transported them overseas.

**EXHIBIT 6.1**   *Continued*

*Frente Farabundo Marti De La Liberacion Nacional (FMLN)*

On May 24, 1993, El Salvadoran authorities hastily released two FMLN members despite strong U.S. objections. The U.S. Government is actively seeking to have these two individuals stand trial in El Salvador on charges relating to the murders of two U.S. servicemen.

Two years previously, on January 29, 1991, members of the FMLN shot down a U.S. military helicopter in El Salvador. A joint FBI/Salvadoran police investigation subsequently determined that two U.S. servicemen survived the crash of the helicopter, but were subsequently murdered by the FMLN.

Through the efforts of the FBI, the U.S. Ambassador in El Salvador ensured that this incident received priority attention by Salvadoran authorities. The FBI assisted in identifying the perpetrators. Evidence developed by the FBI investigation was then presented before the federal grand jury, in Washington, D.C.

On July 11, 1991, an indictment was returned by the federal grand jury charging Fernan Hernandez-Arvalo, also known as Porfirio, with the murder of the U.S. servicemen. On March 17, 1992, two FMLN suspects surrendered to El Salvadoran authorities. However, the El Salvadoran Assembly enacted an amnesty law on March 20, 1992, relative to political murders which occurred during the 12-year civil war. This law led to the release of the two FMLN members.

*Sendero Luminoso (SL)*

In May, 1993, Jose Antonio Manrique Vega was found guilty by a Peruvian court of terrorism against the state and aggravated homicide of Todd Carter Smith, a U.S. citizen. Smith was found murdered on the side of the road in the town of Uchiza, Upper Huallaga Valley, Peru, on November 20, 1989.

The presiding judge recommended that Vega be sentenced to 30 years' incarceration, fined $100,000 soles (U.S. $51,000), and an additional fine of 70,000 soles (U.S. $36,000), to be paid to Smith's relatives.

Attached to Smith's body was a note which espoused rhetoric endemic to the Sendero Luminoso (SL), one of Latin America's most notorious and violent terrorist groups. However, to date, the SL has not claimed responsibility for Smith's murder.

During the investigation of Smith's murder, a cooperating witness positively identified Jose Antonio Manrique Vega, reportedly an SL member, as being one of the individuals who beat Smith to death. On August 30, 1992, based on FBI information, Vega was arrested by the Peruvian National Police.

*Ejercito Popular de Liberacion (EPL)*

On May 25, 1993, Scott Heimdal, a U.S. citizen, and an FBI Agent testified before a federal grand jury in Washington, D.C., regarding Heimdal's kidnapping in South America in 1990. Upon completion of these testimonies, the Assistant U.S. Attorney confirmed that a U.S. indictment of two individuals involved in the kidnapping will be sought for violation of the Federal Hostage Taking and Weapons Statutes.

On April 28, 1990, Heimdal was working along the border of Ecuador

*Continued*

**EXHIBIT 6.1**  *Continued*

and Colombia, when he was forcibly kidnapped. The kidnappers claimed to be members of the EPL, a Colombian terrorist organization.

In furtherance of extraterritorial responsibilities, the FBI deployed personnel to Ecuador to work closely with Ecuadoran authorities and secure the safe release of Heimdal. During early May 1990, a ransom demand was received from the EPL. The Heimdal family subsequently decided to pay a ransom to the kidnappers in an attempt to gain their son's release. On June 29, 1990, Heimdal was released unharmed by his captors. The kidnapers fled into the guerrilla-controlled jungle near the Ecuadoran and Colombian border.

*Abu Nidal Organization (ANO)*

On April 1, 1993, ANO member Saif Nijmeh was arrested in St. Louis County, Missouri, following his indictment by a federal grand jury in the Eastern District of Missouri on March 31, 1993. This indictment culminated an investigation which began in 1986. Three other ANO members, identified as Luie Nijmeh, Zein Isa, and Tawfiq Musa, were also indicted.

Luie Nijmeh and Tawfiq Musa were also arrested on April 1, 1993, by FBI Agents in Dayton, Ohio, and Racine, Wisconsin, respectively. Zein Isa is presently incarcerated in the State of Missouri Correctional System after receiving a death sentence for the murder of his 16-year-old daughter Tina in 1989.

The Nijmehs, Musa, and Isa were all charged with violation of the Racketeer Influenced and Corrupt Organizations (RICO) Statute, based on their illegal activities in connection with their association with the ANO.

The six-count indictment includes a substantive violation of the RICO Statute, Title 18, U.S. Code, Section 1962 (d), three counts of traveling in interstate and foreign travel in aid of racketeering enterprise; Title 18, U.S. Code, Section 1952; and one count of conspiracy to commit passport fraud, Title 18, U.S. Code, Section 371. The maximum sentence upon conviction of all charges is life in prison, with no possibility of parole, plus 20 years.

*Palestinian Terrorism*

Khalid Al Jawary was convicted on March 8, 1993, for his part in the March 4, 1973, attempted bombing of three vehicles in New York City. Pamphlets from the Black September Organization (BSO) were located inside the vehicles at the time. The BSO was an operational terrorist wing of the Palestine Liberation Organization created by Yasir Arafat. Additionally, BSO terrorists were responsible for the 1972 massacre at the Munich Olympics.

On April 16, 1993, sentence was imposed in the Southern District of New York. Al Jawary was sentenced on three counts of violating Title 18, U.S. Code, Section 844 (i), Attempted Destruction of Buildings Used in Interstate Commerce. He was sentenced to 10 years' imprisonment and a $10,000 fine on each count, consecutively, for a total of 30 years' imprisonment and a $30,000 fine.

*Mohammed Ali Rezaq*

On July 15, 1993, Mohammed Ali Rezaq was taken into custody in Nigeria, flown to the United States, and charged with air piracy in violation of Title 49, U.S. Code, Section 1472(n). Rezaq is charged with the hijacking of Egypt Air Flight 648 on November 23, 1985, en route from Athens,

**EXHIBIT 6.1** *Continued*

Greece, to Cairo, Egypt. During the siege, which ended in Malta, Rezaq shot three Americans and two Israelis in the head at point-blank range, dumping their bodies onto the tarmac. Two of these shooting victims, one American and one Israeli, died.

*International Radical Fundamentalism*

During September, 1993, the trial for World Trade Center (WTC) bombing suspects Mohammed Salameh, Nidal Ayyad, Mahmud Abouhalima and Mohammed Ahmad Ajaj, commenced in the Southern District of New York.

Previously on March 4, 1993, Salameh was arrested in Jersey City, New Jersey, for his involvement in the bombing of the WTC. Ayyad was arrested on March 10, 1993, and Bilal Al-Kaisi and Abouhalima were arrested on March 24, 1993.

FBI investigation subsequently determined that Ajaj and Ramzi Ahmed Yousef were involved in the bombing conspiracy. Ajaj and Yousef entered the United States at New York City on September 1, 1992, on a Pakistani Airline Flight that had originated in Karachi, Pakistan.

At the time of his arrival in New York City, Ajaj was found to have in his possession a fraudulent Swedish passport, as well as books and videos detailing bomb construction. Ajaj was detained by the Immigration and Naturalization Service (INS) until March 2, 1993, and consequently was in custody at the time of the bombing of the WTC. On March 9, 1993, Ajaj was returned to the custody of the INS and was arrested by the FBI on May 6, 1993, on charges related to the bombing.

Following Yousef's September 1, 1992, arrival into the United States, he became Salameh's roommate. Yousef is believed to have departed the United States for Pakistan on the evening of February 26, 1993, immediately following the bombing.

Additionally, it has been determined that Abdulrahaman Yasin, who was an associate of Salameh and Yousef, was involved in the WTC bombing. Yasin departed the United States on March 5, 1993, and he is believed to be currently residing in Iraq.

Salameh, Ayyad, Abouhalima, Al-Kaisi, Ajaj, and Yousef were subsequently indicted on seven counts related to the bombing by a federal grand jury, Southern District of New York. The seven counts included one count of Title 19, USC, Sections 844 (i) (Damage by Means of Fire or an Explosive), 844(d) (Transport in Interstate Commerce of an Explosive), and 33 (Destruction of Motor Vehicles or Motor Vehicle Facilities); one count of Title 18, UCS Sections 844 (i) 34 (Penalty of Death or Life Imprisonment when Death Results) and 2 (Aiding and Abetting); one count of Title 18, USC, Sections 844 (f) (Destruction by Fire and Explosives to Buildings and Vehicles) 34 and 2; one count of Title 18, USC, Sections 844 (d), 34, and 2; two counts of Title 18, USC, Sections 33, 34, and 2; and one count of Title 18, USC, Sections 924 (c) (Commission of a Crime of Violence through the use of a Deadly Weapon or Device) and 2. Ajaj and Yousef were charged with an additional eighth count of Title 18, USC, Sections 1952 (Interstate and Foreign Travel or Transportation in Aid of Racketeering Enterprises) and 2.

Al-Kaisi has requested that he be tried separately. Yousef and Yasin have been designated fugitives. Yousef has been placed on the FBI's TEN MOST WANTED FUGITIVES LIST.

## *Brief History of Terrorism*

The assassins of Persia were the best known early terrorist group, although their attacks were confined to officials and authorities. The Jacobin period of the French Revolution and its reign of terror provided the name, while the Russian nihilists and bomb throwers of the late nineteenth century provided the classic vision of the terrorist. Russian terrorists with their eschatological hope for a utopian society were described by Laqueur (1987, p. 3): "the popular image of terrorists some 80 years ago was that of a bomb-throwing alien anarchist, disheveled with a black beard and a satanic (or idiotic) smile, fanatic, immoral, sinister and ridiculous at the same time."

Before World War II most terrorism consisted of political assassination of government officials. A new, second form of terrorism was inaugurated in Algeria in the late fifties by the FLN, who popularized the random attack on enemy civilians. This is depicted well in the classic film *The Battle of Algiers*. This film describes state terrorism using torture to attempt to defeat Algerian nationalists and the effective use of targeting innocents by the latter in order to win their independence. A new, third stage of terrorism became popular since the sixties—media terrorism—random attacks on anyone for publicity purposes. The Bush Commission (Vice President's Task Force, 1986) called it "political theatre," an example of "propaganda by deed." The latter assumes since many are illiterate or apathetic that the written word may have little impact, whereas the "philosophy of the bomb" can have an explosive and hard to ignore effect. This modern or media terrorism has sprung from three seeds (Kidder, 1986, pp. 19–20):

1. Broad historical trends which include a nuclear stalemate which makes major conflict prohibitive, the end of colonialism, and a growing emphasis upon human rights in democracies.
2. Ideological shifts which include a resurgent Islamic fundamentalism, radicalization in the post-Vietnam era, and the emergence of urban "guerilla warfare."
3. Technological advances such as television satellites, increased air travel, and better weapons.

Indiscriminate terror has become widespread only in recent times with the invention of more effective explosives and modern mass media. Such action is easier to commit than against hardened targets or well-guarded leaders and, since such actions are unlikely to gain political support, are more likely to be committed against foreigners. Most of this terrorism is targeted against democracies with little against totalitarian states. Much of it represents war by proxy in which, in the nineties, countries such as Libya, Iran, or Iraq could wage "war on the cheap."

In the late nineteenth century the fate of captured terrorists spelled condemnation and execution, but few since the sixties have suffered such a fate. More likely capture sets off a self-perpetuating cycle with new operations to effect the release of political prisoners. Fearing retaliation, after World War II the punishment of terrorists became permissive. Terrorism has almost become respectable with a substantial majority at the United Nations opposing any significant action against it. The rules of international diplomacy were established by the European colonial powers and are not entirely shared by Third World countries or by the foreign powers in the shadows of the new species of terrorism.

Russian anarchist Peter Kropotkin (1842–1921) viewed terrorism as "propaganda by deed." Carlos Marighella, the Latin American author of a handbook on urban guerilla warfare, viewed one purpose of terrorism as to provoke repressive responses by the state and, subsequently, public opposition to the state. Such tactics have in the past destroyed democracies and created more repressive regimes in Argentina, Uruguay, and Turkey; but recent brands of terrorism have to date failed to topple any government. Terrorists often assume for themselves a higher morality in which they reject moral limitations and embrace the conviction that "righteous homicide justifies killing innocents" (Nettler, 1982, vol. 2, p. 231). Although members or defenders of a status quo under siege are apt to define any revolutionary or guerilla activities as terrorism, the term should be restricted to indiscriminate attacks on civilians and innocents. Although this type of terrorism may never have toppled governments as Nettler suggests, more conventional terrorism aimed at governmental targets certainly has.

Frederick Hacker (1976, p. 69) in *Crusaders, Criminals and Crazies* points out:

> *Contrary to widespread belief, terroristic violence is not always futile and ineffective in transforming reality. If it had not been for IRA terrorist activities, the Republic of Ireland never would have come into being. This is also true of independent Cyprus, Algeria, Tunisia, and possibly Israel. . . . Terrorism often is not confined to outlaws and the dregs of society (riffraff theory); it is supported by responsible citizens and organizations, either openly or in secret. . . . Terrorists are not all part of a Leninist-Marxist conspiracy. The IRA, particularly its activist Provisional branch, is actually conservative, patriotic, nationalistic, and rightist, and is denounced by opponents as a bunch of fascists and "crazy drunkards."*

Some terrorists become, to use Sterling's (1981) concept, "retail terrorists"—a travelling circus of mercenaries such as Carlos the Jackal, Abu Nidal's group, or Rengo Sekigun (the Japanese Red Army). Exhibit 6.2 describes two of the most infamous terrorists of the late twentieth century—Carlos the Jackal and Abu Nidal.

Some terrorist groups active in the nineties include the Basque ETA, which was viewed as a major security threat during the Barcelona Olympics. They are a nationalist/separatist group that attack Spanish targets in the quest for a separate Basque homeland in Northern Spain.

Sikh extremists seek independence for India's population in the Punjab. They are responsible for the assassination of Indian President Indira Gandhi and other bombings in India. Tamil separatists seek independence for the northern part of the

---

**EXHIBIT 6.2    Carlos the Jackal and Abu Nidal**

Perhaps the most notorious and legendary terrorists of the latter part of the twentieth century were Carlos the Jackal and Abu Nidal. Carlos, whose real name was Ilich Ramirez Sanchez, was a globetrotting, freelance terrorist. A product of the extreme left in the sixties, his sponsors (Syria, Iraq, and Libya) abandoned him with the collapse of European Communism in the early nineties. Seized by French agents in 1994, he had often been the leader of a flying circus of terrorist operations. His most notorious operation involved the kidnapping of eleven OPEC (Organization of Petroleum Exporting Countries) oil ministers in Vienna in December 1975. He was credited with orchestrating assassinations and other terrorist activities by a variety of radical groups including the Popular Front for the Liberation of Palestine, Japanese Red Army, the Baader-Meinhoff Gang, and Turkish Liberation Front.

Abu Nidal, whose real name is Sabri Khallil al-Banna, is the head of the Fatah Revolutionary Council and has been involved in terrorist activities for over two decades and responsible for over 100 attacks and over 280 deaths since 1974 (Seale, 1992; Ignatius, 1992). His organization was responsible for massacres in 1985 on El Al Airline ticket counters in Rome and Vienna. It is alleged that Abu Nidal practiced extortion and received millions from governments such as France, Belgium, and Saudi Arabia in return for not attacking them. He has essentially functioned as a mercenary for various Arab sponsors. Expelled by Arafat from Fatah in 1994, he was sheltered by Iraq from 1974 to 1981, Syria from the early to mid-eighties, and has been holding up in Libya from 1987.

---

island of Sri Lanka, which is currently controlled by the Sinhalese. Both sides in this conflict have routinely massacred civilians. In 1992 Abrinael Guzman Reynoso, head of Sendero Luminoso (the Shining Path) was captured by police in Peru. This Maoist group had been waging a nearly 22-year period of insurgency and terror, killing more than 120 mayors and officials. The most protracted separatist/nationalist terrorist campaigns have been those in Northern Ireland and Palestine.

*"26 + 6 = 1"*
*(Slogan for a United Ireland: 26 counties of the Republic + 6 northern counties = 1 Ireland).*

## The Troubles

"The troubles" refer to periods of sectarian, civil strife in Ireland. Recent troubles between Irish Catholics and Irish Protestants in Northern Ireland are a religious, ethnic, and class struggle reflecting centuries of conflict between the Irish and their British conquerors. Protestant Britain completed its conquest of Ireland in the seventeenth century and set up a system of repression which made Irish Catholics second-class citizens in their own country. Scotch Presbyterians, who viewed themselves as British, were encouraged to settle in Ulster, Northern Ireland. A system of absentee English landlords, trade laws, and retarded industrial growth kept Ireland an impoverished agricultural state. In the late eighteenth century, patriot Wolfe Tone (the father of Irish independence) called for independence as did patriot Charles Parnell in the late nineteenth century.

The Easter Rebellion began in Dublin on Easter Sunday, 1916, led by Patrick Pearse; and after 6 years of violence the country was partitioned into the Republic of Ireland (the lower twenty-six counties) and Northern Ireland (six counties). The latter was two-thirds Protestant and retained as part of the United Kingdom. Catholics in Northern Ireland continued to suffer discrimination and second-class treatment.

In 1969 using the U.S. Civil Rights movement as a model, Irish Catholics in the North began marches and demonstrations demanding fairer treatment in jobs, education, and housing. Loyalists attacked demonstrators and burned a Catholic neighborhood. British troops were sent to provide protection and the IRA (Irish Republican Army) reorganized to protect Catholics. The IRA had been outlawed since 1922 and had refused to recognize the partition of Ireland. Although initially greeted favorably by Catholics, the British army became detested after they killed thirteen unarmed civilian Catholic protesters on Bloody Sunday, January 30, 1972. In 1973 London declared emergency measures to control the IRA, suspending civil liberties and using one judge, no jury trials. Attempts to compromise, such as a proposed power-sharing plan, were abandoned after general strikes and violence by Protestants led by the Reverend Ian Paisley.

In 1976 Mairead Corrigan and Betty Williams organized Protestant and Catholic women into a peace crusade, for which they received the Nobel Peace Prize; but nothing changed. An IRA bomb assassinated Lord Mountbatten, a member of the British royal family, in 1979 escalating violence on both sides. Ten IRA political prisoners, including Bobby Sands, held on H block in a Northern Ireland prison staged hunger strikes in 1981; and their deaths inspired further IRA activity. In 1984 bomb assassination attempts against British Prime Minister Margaret Thatcher and other officials failed, but brought the battle to the heart of London. By the mid-eighties renewed attempts at power-sharing were greeted with some reception but bitter opposition by Ulster loyalists as well as Sinn Fein ("Ourselves Alone"), the political wing of the IRA.

Violence by the Provisional Irish Republican Army (PIRA) or "Provos" was continually met by similar activities of Protestant loyalist rivals, the Ulster Volunteer Force and the Ulster Defense Association. A vendetta of brutal murders, often involving innocents, characterized both sides of the conflict. In 1991 for example, the IRA bombed a Belfast hospital killing two soldiers and wounding others. A Protestant hit man shot randomly into a Catholic pub and also executed an 8-year-old boy.

In August 1994 the IRA announced a cease fire, and a truce was declared by Great Britain and the Republic of Ireland. Despite the fact that violations of the cease fire continued, in September 1994 the IRA announced complete cessation of military operations and Sinn Fein was offered a seat at the bargaining tables. Perhaps "the troubles" that for so long had plagued Northern Ireland were about to be played out, or was this an intermission in a centuries-old vendetta without end?

## The Palestinian Movement

Resurgent Islamic fundamentalist groups have for the most part surpassed larger and traditional Palestinian organizations that were dominant from the sixties to the eighties. The Palestinian Liberation Organization (PLO) is the parent, traditional organization consisting of a variety of groups with divergent ideologies but a common goal of a Palestinian state. Traditionally PLO policy was set by the Palestinian National Council (PNC), a parliament in exile made up of PLO constituent groups and independent, nonmember Palestinian groups. Palestinian dissident groups (rejectionists) are those who defected from the PLO since 1984 and boycotted the seventeenth meeting of the PNC in 1984 to reject leader Yasar Arafat's more moderate policies which would eventually lead to a recognition of Israel. Dissidents are also groups that have never been PLO members ("Palestinian Organizations," 1990). Palestinian organizations have included:

### PLO Member Groups:

Fatah
Popular Front for the Liberation of Palestine (PFLP)
Democratic Front for the Liberation of Palestine (DFLP)
Palestine Liberation Front (PLF)—Abu Abbas Faction
Arab Liberation Front
Palestine Communist Party

### Palestinian Dissident Groups:

Popular Front for the Liberation of Palestine—General Command (PFLP—GC)
Sai'qua (aka The Thunderbolt—Vanguard of the Popular Liberation War)
Popular Struggle Front
Fatah Dissident Groups
Abu Nidal Organization
Popular Front for the Liberation of Palestine— Special Command (PFLP—SC)
Palestine Liberation Front—'Abd al-Fatah Ghanim Faction

Exhibit 6.3 lists some significant events in the history of Arab-Israeli conflict.

Arab and Palestinian terrorism has had its mirror image in episodes of Israeli terrorism. The Kach and Kahane Lives groups have been responsible for terrorist acts in the nineties. On February 25, 1995, Dr. Baruch Goldstein, an American settler, killed over thirty Palestinian worshippers in a mosque in Hebron, West Bank.

**EXHIBIT 6.3   Significant Events in Palestinian-Israeli Conflict**

70—The Second Temple is destroyed and Jewish Diaspora begins

600s—Arabs conquer Palestine, Mohammed dies

1897—First Zionist Congress convened in Switzerland

1917—Balfour Declaration gives Great Britain mandate over Palestine

1937—British propose partition of Palestine

1947—United Nations proposes partition of Palestine

1948—State of Israel declares its independence; First War in Palestine

1950s—Continuing violence

1956—Second War in Palestine and Suez Crisis

1957—Arafat forms Palestinian Liberation Movement and Al Fatah

1964—Palestinian Liberation Organization established

1967—Third War in Palestine

1968–70—Terrorism escalates, Fourth War in Palestine

1972—Munich Olympics massacre of Israeli team members by Black September

1973—Yom Kippur War (Fifth War in Palestine)

1975—Lebanese Civil War

1976—Entebbe hijacking foiled by Israeli commandoes

1978—Thirty killed in bus attack by PDFLP; Israel retaliates and invades Lebanon and terrorist staging areas

1980—Camp David Peace Accords between Israel and Egypt

1981—Annexation of Golan heights (from Syria)

1982—Israel leaves the Sinai; Invasion of Lebanon disperses the PLO; Massacres by Christian allies of Israel in two Palestinian camps

1983–84—Lebanon Civil War continues; U.S. Marines killed by terrorist bomb in Beirut

1985—Abu Nidal attacks Rome and Vienna airports; Abu Abbas seajacks Achille Lauro; Israel bombs PLO headquarters in Tunisia

1986—United States bombs terrorist training centers in Libya

1987—PLO Reconciliation

1992—Hezbollah bombs Israeli embassy in Buenos Aires

1993—Israeli-Palestinian peace pact grants limited Palestinian autonomy over Gaza and the West Bank

1994—Hezbollah bombs Argentine Jewish Community Center; Hamas steps up terrorist attacks in Israel

1994—Israel signs a peace treaty with Jordan

1995—Terrorist bombings continue to attempt to disrupt Arab peace with Israel

Portions adapted from James M. Poland. *Understanding Terrorism.* Englewood Cliffs, N.J.: Prentice-Hall, 1988.

Both organizations were inspired by the late Jewish-American Rabbi Meier Kahane, who advocated and used terrorist activity as a means of gaining the biblical Jewish homeland. Israeli-Palestinian accommodation seems to have created a vacuum for Islamic fundamentalist extremists; the best known of these groups in the nineties were Hamas and Hezbollah.

### Hamas

Hamas (the Islamic resistance movement) was an outgrowth of the "intifada," a Palestinian revolt against Israeli occupation that began in 1987. The word "Hamas" in Arabic means fervor or zeal. Beginning as an Islamic social organization in 1989, it later started to use violent tactics as its support among Palestinian nationalists seemed to wane. Quadriplegic Sheikh Ahmed Yassin was the original leader, but by the 1990s Hamas received assistance and training from more militant groups including fundamentalist veterans of the Afghan War. Being a collection of largely independent and secretive cells, Hamas has been very difficult for counterintelligence services to infiltrate (Bartholet, 1994). Bent on preventing peace between Israel and the Palestinian Liberation Organization, Jordan, and other Arab neighbors, Hamas has resorted to recruiting young boys and indoctrinating them into becoming suicide bombers and martyrs for Allah. One 14-year-old who was released to his family when his Hamas cell was arrested described his indoctrination as consisting of promises of eternal heavenly pleasures, "rivers of sweet honey and holy wine, seventy-two virgin brides, and free passes to Paradise for seventy of his friends and relatives" (Bartholet, 1995) if he were to serve as a martyr, a holy warrior for Allah. On October 19, 1994, a suicide bomber set off a bomb on a crowded bus in Tel Aviv killing twenty-two and wounding forty-six. Such bombers are idolized in the Gaza Strip the same way sports heroes are in other cultures. A publisher of a Hamas newspaper explains:

> We don't call this suicide, which is forbidden in Islam. . . . These are martyrdom operations. We are commanded to wage holy war for the sake of God. Here the attacker is assured success, he avoids arrest, inflicts heavier casualties on the enemy and gains martyrdom (Greenberg, 1995, p. A6).

Hamas receives money and supplies from Iran and refuge and training grounds from Syria. Outmaneuvered by more zealous religious terrorists, old-line rejectionists (those rejecting PLO detente with Israel) such as the Popular Front for the Liberation of Palestine, the Democratic Front, and the General Command have reluctantly entered into alliance with Hamas. Wanting an Islamic theocratic state, Hamas opposes a two-state solution for Palestine and is against Israel's very existence ("Hamas Way of Death," 1993). Israeli intelligence (Mossad) is having a difficult time vetting Hamas and its more radical military wing, the Izzedin al-Qassam brigade. It is estimated to consist of only about eighty members with independent cells of only two or three members each. Rivalling Hamas in fanaticism has been Hezbollah.

## Hezbollah

Hezbollah, the "Party of God," and its action arm, Islamic Jihad, is a Lebanon-based, Iranian-backed, Shiite fundamentalist terrorist group. It has been the principal tool since 1979 by which the theocratic regime in Iran has pressed its jihad (holy war) against the West. The best known operation of Islamic Jihad was the suicide truck bombing of U.S. Marine and French troop barracks in Beirut on October 23, 1983, in which 241 U.S. servicemen were killed. This was the largest single loss of U.S. troops since the Vietnam War. This organization has been involved on numerous occasions in assassinations and bombings of perceived enemies of the Iranian regime. On June 14, 1985, they skyjacked TWA flight 847 and forced it to fly to Beirut. After murdering a U.S. Navy Seal on board, the hostages were released in return for Israel releasing 735 prisoners taken captive in Lebanon. Other operations included killing sixty-three in a truck bombing of the U.S. embassy in Beirut and holding American hostages including CIA Station Chief William Buckley, whom they tortured and murdered. Hezbollah's operations are an example of Iranian state-sponsored terrorism. On March 17, 1992, Hezbollah is believed to have been responsible for bombing the Israeli embassy in Buenos Aires killing twenty-nine, and on July 18, 1994, killing ninety-five Argentine Jews by bombing a Jewish community center. The truck bomb had become the signature of many Mideast terrorist groups and all too common in later operations by other groups such as at the World Trade Center and in Oklahoma City. Easily available commercial ingredients, fertilizer, and fuel oil were used. Claims of responsibility for the Buenos Aires bombings and others have been made by a group calling itself Ansar Allah ("Followers of God"), a splinter group of Hezbollah or perhaps a flag of convenience name to confuse and mislead investigators.

## Fallacies/Assumptions and Research Issues

### Fallacies

A number of fallacies exist in interpreting the modern version of terrorism:

- "One man's terrorist is another's freedom fighter" is a "false symmetry" (Netanyahu, 1986). It confuses the modern brand of terrorism with its pre-World War II progenitor. Guerillas and "freedom fighters" concentrate on military targets and do not willfully choose innocent victims in a calculated manner. Terrorists focus almost entirely on democracies rather than totalitarian systems. During World War II, the partisans did not systematically kill German women and children in occupied France.
- Terrorism is not a new and unprecedented phenomenon.
- Terrorism is not always left wing. Between World War I and II, and in the nineties, it was predominantly right wing.

- Contrary to popular myth cases of suicidal terrorism appear to be rare. Most perpetrators wish to live and escape punishment.
- There is a tendency to exaggerate the impact of terrorism out of proportion to its actual danger. Compare its results for instance with the domestic murder rate in the United States.
- Terrorism is not simply a response to legitimate grievances. Bad conditions alone are not the cause. Even separatist/nationalist groups such as the provisional IRA and Puerto Rican nationalists are attempting to win through terror that which they cannot obtain through the ballot box.
- Terrorism is erroneously assumed to be highly effective. Most groups are not successful unless their activities are part of a larger revolution such as in Ireland, Algeria, or South Africa.
- Terrorism is believed to be a weapon of the poor. With state sponsorship many groups such as the Hamas and Hezbollah are well financed. Terrorism was a weapon of the weak in the nineteenth century, which saw oppressive rule as targets; but the current attack on parliamentary democracies is often "war on the cheap" by proxy or carried on by wealthy middle-class leadership.
- Terrorists are not always those in opposition to government. Some observers feel the real growth in terrorism since World War II has been in state terrorism such as in Indonesia, Thailand, El Salvador, China, Zaire, Cambodia, or previously, Hitler's Germany and Stalin's Russia.

## Assumptions

If these fallacies are indeed myths, then a number of assumptions or hypotheses present themselves: most international terrorism is not a sporadic phenomenon born of social misery and frustration, but politically ambitious designs of expansionist states and allies. Why, for instance, had there been little anti-Soviet terrorism by Islamic fanatics even when the Soviets were the only European state attacking an Islamic country (Afghanistan) in the eighties? Media terrorists require publicity. "If a tree falls in the forest and no one hears it, has a tree fallen?" In the case of terrorism—no. Terrorism is aimed at the viewing public and not the actual victims. The massacre of over 20,000 people at Hama by Syrian troops in the eighties was hardly reported in the Western press, while Israeli responsibility for Christian massacres at PLO camps was widely reported. The names of obscure groups claiming responsibility for terrorist actions reflect a strategy established by Fetrinelli, a 1960s Italian terrorist—the "name scam" in which different names are concocted for each operation. For example, Black September was Al Fatah which was the PLO.

Terrorism cannot be explained by simplistic, psychological theories. Criminologist Cesare Lombroso once seriously suggested that bomb-throwing by Mediterranean populations was due to a diet deficiency which caused pellagra (Laqueur, 1987, p. 134). For many terrorists terrorism becomes a way of life, the only employment and way of life they know, complete with high income and vacations to "love camps." The Iranians, a la Orwell's *Animal Farm* (1954), train war orphans as mujahedin. Many terrorists have become, to use Sterling's words, "retail terrorists," a travelling circus of performers such as Carlos the Jackal, or Abu Nidal's group, or Japanese Red Army, the Rengo Sekigun. Foreign support keeps terrorist groups operating long after any rational objective appears possible or their 3- to 4-year life span. Prolonged subvention by foreign sponsors seems to have a demoralizing effect on the leadership and rank and file of the terrorist movement. It is more difficult for offended governments to respond outside their own territory, and countermeasures are not without cost. For example, Israeli vengeance after the Munich Olympic massacre mistakenly killed an innocent victim; and a U.S.-commissioned car bombing in Lebanon backfired, killing many innocent civilians. Democratic societies cannot violate their own morals and values in fighting terrorism lest they become the very monster they are fighting.

## Research Issues

All of these fallacies and assumptions may also be viewed as research problems or questions. The social sciences and criminology can assist social policy in critically examining and providing empirical assistance with respect to these and other questions. Why have some democratic societies been relatively unaffected by terrorism, for example, Scandinavia, Australia, New Zealand, Switzerland, Belgium, and Holland? They are all small in population, peaceful, mainly Protestant, and often neutralist or minor league powers. What about rehabilitated terrorists? Regis Debray (who was later a member of the French Mitterand government) was captured in Bolivia as part of the Che Guevara debacle. Menachem Begin, Anwar Sadat, and Yasir Arafat were former terrorists. More study is needed of successfully eliminated terrorist groups or sponsors, for example, Cuba after the U.S.-Cuban antiskyjacking treaty or Algeria, a former major sponsor of terrorism. How much are we using in the way of counterpropaganda in media-controlled areas? Do we have the equivalent of Radio Free Iran or Iraq to communicate the real operations of the terrorists these populations regard as heroes?

A time-series analysis should be done of counterterrorism operations, such as the impact of the U.S. raid on Libya, in culling terrorism. Prior advice had been mixed on the impact of bombing. Why is it so hard to pinpoint terrorist groups responsible for particular actions? Where are all the truth serums and other techniques used in spy fiction? Does the European model of profit/trade before morality in these matters explain it?

## Public Policy and International Terrorism

Public policy initiatives to deal with the problem of terrorism are invariably beyond the framework of counterterrorism and discussions of it. The strengthening of the social and economic order and alleviation of extreme distributions of wealth, status, and power addresses root conditions which spawn terrorism. To lump all terrorists together, however, is a mistake; and actions against one type may not work against another.

The terrorist threats of the future promise to be more nuclear, more urban, involving wealthier and more skilled terrorists. There is also likely to be an increase in terrorism by proxy. It remains a problem to be managed rather than solved. The Tokyo summit on terrorism in 1986 proposed a number of measures including diplomatic sanctions against sponsoring nations, improved intelligence and security measures, uniform legal and social measures, increased public awareness, greater control of traffic in arms and explosives, military/police action, and media self-regulation.

The single person and event that made large-scale terrorism a possibility was Alfred Nobel and the invention of dynamite in 1867. Now terrorist attacks could target large numbers anonymously and in a way that could hardly be ignored. The potential of such chemical compounds is well illustrated in the bombing of airlines such as Pan Am 103 over Lockerbie, Scotland in 1988 or in both the World Trade Center attack in 1993 and the Oklahoma City bombing in 1995. In both the World Trade Center and Oklahoma City incidents a truck bomb was used utilizing a simple, but lethal, mixture of fertilizer and fuel oil. The use of poisonous gas as a weapon of terrorism against innocent civilians debuted in the cult attacks on Tokyo subways and Yokohama shopping sites in 1995.

With the dawn of the twenty-first century, the likelihood that a terrorist group will utilize some form of chemical, biological, or radiological warfare against civilians increases. Stinger antiaircraft missiles, originally supplied by the United States to Afghani mujahedin in their war against the Soviets, have made their way onto the black market, as have parts of the former Soviet Union's nuclear arsenal. Stingers have already been used to shoot down civilian airliners. Plastic explosives such as semtex, which was most likely used in the downing of Pan Am 103, is cheap and easily transportable. Such weaponry makes the terrorist threat even more sinister.

While European nations with a history of domestic terrorism see it as a crime problem, Israel and increasingly the United States see domestic terrorism as a form of warfare. What of the role of the media in controlling terrorism? If terrorists want publicity, give it to them before the fact. Let them air grievances and urge dialogue between them and responsible governments. Give them air time to express views and maybe they will not have to bomb in order to get attention. The world press could reveal state terrorism, which may lessen the need for desperate groups to seek publicity through terrorism on their own. If the world knows about it, terrorists may have less need to call attention. Media self-regulation rather than censorship is needed. As an illustration, the media no longer focuses cameras on "goofs" at sporting events who run onto the field and disrupt play in order to get attention.

Sanctions must be imposed on regimes that sponsor terrorism. This could include withdrawal of aid and diplomatic recognition and the invocation of strict liability rather than business as usual. Because terrorism is a problem to be managed rather than controlled, there is ultimately no magic bullet. Chapter 8 will explore in more detail some possible strategies for controlling the future threat of terrorism.

# 7

Crime against
Government:
Domestic Terrorism

## The World Trade Center Bombing

In the seventies and eighties Americans overseas were a major target of international terrorism, while domestic terrorism within the United States was rare and even declining. The truck bomb attack on the World Trade Center in February 1993 reminded Americans of the danger of complacency or assuming that it cannot happen here. The World Trade Center attack and subsequent aborted scheme to simultaneously blow up the United Nations, Federal Bureau of Investigation Headquarters, and the Holland and Lincoln Tunnels at rush hour resembled improbable plots from some B-grade disaster movie. Constituting at the time the worst terror attack ever committed on American soil, the World Trade Center bombing involved the detonation of explosives in a Ryder van rented by Palestinian immigrant Mohammed Salameh. The massive explosion ripped through six underground floors and killed six people and injured another thousand. Those behind the diabolical plot had incredibly hoped to topple one giant tower into the other. While the apparent ringleader, an Iraqi using the name Ramzi Ahmed Yousef, fled the country, the four conspirators in the bombing—Salameh, as well as Nidal Ayyad, Mahmed Abouhalima, and Ahmad Ajaj—were all convicted. Yousef had originally been permitted to come to the United States when he applied for political asylum on September 1, 1992. After his flight he was subsequently caught and extradited to the United States. Others were also believed to have been involved in the plot and continued to be investigated.

The Trade Center bombers were described as not particularly professional in their operations. They failed to use aliases; kept incriminating evidence in their homes; and worshipped, lived, and protested together as devoted followers of an Egyptian blind sheik, Omar Abdel Rahman. Rahman, an Islamic fundamentalist and bitter opponent of assassinated Egyptian leader Anwar Sadat and his successor Hasni Mubarek, was the believed inspiration for both attacks. A subsequent plan by fifteen of Rahman's followers to bomb the United Nations and other targets, including the Lincoln and Holland tunnels, was aborted by FBI informer Emad Salem, who had infiltrated Rahman's organization. Speculations were raised as to whether either or both of these terrorist operations were the work of amateurs or professionals as an example of state-sponsored terrorism. Proponents of the latter point to Yousef as an Iraqi agent and Saddam Hussein's call for revenge for his bitter defeat by the United States led U.N. troops in the Persian Gulf War. On the other hand, fundamentalist Rahman, a veteran of the Afghani war against the former Soviet Union was described as not on friendly terms with Hussein. Islamic fundamentalists after Khomeini's takeover in Iran in the late seventies were strong advocates of a crusadelike jihad or holy war against the secular West and infidels such as the "Great Satan" (their name at the time for the United States). It is ironic that Sheik Rahman traveled to the United States on a CIA visa, even though he was a militant on the State Department's list of undesirables. The CIA needed support for its covert war against the Soviets in Afghanistan and had unwittingly stoked up Islamic fundamentalist fanaticism in the Brooklyn headquarters of Rahman. Unfortunately, the agency failed to consider that such extremists might also hate the United States and never dreamed that this enmity would be strong enough to lead them to blow up the World Trade Center and plot their reign of terror on New York City. Secret CIA support and training for Afghani operations had created a "blowback," an unanticipated public policy recoil which is hard to head off (Friedman, 1995; Weiner, 1994a). They had literally created a monster without considering all the consequences beforehand.

## Jihad in America

While the public is often critical of the press' role in covering terrorism, it was journalist Steven Emerson who first raised the possibility of a holy war by Mideast terrorist groups such as Hamas, Hezbollah, and Islamic Jihad units in the United States itself (Rosenthal, 1995). He was the executive producer of the PBS documentary *Jihad in America,* which was broadcast on November 21, 1994. Exhibit 7.1 details Emerson's views on Islamic fundamentalist extremism.

**EXHIBIT 7.1    Islamic Fundamentalist Extremism**

In speaking of militant Muslim fundamentalist groups Emerson (1993) noted that, despite brilliant detective work by law enforcement agencies in catching the World Trade Center terrorists as well as heading off the plan to blow up the United Nations and other facilities, the Islamic terrorist problem cannot be viewed as simply one to be addressed by law enforcement alone. It must be perceived in a larger context of a comprehensive approach using legislative, diplomatic, and intelligence agencies. Emerson (1993, p. A10) offered seven important lessons in dealing with Islamic fundamentalists:

1.  Radical Islamic fundamentalism cannot be reconciled with the West.
2.  The terms "foreign" and "domestic" [terrorism] do not apply.
3.  There is no one ringleader or country orchestrating the attacks.
4.  Members of the Islamic fundamentalist network cannot be classified under one nationality or political alliance.
5.  The political and religious arms of radical Islamic fundamentalism are one and the same.
6.  The United States needs to adopt a coordinated antiterrorism strategy involving the entire West and our many domestic law enforcement and intelligence agencies.
7.  The United States must lend support to the overwhelming vast majority of moderates in America's Muslim community.

Islamic fundamentalist ideology assumes that the very existence of the "godless" secular West is an abomination and an insult to Islam. This leaves little room for compromise. Although the FBI was unable to prove foreign involvement in the two New York City attacks, Emerson (ibid.) indicated:

> For all practical purposes, this is a meaningless statement. Militant Islamic fundamentalism transcends all borders. Increasingly, radical organizations—such as the Jihad Group (centered around Sheik Abdel-Rahman), the Palestinian Hamas, and the Lebanese Hezbollah have established infrastructures in the United States, Germany, and Britain in addition to their base of operation in the Middle East.

Although sponsoring states such as Iran or the Sudan may supply support, many of the Islamic fundamentalist groups are part of a loose confederation of terrorist groups who lack centralized command. These militants collaborate with each other united by fundamentalism and not nationalism, religious rather than political ideology. "Radical Islamic fundamentalists, however, use their mosques and their religious leaders to form the nucleus of their terrorist infrastructure" (ibid.). There is a need for an international database on terrorists as well as attention to the fact that some members of America's Muslim community have been intimidated in the past by militant fundamentalists. Protections, such as those given against mafia threats in the past, must be afforded this community.

## *The Oklahoma City Bombing*

Terrorism in the United States may reflect ideological cycles or pendular shifts such as those described by historian Arthur Schlesinger in his *Cycles of American History* (1986), in which he proposed that in every generation the American political mood undergoes ideological shifts. Terrorism prior to World War II was predominantly right wing, after the war left wing, and since the seventies right wing once again. The latter is no better illustrated than the April 19, 1995, bombing of the federal building in Oklahoma City, the worst single terrorist incident ever committed on American soil, superseding the World Trade Center bombing of 2 years before. Timothy McVeigh rented a truck, filled it with 4,800 pounds of explosives, and murdered 191 men, women, and children. Alleged accomplices in the scheme were former army buddies Terry Nichols and Michael Fortier. Nichols was a member of one of the groups of militias calling themselves "Patriots" who are "true believers" in a federal government conspiracy.

The Oklahoma bombing was, in part, apparently in revenge for the deaths of seventy-nine members of David Koresh's Branch Davidian sect in Waco, Texas, who died when their compound was stormed by federal agents. The Oklahoma bombing took place exactly 2 years to the day of the Branch Davidian incident. Federal investigators concluded that, while federal agents were not without fault in managing the Waco incident, most of the casualties were due to Koresh and his followers, who had started the fire themselves in a mass suicide as federal agents stormed the compound. Koresh had accumulated a huge illegal arsenal of weapons which led to confrontation with federal agents. The Waco incident, as well as a federal siege of white separatist Randy Weaver's cabin in Ruby Ridge, Idaho, in which his wife and young son were killed by snipers, became battle cries for right-wing militia movements in the United States.

Further paranoia was whipped up by militant "patriot" leaders such as Mark from Michigan—Mark Koernke—and other practitioners of "hate radio" such as Gordon Liddy, who advised listeners to shoot any invading ATF (Alcohol, Tobacco and Firearms) agents in the head since they wear bulletproof vests. Paranoia has always been a factor in American political history (Hofstadter, 1965), but the Oklahoma bombing represents a critical departure: the worst terrorist incident ever committed on American soil in which large numbers of innocent persons were slaughtered by apparently remorseless fanatics and their zealous supporters who were fellow Americans. Extremist militia groups introduced another wrinkle into the "craft of terrorism" with their extensive use of Internet, fax machines, shortwave radios, and talk radio for communicating their views.

## *Right-Wing Extremist Doctrine*

Much of the catechism of right-wing militia groups seems to resemble the script from a B-rate, 1980s, made for television movie entitled *Red Dawn,* in which militia groups called Wolverines fight U.N. troops that have taken over the United States. Some of the beliefs of extreme elements of militia groups include:

- The Waco incident and the Randy Weaver shooting (Ruby Ridge) in Idaho are part of an effort by the federal government to declare war on gun owners.
- The United Nations wants to create a "New World Order" and takeover of the United States using U.N. troops.
- Foreign troops under U.N. command are training on U.S. soil and stocking supplies for the takeover.
- Jews control the banking system and the economy of the United States.
- "Patriots" must prepare for an inevitable conflict with the federal government.
- The United States is secretly building concentration camps to incarcerate those who oppose the New World Order.
- Small microchips are being secretly planted in people's bodies in order to monitor them.
- Bar codes will later be branded on citizens for the same purposes.
- The back of stop signs contain such bar codes for directing invading U.N. troops. Color-coded detours on interstate highways are also directions for the invading troops.
- Los Angeles street gangs such as the Crips and Bloods are being recruited to serve in the New World Order army (Shapiro *et al.,* 1995, p. 38).

Exhibit 7.2 describes *The Turner Diaries,* a fictionalized blueprint for right-wing revolution in the United States.

True believers in these movements would appear to check their IQs at the door before entering; however, their paranoia represents a basis for dangerous actions and they should be taken seriously no matter how absurd their views.

The militia movement is not made up entirely of such extremists, but has managed to combine a variety of movements which includes racists, anti-Semites, traditional hate and supremacist groups with tax resisters, antiabortion advocates, antigun control groups, and opponents of big government. Figure 7.1 contains a list of the various terrorist groups operating in the United States since 1982.

Domestic, radical, leftist terrorist groups declined in the eighties. "New left" groups such as the SLA (Symbionese Liberation Army), the SDS (Students for a Democratic Society), Weathermen, and Black Panthers were quite visible in the sixties and seventies. Right-wing groups such as the Sheriff's Posse Comitatus, which advocates a tax moratorium and disregard for federal and state authority, as well as white hate groups, militias, neo-Nazi skinheads, and patriot groups became more critical concerns. In a class by itself as the most prominent terrorist-hate group in the United States has been the Ku Klux Klan, whose cross burnings, arson, bombing, vandalism, intimidation, shootings, and assaults continue, although their movement may have also gone more underground (Klanwatch, 1985) or melded with other newer groups.

## EXHIBIT 7.2    The Turner Diaries

Small groups of alienated white supremacists and anti-Semites explode a massive bomb made from fertilizer chemicals, destroying a federal building and killing hundreds. More than two weeks pass before enough rubble has been cleared to find all the victims. A shocked president warns Americans to stay alert and calls on Congress to pass new laws to stamp out domestic terrorism. It is 18 months after the Cohen Act has outlawed all private ownership of guns in the United States, and a shadowy group called the Organization has launched its first attacks, the start of a campaign to bring down the System by blowing up federal buildings, executing federal judges and assassinating newspaper editors and legislators (Fisher and McCombs, 1995, p. 9).

The above describes a hate novel, *The Turner Diaries* by Andrew MacDonald, the pen name of neo-Nazi, right-wing extremist William Pierce. This and other right-wing literature and pamphlets act as blueprints and inspire extreme elements of militia groups and others and have a self-fulfilling prophecy element about them (see "The Secret Army," 1985; Sapp, 1986; and Wiggins, 1986). *The Turner Diaries* is a roman a' clef and is really a handbook for a fictional revolution and right-wing takeover of the United States. In the year 12 BNE (Before the New Era) or 1987, an organization was formed to settle the race question and prevent destruction of the country by blacks and

Jews. It proposes violent guerrilla and terrorist operations against the federal government (ZOG, which stands either for "Zombies of Government" or "Zionist Occupied Government"). The secret police of ZOG are the "Feebees" (FBI) and are particularly hated targets. The construction of bombs and their detonation are detailed in the book as are objectives such as blowing up the U.S. Capitol building. Key administrative figures are assassinated such as members of Congress, federal judges, secret police, and media figures. Synagogues, power stations, fuel depots, industrial plants, and missile silos were also to be targeted. After seizing nuclear facilities, New York, Israel, and the Soviet Union would be attacked.

The document explains that innocent victims were lamentable but necessary. The organization supports itself through armed robbery and counterfeiting. Once in power they plan to kill Jews, blacks, liberals, and other minorities (Klanwatch, 1985, p. 6). Extremist right-wing groups such as the Order, Aryan Nations, Bruder Schweigen (The Silent Brotherhood), and CSA (the Covenant, Sword and Arm of the Lord) and similar groups are linked by "identity theology," an anti-Semitic ideology that views Aryans as God's children and Jews as Satan's. Survivalism, a self-sufficient stocking of arms and supplies, is also practiced in preparation for some final Armageddon. In the eighties members of these groups killed Jewish talk-show host Alan Berg in Denver in 1984, robbed armored cars and banks, killed federal agents, and attacked minorities—all according to the *Turner*

---

**EXHIBIT 7.2** *Continued*

*Diaries* script. In the nineties extreme elements of militias and self-described Patriot movement devotees such as Timothy McVeigh and Terry Nichols blew up the federal building in Oklahoma City.

In *Lord of the Rings* novelist J.R.R. Tolkien drew an allegory to the rise of Nazi Germany. Gandalf, the wizard, tutors Frodo, the Hobbit, of the nature of such evil: "Always, after a defeat and a respite, the Shadow takes another shape and grows again." The Order, neo-Nazi hate groups, and Ku Klux Klan appear at times defeated yet reappear in new forms under new names. Skinheads, white supremacists, Patriot extremists, and the Identity Movement continue to weave webs of paranoia and hate. Timothy McVeigh carried copies of *The Turner Diaries* and passed out free copies to others. He also mentioned that he rented on a number of occasions a film entitled *Red Dawn.*

---

Some terrorist groups in the United States are either international or strongly identified with separatist or leftist movements. Puerto Rican independence, Armenian nationalism, anti-Castro groups, the Jewish Defense League, and similar groups are examples. Puerto Rico is a United States commonwealth that was ceded to the U.S. by Spain in 1898 as part of the Treaty of Paris ending the Spanish-American War. Numerous public opinion polls as well as a plebiscite in 1993 have all indicated that the majority of Puerto Ricans reject seeking U.S. statehood as well as total independence, but prefer to retain this commonwealth status.

Historically, Puerto Rican independence groups have been very active. In 1950 one such group attempted to assassinate President Truman and in 1954 opened fire on the U.S. House of Representatives while it was in session. Such groups want a separate and independent Puerto Rico (which has been a commonwealth of the United States). The two most active groups are the FALN and the Macheteros (Puerto Rican People's Party.) The FALN (Fuerzas Armadas de Liberacion Nacional—Armed Forces for National Liberation) has been responsible for over 200 bombings in the United States and Puerto Rico. The Macheteros (Machete Swingers) have attacked U.S. military personnel and bases in Puerto Rico (Harris, 1987). They were also responsible for a Wells Fargo robbery in West Hartford, Connecticut, that netted $7.3 million.

Exhibit 7.3 presents an advertisement which appeared in the *New York Times* in 1994 pleading for the release of Puerto Rican "political prisoners." Members of Puerto Rican independence groups view themselves as patriots and anticolonial freedom fighters, prisoners of war and not terrorists.

Armenian nationalist groups such as ASALA (Armenian Secret Army for the Liberation of Armenia) wish to avenge the Turkish genocide of a claimed over 1.5 million

Justice Commandos of the Armenian Genocide
Jewish Defense League
Omega 7
Antonia Martinez Student Commandos
Armed Forces of National Liberation
Provisional Coordinating Committee of the Labor Self-Defense Group
Boricuan People's Army—Macheteros
Armed Forces of Popular Resistance
Croatian Freedom Fighters
Boricuan Armed Anti-Imperialist Commandos
Guerrilla Column 29 September
The Star Group
United Freedom Fighters
United Jewish Underground
People of Omar (Anti-Khadafi Libyans)
Revolutionary Fighting Group
Sheriff's Posse Comitatus
Republic of Revolutionary
Armed Resistance Unit
Ejercito Popular Boricua—Macheteros
Ejercito Revolutionario del Pueblo
Red Guerrilla Resistance
Organization of Volunteers for the Puerto Rican Revolution
National Revolutionary Front of Puerto Rico
Aryan Nations
Animal Liberation Front
Guerrilla Forces of Liberation
Evan Mechan Eco-Terrorist International Conspiracy (EMETIC)
Pedro Albizu Campos Revolutionary Forces
Organization Alliance of Cuban Intransingence
Brigada Internacionalista Eugenio Maria De Hostos de las Fuerzas
    Revolucionaries
    Pedro Albizu Campos Revolutionary Forces
Up the IRS, Inc.
Earth Night Action Group
Popular Liberation Front
Mujahedin-E-Khalq (MEK)
Mexican Revolutionary Movement

---

**FIGURE 7.1    Terrorist Groups Active in the United States Since 1982**

Source: Federal Bureau of Investigation. *Terrorism in the United States: 1982–1992.* Terrorist Research and Analytical Center, Counterterrorism Section, Intelligence Division, Washington, D.C.: Government Printing Office, 1993.

## EXHIBIT 7.3 Open Letter to President Clinton: Free Puerto Rican Political Prisoners

As citizens engaged in business, industry, civic activities and as Puerto Rican leaders, we call upon you to release the fifteen (15) Puetro Rican men and women imprisoned in the United States for their activities seeking independence for Puerto Rico. They are serving disproportionately lengthy sentences, with no hope for parole, while social prisoners routinely serve a fraction of the more than fourteen (14) years most of these women and men have already served. Regardless of what we may think about the status of Puerto Rico or efforts to gain its independence, we urge you, in the best spirit of reconciliation and the search for peace which is prevailing in the world today as reflected in your initiatives towards inhanced understanding among the people of South Africa, Haiti, the Middle East and Northern Ireland, to exercise your constitutional power of pardon, as have so many presidents before you, to free these incarcerated Puerto Ricans.

**From Puerto Rico:**
Sen. Roberto Rexach Benitez, (New Progressive Party, PNP), President, Puerto Rican Senate
Rep. Zaida Hernández Torres, (New Progressive Party, PNP), Speaker of Puerto Rico's House of Representatives
Sen. Miguel Hernández Agosto, Popular Democratic Party (PPD), Senate Minority leader, Puerto Rican Senate
Sen. Ruben Berrios, Puerto Rican Independence Party (PIP)
Rep. David Noriega, Puerto Rican Independence Party (PIP)
Gov. Rafael Hernández Colon, ex-governor, Popular Democratic Party (PPD)
Gov. Roberto Sánchez Viella, ex-governor, Popular Democratic Party (PPD)

**Puerto Rican Federation of Labor (AFL-CIO) and its Executive Committee:**
Valentín Hernández, President
José M. Torres, Sectretary-Treasurer
José E. Cádiz, 1st Vice-President
Carmen Fanny Valdes, Vice-President
José Feliciano, Vice-President
Carlos Ortíz, Vice-President

**Puerto Rican Manufacturers Association**

**Puerto Rican Bar Association and Present and Past Presidents:**
Harry Anduze Montano 1994–96
Carlos Noriega 1992–94
José M. Sagardia Perez 1990–92
Hector Lugo Bougal 1986–88
Luis F. Camacho 1980–82
Angel Tapia Flores 1978–80
Graciany Miranda-Marchand 1976–78
Fransisco Aponte Perez 1970–72
Rodolfo Cruz Contreas 1968–70
Noel Colón Martinez 1964–66

**From New York:**
Congressman José E. Serrano (D-NY)
Congresswoman Nydia M. Velázquez (D-NY)
Sen. Efrain González, New York State Senator
Councilman José Rivera
Councilman Adam Clayton Powell
Roberto Ramy, Bronx Democratic Party Chairman
Fernando Fuentes, Councilman, 2nd District, Yonkers
Willie Conlon

**From Chicago:**
Congressman Luis V. Gutierrez (D-IL)
Alderman Billy Ocasio

**From Philadelphia:**
Councilman at Large Angel L. Ortíz

Source: New York Times, December 9, 1994, p. A19. Used with permission of the National Committee to Free Puerto Rican Political Prisoners.

Armenians during World War I as well as regain an Armenian homeland. They primarily attack Turkish diplomatic and economic targets. Poland (1988, pp. 79–80) explains:

> *Despite the fact that the Ottoman Empire no longer exists, the nationalists insist the present Turkish state must pay for the crimes of the past. The fact that their political goals seem unrealistic does not dim their determination. Armenians cite the creation of the state of Israel, the influence of the Zionist movement, and the struggle for the recovery of Palestine as comparable examples. . . . Attempts to raise the issue [Armenian genocide] have been blocked by Turkish supporters on the U.N. Commission on Human Rights. . . . This sense of Armenian identity and nationalism has been reawakened by terrorism and violence. The voice of terrorism, the bomb and the gun, speak for the Armenian.*

Croatian separatist groups with various names are nationalist and anticommunist with fascist tendencies. They attacked Yugoslavian targets. Croatia was part of Yugoslavia (Poland, 1988, p. 84). These groups have waned since the 1980s with the collapse of the former Yugoslavia.

While anti-Castro Cuban groups such as Omega 7 and Alpha 66 still exist, their activism fades as their leadership (former Cold Warriors and veterans of the Bay of Pigs invasion) ages. Their main targets have been Soviet and Cuban diplomats. Most of their activities have been raids into Cuba rather than activities within the United States itself, although Omega 7 has been involved in bombings and assassinations including a Cuban airline bombing in 1976 which killed seventy-six people. Once heavily financed by the CIA as late as 1993, these groups were targeting tourists in Cuba as a means of destroying Castro's economy.

The Jewish Defense League is an anti-Arab, anti-Soviet group of religious zealots who support a militant Zionism. Through bombing campaigns and harassment they attack targets that they feel are anti-Jewish (Poland, 1988, p. 89). The organization was founded in 1968 by Rabbi Meier Kahane in New York City to defend the rights of Jews. The organization's battle cry is "Never Again," a reference to the holocaust. Kahane, who was assassinated by Islamic extremists in New York City, had rabid support of Zionist extremists who supported the total expulsion of Arabs from the biblical land of Israel.

## Single-Issue Terrorists

Schmid and de Graaf (1982) used the term "single issue terrorists" to refer to those groups who use extremist tactics in support of one issue. Examples include animal rights activists as well as pro-life and pro-choice activists. Exhibit 7.4 describes the bizarre operations of a serial bomber with fifteen bombings in 17

## EXHIBIT 7.4 The Unabomber

On April 20, 1995, the Unabomber struck again when a California timber industry lobbyist opened a package which exploded in his face. Since 1978 this lone assassin has killed three and injured and maimed twenty-three others in sixteen bombings and is believed to have a grudge against technology. Called the Unabomber because his earliest targets were universities and airlines, his sporadic 17 years of serial bombing as of 1995 have defied investigators. Signing his letters "F.C.," the Unabomber left behind the following bizarre message:

> It's no fun having to spend all your evenings and weekends preparing dangerous mixtures, filing trigger mechanisms out of scraps of metal or searching the sierras for a place isolated enough to test a bomb.

On June 18, 1995, airports in California took extra precautions having received a warning from the believed Unabomber that he might blow up an airline. When nothing happened, they received word that he had been only kidding. Two days later he delivered a "revolutionary manifesto," that he demanded be published by either the *New York Times* or the *Washington Post* in order to end his campaign of terror. Both eventually published only portions of his very lengthy treatise attacking modern technology.

### FBI Profile of Unabomer

A recluse, white man in his late 30's or 40's with at least a high school education. He is familiar with university life, too. He is a neat dresser with a meticulously organized life, probably likes to make lists, and is probably quiet and an ideal neighbor. He has low self-esteem, most likely has had problems dealing with women—because of his physical flaws, either real or perceived. If he does have a relationship, it would be with a younger woman.

He fashions his bombs from makeshift material and scrap, and prides himself on the intricate construction of his bombs. He crafts and polishes parts by hand, even though they can be bought at a hardware store. He normally mails the bombs out of Northern California.

He scratches "FC" on most of his bombs.

The suspect seen moving the bomb in the February 20, 1987, Salt Lake City bombing is the one seen in the sketches of the Unabomer. The description given at that time was:

White male, 25–30
5'10–6" tall Weight 165
Reddish-blonde hair, a thin mustache, and
 a ruddy complexion

FBI sketch Use "Back" to return here.

He would now be in his 30's to 40's, and his physical description could have changed since then. This suspect is who the FBI sketch of the Unabomer that has appeared everywhere [*sic*].

Also, it may be a group responsible for the bombings, and not just one person.

years, the longest known such case in American history. The motivation of the Unabomber appears to be disaffection with technology.

Although activities of animal rights and antiabortionists were discussed in our earlier coverage of social movements, extreme elements of these movements resort to terrorism as a means of getting their message across.

Antiabortion terrorism is illustrated by the 1993 killing of abortion doctor David Gunn in Florida by abortion activist Michael Griffin. John Salvi's murders of two abortion clinic workers in Boston that same year, as well as Paul Hill's murders of Dr. John Bulton and his escort James Barrett in Florida in 1994, represent a fanatic fringe who insist that their religious/moral views be adopted by others: "Be pro-life or I will kill you." Such extreme tactics may in fact backfire. Paul Hill had previously appeared on a number of television talk shows making it clear that his reading of the Bible justified his actions—justified murder to prevent the killing of innocent children. He was convicted and received a life sentence.

## Hate Crime

In 1993 the U.S. Senate passed a bill increasing the length of federal criminal sentences for hate crimes by an average of one third. Hate crime was defined as "criminal attack targeted on a person or his [or her] property on the basis of the victim's race, color, religion, national origin, ethnicity, sex, or sexual orientation" (Krauss, 1993b). Although the Senate bill covers only crimes committed on Indian lands or federal property, it will also serve as an example to state and local governments. Massachusetts was one of the first states to attack hate crimes defining them as "acts which are motivated, in part or whole, by bias or bigotry directed at a victim due to that victim's race/ethnicity/national origin/religion/sexual orientation or handicapped status" (Executive Office of Public Safety, 1992, p. 3). Groups such as skinheads, identity theology groups, neo-Nazi, or KKK groups have been known to vandalize, intimidate, attack, and murder individuals out of hatred. State and federal hate crime legislation is an effort to track such behavior on a more uniform basis. Hate crimes have recently become the focus of international attention as well (Hamm, 1993 and 1994). The return of anti-immigrant neo-Nazi groups in Germany and Russia raises the haunting specter of the thirties and Fascism. Exhibit 7.5 reports on FBI investigations of domestic terrorist groups including the World Trade Center investigation.

## Controlling Domestic Terrorism

In the wake of the Oklahoma City bombing, Congress gave more hurried consideration of President Bill Clinton's proposed Omnibus Counterterrorism Act of 1995. Some key features of this act included:

- Hiring 1,000 new agents, prosecutors, and other personnel to fight terrorism.
- Creating a national domestic counterterrorism center headed by the FBI.

## EXHIBIT 7.5 FBI Investigation of Domestic Terrorist Groups

### *The Increase in Right-Wing Terrorism*

#### *Domestic Terrorism*

The FBI describes domestic terrorists as those who operate entirely within the United States or Puerto Rico without foreign direction. They generally direct their activities against the U.S. Government or some element of our society. Traditionally, domestic terrorist groups are separated into three broad categories.

Left-wing groups generally strive to bring about armed revolution in the United States and profess a socialist doctrine. They believe that change can only be effected through armed conflict. Examples of these groups include the United Freedom Front, the Puerto Rican Armed Forces of National Liberation—or FALN—and the Macheteros. Although many of the leaders of these groups are in jail, there remain individuals who operate on their own who are willing to commit terrorist attacks in furtherance of their beliefs. Consequently, they continue to pose a threat.

The next category are right-wing terrorists. They are guided by a racist or anti-Semitic philosophy and advocate the supremacy of the white race. According to this view, all ethnic minorities are inferior in every way. Many right-wing terrorist groups also espouse antigovernment sentiments and engage in survivalist and/or paramilitary training to ensure the survival of the white race and/or the United States. Examples of this include groups like the Aryan Nations, The Order, and Posse Comitatus.

Posse Comitatus and Arizona Patriots members also advocate nonpayment of taxes and regard federal and state laws as unconstitutional.

---

*The FBI is committed to eliminating hate groups and terrorists, regardless of their political or racial orientation, whenever they engage in criminal activities to further their political or social goals.*

---

The final category of domestic terrorists falls into the "special interest" category. While both left- and right-wing terrorist groups want to change the existing, lawfully elected U.S. Government, special interest terrorist groups are committed to a specific cause. They focus on the resolution of particular issues. An example of these individuals is those who commit terrorist activity in order to advocate environmental causes. While the causes themselves are not illegal, perpetrating acts of terrorism in furtherance of their goals is illegal.

#### *Animal Liberation Front*

During 1993, 11 out of 12 terrorist incidents in the United States were perpetrated by domestic terrorist groups. One terrorist incident was defined as an international terrorist incident. The majority of the domestic terrorist incidents (nine incidents) were perpetrated by individuals

*Continued*

Source: Federal Bureau of Investigation. *Terrorism in the United States,* 1993. Washington, D.C.: Government Printing Office, 1994, excerpts from pp. 9, 21–29.

**EXHIBIT 7.5**   *Continued*

who claimed to be representatives of the Animal Liberation Front (ALF) in Chicago. Individuals claiming to be representatives of ALF placed nine incendiary devices in four department stores. They were intended to ignite flammable material near the devices.

### Skinheads

The remainder of the domestic terrorist incidents (two incidents) were perpetrated by the American Front Skinheads. They targeted the National Association for the Advancement of Colored People (NAACP) headquarters in Takoma, Washington, and a bar frequented by homosexuals in the Seattle, Washington, area. Skinheads in the United States are broken into various factions, and the American Front Skinheads are located on the West Coast.

Skinheads are generally young, ranging in age from fifteen to twenty-five. The Skinhead movement originated in England in the 1970s as a protest to social unrest and high unemployment. They emphasized racial (white) pride, patriotism, and support of the working class. Many of the Skinheads in England follow British punk rock groups, some of whose members are racist. Neo-Nazi groups in England took notice and successfully began to recruit them.

Skinheads first appeared in the United States around 1980 as these British rock groups gained followers here. While some Skinheads in the United States kept the dress and music but not the racist philosophy, others continued to believe in racism, neo-Nazism, and hatred of minorities. The racist Skinheads in the United States are becoming more of a concern to law enforcement

because of their increasingly violent behavior and criminal activity.

### Increase in Violence

During the past few years there has been an increase in right-wing terrorist activity in the United States. The FBI remains concerned about the level of right-wing violence in this country. This activity has been particularly prevalent on the West Coast. Since 1987 in the Los Angeles, California, area there has been a rise in the Number of racially motivated crimes perpetrated by various factions of Skinheads.

Once the line has been crossed from believing in racist or anti-semitic philosophies to actually using force or violence in furtherance of these beliefs, these activities become illegal and criminal in nature. Right-wing groups often resort to robbery, murder, and other crimes to fulfill their particular goals. Despite numerous recent arrests and trials, groups employing these tactics remain a threat.

FBI Agents and other federal and local law enforcement officers arrested eight people on July 15, 1993, who were about to launch an anti-black "revolution." All were Skinheads from the Los Angeles area. They were arming themselves in preparation for the riot they expected to occur following the Rodney King verdict. King gained national media attention when he was assaulted during his arrest by members of the Los Angeles Police Department. When that riot did not occur, the Skinheads—members of the Fourth Reich Skinheads—plotted to assassinate prominent members of the black and Jewish communities in Los Angeles. Fortunately, law enforcement stepped in before the group began their

**EXHIBIT 7.5** *Continued*

"revolution." All of those arrested either pled guilty or were convicted of the charges against them.

There was an increase in anti-semitic incidents in the United States during 1993. The latest statistics reveal an upswing in hate violence, such as assaults and cross burnings in America. Clearly, this level of hate and violence is intolerable in American society. The FBI is committed to eliminating hate groups and terrorists, regardless of their political or racial orientation, whenever they engage in criminal activities to further their political or social goals.

*PRTP-EPB-Macheteros*

On December 13, 1993, the U.S. Government prevailed in its appeal of San Juan District Court Judge Hector Laffitte's decision to dismiss weapons and explosives charges against Luis Alfredo Colon-Osorio, in connection with his March, 1992, arrest. Colon-Osorio, is a high-ranking member of the Macheteros, a Puerto Rican terrorist group. Once this case returns to the District Court, the U.S. Attorney's Office in San Juan, Puerto Rico, will proceed with the retrial of Colon-Osorio.

On March 17, 1992, Colon-Osorio was arrested by the FBI in San Juan, Puerto Rico. He was wanted for bond default in connection with the September 12, 1983, $7.2 million armed robbery from a Wells Fargo depot in West Hartford, Connecticut. He became a federal fugitive on September 22, 1990, after going underground with Filiberto Ojeda-Rios, the self-proclaimed leader of the Macheteros. Ojeca-Rios remains a fugitive.

### The Bombing of the World Trade Center: Conducting the Crime Scene Investigation

Within one week of the bombing of the World Trade Center (WTC), investigators had sifted through the rubble and pieced together evidence in the largest crime scene ever conducted on U.S. soil.

The explosion created a crater 150 feet in diameter and five stories high beneath the twin towers. After a preliminary search for minute fragments of evidence in this devastated area, it became clear to law enforcement officials that the explosion was caused by a bomb, rather than an accident such as a gas leak. As a result of damage to materials such as concrete, structural steel and automobiles, an assessment of the explosive used suggests that it had a velocity of detonation of around 14,000 to 15,500 feet per second.

*Initial Assessment*

Additionally, due to the extent of damage and size of the crater, it was determined that the bomb consisted of approximately 1,200 pounds of explosives. When making this type of extrapolation, explosives investigators must consider external factors such as confinement by the target itself, debris materials and the structural integrity of the building.

As the lead agency for investigating acts of terrorism in the United States, the FBI assumed the responsibility for the management of the crime scene investigation at the WTC. Immediately after the bombing, a total of 300 law enforcement

*Continued*

**EXHIBIT 7.5**   *Continued*

officials were assigned to conduct forensic examination of the crime scene. Cooperating with the FBI in the investigation were the New York City Police Department (NYPD); the United States Secret Service; the United States Immigration and Naturalization Service; the United States Customs Service; the United States Department of State; the Bureau of Alcohol, Tobacco and Firearms (BATF); and the Port Authority of New York and New Jersey, as well as other local law enforcement entities.

Despite the most adverse conditions ever experienced by U.S. law enforcement officials conducting a crime scene investigation, a coordinated effort between law enforcement agencies was launched immediately after the explosion. This was necessary in order to expeditiously process the crime scene and determine who was responsible for this terrorist attack.

*Investigative Safety*

For the duration of the crime scene investigation, law enforcement officials were faced with a very difficult and dangerous task. The first and most important problem investigators faced was determining whether the blast area was safe enough of conduct forensic analysis.

During the initial assessment of explosive damage to the complex, it became very clear to law enforcement officials that the structural integrity of one of the WTC's twin towers, along with the adjoining Vista Hotel, was in jeopardy and faced the risk of collapse. This collapse could have occurred within days if structural steel supports were not added. Within the crater, pieces of concrete 14 inches thick and as large as five feet in length were falling from 70 feet above. To

make the WTC structurally sound, three private contracting firms employing over 250 engineers and laborers were called upon to reinforce the building in order to enable the search to begin and to collect physical evidence. This was accomplished by dumping tons of rubble back into the crater before the investigation could begin. The rubble was then methodically sifted.

Safety concerns required that significant logistical issues had to be immediately addressed. A voluminous amount of dust and carcinogens had been deposited into the air by the explosion. Among the biological hazards present were asbestos, mineral wool (a level 2 carcinogen), acid and fuel from automobiles, and small fires caused by short circuits. The necessary safety gear and equipment for all law enforcement personnel working within the crime scene had to be procured and issued to allow processing of the blast area.

To ensure workers could breathe safely, the Occupational Safety and Health Administration (OSHA) fitted investigators with protective clothing, boots, gloves and safety equipment, such as hard hats, eye protection, and respirators. The most modern equipment available was purchased to process the crime scene. OSHA also provided numerous air quality monitors to determine whether the crime scene effort disturbed any hazardous materials. This equipment enabled the search teams to process evidence much more quickly than would have otherwise been possible.

Investigators were also plagued with the fact that no electricity was available to provide lighting in the damaged area. This was compounded by fires which resulted from vehicle gas tanks being

**EXHIBIT 7.5**   *Continued*

breached, broken water mains, and the overflow of raw sewage. All of this caused further structural instability of the areas surrounding the main crater and made assessment and planning a major task. More than two million gallons of water and sewage were pumped out of the crime scene.

*Logistical Matters*

Not only was the investigation dangerous, but it was also formidable and complex. Law enforcement officials removed and sifted through 2,500 cubic yards of rubble weighing about 4,800 tons. More than 3,000 pounds of this material were transported to the FBI Laboratory in Washington, D.C., for further analysis.

---

*The dedication and experience demonstrated by all law enforcement personnel involved allowed for a swift and professional integration of manpower into a very dangerous situation.*

---

Thousands of items of evidence were recovered, more than in any other investigation in the history of FBI bombing investigations. To facilitate the on-site evidence collection effort, an evidence collection effort, an evidence control center was established approximately one block from the crime scene. This center incorporated telephones, facsimile, photocopiers, radio communication equipment, computers, and photo telesis. This control center served as the central clearinghouse and coordination point for the processing of the crime scene by the various law enforcement agencies involved in the investigation.

*Investigative Team Approach*

During the search of the crime scene, bomb technicians were required to determine the immediate importance of many items of potential evidence and determine what items were of investigative lead value. To facilitate this complex task, a vehicle identification team was created for the duration of the investigation. This team removed and searched over 1,600 damaged or destroyed cars from the parking garage. A total of 250 destroyed vehicles were identified in the immediate area of the blast site by serial numbers.

This team of law enforcement individuals served a crucial role in identifying component parts of the vehicle used as the container and delivery vehicle for the bomb. Based on the type and amount of explosive used, investigators surmised that the bomb was too large to transport in a sedan type automobile. Additionally, the ceiling clearance in the parking area limited the height and size of the vehicle. By this method of reasonable deduction, it was estimated that the explosive device was transported into the WTC with either a pickup truck or a van.

*Specialized Support*

To further facilitate the crime scene investigation, a temporary laboratory was established in the already-existing NYPD Laboratory. This laboratory, which was staffed by chemists from the FBI, the BATF and the NYPD, provided a repository for the collection of samples from the crime scene for rapid analysis. This approach to crime scene operations proved extremely valuable and

*Continued*

---

**EXHIBIT 7.5**    *Continued*

resolved many issues of immediate importance during the investigation.

It was during this phase of residue collection that a bomb technician discovered a fragment from a vehicle frame which displayed massive explosive damage. This 300-pound fragment was transported to the laboratory for analyses. A laboratory inspection of the fragment displayed a dot matrix number. The number was identified as the confidential vehicle identification number of a van reported stolen the day before the bombing. The vehicle was a 1990 Ford, F-250 Econoline van owned by Ryder Truck Rental, Inc., and rented in New Jersey.

*Investigative Result*

As the investigation progressed, the laboratory staff was called upon to conduct on-site analysis and sampling at various arrest and search sites. As a result of these analyses, significant facts were established which linked the crime scene with other safe-house locations used by the subjects in this bombing.

During this investigative phase the remains of three high-pressure gas cylinders belonging to a welding supply company were identified. A small particle of red paint with a gray primer was located on one of the metal fragments of the gas cylinder. This paint fragment was compared with the red paint used by the welding company on their hydrogen tanks and was found to be the same. It was learned

that on February 25, 1993, that a welding company in Clifton, New Jersey, delivered three hydrogen tanks to the storage space used by the subjects.

Among other items discovered were 300 pounds of urea, 250 pounds of sulfuric acid, numerous one-gallon containers; some filled with nitric acid, sodium cyanide, and two fifty-foot lengths of hobby fuse. Additionally, the inventory of these materials revealed six two-quart bottles of brown liquid. The liquid was identified as homemade nitroglycerine. This unstable nitroglycerine was subsequently transported and destroyed by the New Jersey State Police Bomb Squad.

Despite the hazards, the dangers and the difficulties encountered in this operation, by March 24, 1993, less than a month after the explosion, the FBI completed its investigation of the crime scene. The dedication and experience demonstrated by all law enforcement personnel involved allowed for a swift and professional integration of manpower into a very dangerous situation.

The result was the accomplishment of a safe and successful processing of the crime scene. The initiative shown by this multiagency team in coping with the ever-increasing demands of the investigation as it rapidly developed, directly contributed to the success of conducting the most complex crime scene investigation in the history of terrorist bombings in the United States.

---

- Placing telltale "taggants" in particles of explosive materials.
- Amending the Posse Comitatus Act of 1878 which would permit the use of the military in helping with investigations of crimes involving chemical, biological, or nuclear weapons.
- Amending the Electronic Communications Privacy Act of 1986 permitting wider electronic surveillance to fight terrorism.

- Granting new authority to federal agents to check credit, hotel and travel records of suspected terrorists.
- Requiring telephone companies to provide easy opportunity for court-approved wiretaps of new digital computer lines.
- Increasing the penalty to a 10-year mandatory minimum for knowingly transferring firearms or explosives that will be used in drug trafficking or crimes of violence.

FBI Director Louis Freeh as well as other Department of Justice officials indicated that a more broad reinterpretation of existing guidelines permitting a more proactive investigatory approach to potentially terrorist groups would be helpful. The ghost of J. Edgar Hoover in the form of abuses by investigating groups, particularly in the sixties, had led to strict guidelines in the seventies which required that a group be involved in committing crime before an investigation could be authorized. Columnist William Safire (1995, p. A13) reflects the wariness of carte blanche approval of wider investigations and a return to programs such as Cointelpro, "black bag jobs," illegal surveillance and wiretaps that took place against legitimate groups in the sixties:

> *FBI penetration of legal organizations, then of dissident groups, then of mainstream opposition—all this happened within living memory. As a nation, we're ashamed of those transgressions which led directly to Watergate. After two decades, as fear of the far right replaces fear of the far left, do we really want our FBI to become "proactive" again.*

Freeh indicated that a broad interpretation would enable the investigation of groups that advocate the use of violence or force to achieve political or social ends, while groups such as the American Civil Liberties Union see dangerous ground in not requiring a criminal predicate before launching investigations. Assuming the ghost and manner of J. Edgar Hoover has been laid to rest, preliminary investigation of groups could be undertaken, informants used, and intelligence gathered, and then a determination made as to whether there is a reasonable indication for a full-fledged investigation. This is basically already permitted under existing legislation and guidelines.

Some additional policy tools for managing domestic terrorism include the U.S. State Department's lookout system for undesirables. This hopefully prevents the issuance of visas to suspected terrorists such as Sheik Abdel Rahman. Other policy options include increased financing for the use of informants and intelligence-gathering operations. A proposal for a federal ban on paramilitary training not authorized by state laws would recognize the fact that organized and trained armies of paranoid hate groups represent an a priori danger. Better control of illegal aliens including quicker deportation proceedings for those who organize, recruit, or in other ways support terrorist activities is a policy priority as well.

All of these proposals pose a balancing act between preventing terrorism while preserving civil liberties. New shifting coalitions of terrorist groups and threats involving new tools pose a constant challenge to counterterrorism strategies. The new terrorism will increasingly pose nuclear, chemical, environmental, and electronic sabotage threats. Should the FBI wait until a crime is committed before they vet a potentially terrorist group that is likely to utilize chemical, biological, or radiological weapons?

Finally, without violating First Amendment freedom of speech guarantees or unnecessarily censoring radio and television, the media does have a responsibility to see to it that the lively debate and entertainment of the predominantly conservative talkshow hosts not feed the paranoid fears and fantasies of the ignorant and imbalanced searching for the simplistic conspiracies and answers supplied by demagogues.

# 8

---

# Social Control
# and Political Crime

In 1994 Nelson Mandela, a former political prisoner in South Africa for 27 years, was elected president of a new, non-apartheid South African government (Mandela, 1995). Mandela's status from pariah to patrician well illustrates the shifting sands of the status of the political criminal. For political criminals, crime is instrumental; it is a means to an end that they view as being a higher moral goal. Schafer (1974, p. 139) indicates:

> *The convictional criminal, with his altruistic moral ideology, places less emphasis upon secrecy and even seeks publicity for his cause. Dramatic publicity, moreover, is almost a necessity for the convictional criminal in order to make the public understand his actions; his crime may serve as an example to would-be followers and generate further convictional crimes. His punishment is not a deterrent and may serve to interest others in the given ideal and to recruit other convictional violators of law.*

Exceptions to this publicity-seeking behavior are government criminals who often prefer secrecy. Political criminals from the left or right tend to be convinced of the rectitude of their cause and their actions. Rather than viewing their behavior as criminal, political criminals either deny the legitimacy of existing laws or view their violation as essential in preserving the existing social order (crime by government) or in bringing about change in the existing system (crime against government).

Many revolutionaries are drawn from educated and middle-class backgrounds rather than from the ranks of the proletariat, as Marx had predicted. Similarly Laqueur (1987, p. 207) points out that in West Germany in the late sixties and early seventies there were more female terrorists than male terrorists, and the females were more fanatical than the males. Clutterbuck (1975, p. 65) indicates that "terrorist movements seldom have more than very small minority support from the people . . . [and consist of] earnest young intellectuals increasingly frustrated by their lack of response from the ordinary people."

Political criminals operate within subcultures that define their activities as appropriate. Whether it be theories of racial supremacy (the Ku Klux Klan), preservation of law and order (illegal police violence), terrorist bombing of innocent victims, the shooting down of civilian airliners (state violence), or nonviolent passive resistance, political criminals feel that they have support of immediate peers. Being convinced of the rightness of their actions, political criminals also impress others with their resolve and hope that they will see the light and eventually agree with their actions. If proper subcultural support for their actions is not strong, such violators may come to view their actions as illegitimate.

Although some view governmental political criminals as not ideologically committed (Allen *et al.*, 1981, pp. 201–202), they are ideologically committed to preservation of the status quo; and this devotion may be distinct from the quest to preserve personal power (occupational crime) (Ross, 1994). Although governmental political criminals tend to be from more privileged backgrounds, many of their agents (servants of power), such as the police, are not. Political criminals against the government vary considerably in background, although many leaders of the "new left" in the late sixties and early seventies in the West were university educated and drawn from the upper middle class. Even though males dominated numerically, a significant proportion of leaders of radical and terrorist groups during this period were females. Many were status inconsistent; that is, their income and occupational status failed to match their higher educational background.

For many terrorists "the end justifies the means"—the rightness of the cause and actions are viewed as reactions to repression, injustice, or hostile acts of the enemy. It is the latter who must bear the burden of guilt for aggression.

## The Doctrine of Raison d'Etat

For political crimes, government officials historically have sought justification in the "doctrine of *raison d'etat* (reason of state)," usually attributed to Italian political philosopher Niccolo Machiavelli (1469–1527). This doctrine claims that some violations of the law are necessary to serve public utility (Friedrich, 1972, pp. 21–22). This Machiavellian "end justifies the means" is a rationalization of political criminals of all stripes: governmental, religious, or political. Friedrich (1972, pp. 106–107) indicates:

> *The martyrs of Christianity became the saints of a triumphant Christian church; their betrayal of the Roman Empire as seen by its officers was what made them the "functionaries" of a future order. The same may be said of*

*the "saints" of Communism and of national liberation; in the political per-*
*spective the sainthood is measured by the rightness of the cause they*
*served, as seen by the beneficiaries of that cause.*

In cases of crime committed in the act of political policing (by secret police), labels of "official" secrets, "national security," and "reasons of state" shroud many incidents and evidence (Turk, 1982). Political crimes by intelligence agencies often have a "keeping up with the Joneses" quality wherein one must match the extreme measures of one's competitor in order to be successful. "To protect ourselves from the tyrannous, we have slowly built up our own tyranny" (Halperin *et al.*, 1976, p. 236). In the Iran-Contra case, for example, the conspirators invented a new word for lying—"plausible deniability," or being able to say believably that you did not know about something. In pardoning most of the conspirators in the Iran-Contra affair, then-President George Bush felt they had not personally benefitted from their activities. He viewed the whole affair as one of policy differences rather than a question of law or ethics. When accused of wrongdoing in the Watergate affair, former President Nixon adamantly stated, "I am not a crook."

Although much of the literature on terrorists points out their intractability and uncompromising nature, one must also consider the social structural context in which their activities occur. To take but one example, terrorism by the Provisional wing (Provos) of the Irish Republican Army is in part aimed at uniting Ireland. How much terrorism or support would the Provos have, however, if a truly successful civil rights movement were to obtain equal jobs, housing, and political influence for Catholics in the North? Similarly, a Palestinian homeland of some form should remove some of the thunder and support for Palestinian terrorists. Certainly legitimate revolutionary and guerilla warfare barring innocents as targets was a necessary outcome of apartheid, the system of racial separation in South Africa. Although not without its problems, serious acts of terrorism have been greatly reduced with the emergence of a new democratic South Africa.

## *Terrorism and Public Policy*

Terrorist threats of the future promise to be more nuclear, more urban, and to involve wealthier, more skilled terrorists often as proxies for sponsor countries. As indicated previously, terrorism represents a problem to be managed rather than solved. Attempts at international cooperation are hindered by the very ideological disputes that often give rise to terrorism. A precedent does exist. Piracy, a historically common practice, has been fairly eliminated through international agreement. At one time countries hired pirates in a form of "war by proxy"; but for centuries they have been declared *hostis humani generis* (common enemies of mankind), outlaws whose acts fall under the jurisdiction of all states. Perhaps a similar uniform international policy will evolve regarding cross-national terrorism.

Terrorism by "lunatic minorities" in democratic countries that provide legal recourse (for example, the ballot box) must be condemned as crime, and sanctions must be imposed on offending regimes (state terrorism and state-sponsored terrorism). This could include withdrawal of financial aid and diplomatic recognition and invocation of strict liability (holding them legally responsible) rather than conducting business as usual (Martin and Walcott, 1988).

## Societal Reaction to Terrorism

The sociological nature of the concept of political crime is demonstrated by its relativity with respect to time and place. Ideological spies such as the Rosenbergs, who supplied their country's atomic secrets to a foreign enemy, were traitors in the United States but praised as heroes in the Soviet Union. Atrocious acts, such as the slaughter of almost the entire Israeli Olympic team in Munich in 1972, were applauded in many areas of the Arab world. Divergence in international ideology explains the relative ineptness of world bodies such as the United Nations to act in unison in condemning global terrorism and atrocities.

Kidder (1986 and 1983) indicated nine means of countering terrorism:

- Diplomatic measures
- Intelligence gathering
- Security measures
- Legal and social measures
- Public awareness
- Military and police action
- Arms and explosives control
- Media self-regulation
- Maintenance of public composure

Diplomatic measures involve international cooperation in condemning and isolating regimes supporting or harboring terrorists. Terrorism may be not only a crime problem, but increasingly a form of inexpensive warfare. As an example of such measures, in May 1986 the Tokyo summit of seven industrialized nations issued a six-point program. These involved imposing sanctions against nations sponsoring terrorism, the banning of arms sales to such countries, denial of visas to suspected terrorists, improved extradition procedures, tougher immigration rules, and improved cooperation among security organizations. They also called for a reconsideration of diplomatic immunity when embassies are used as terrorist support systems.

Better intelligence gathering and sharing, such as by Interpol's computer capabilities, hold promise in tracking the movement of terrorists and weapons. Improved security measures, such as target hardening, it was hoped would assist in physically deterring terrorists. Beefed up personal security, better airport and embassy security are in order. The United States made a commitment of $4.4 billion to build seventy-nine new embassies and to renovate 175 others in 1993 (ibid.). Exhibit 8.1 at the end of this chapter reports on counterterrorism measures.

Possible legal and social measures include reforms which may encourage reformed terrorists to work within the system. The granting of amnesty, as well as programs to demythologize terrorism, are aimed at making terrorist careers less attractive for alienated youth. Programs to increase public awareness of terrorist atrocities can repulse public support and gain greater cooperation for authorities. Military and police actions may take a myriad of forms with differing degrees of success. The creation of specially trained commando counterterror units such as the then-West German GSG-9, or Britain's Special Air Service (SAS), or the U.S. Delta Force was one weapon. Actions may vary from arrests of terrorists to the invasion of terrorist-sponsoring nations. Such operations have had differing results. In 1995 a French rescue and storming of an Algerian airline was a success, killing all terrorists aboard. The Israeli commando raid at Entebbe, Uganda, in 1976 and the freeing of hostages aboard a Lufthansa airplane hijacked to Mogadishu, Somalia, in 1977 were also stunning successes. A 1980 U.S. effort in Iran to free American hostages was a disaster, as was an Egyptian attempt in 1985 to storm an Egypt Air plane in Malta. Preemptive measures which stop terrorism from happening in the first place through intelligence and undercover operations are important strategies. Retaliation may actually solidify unstable groups, although the U.S. bombing raid of Libya in retaliation for the bombing of a German bar frequented by U.S. troops in April 1986 appeared to result in less sponsorship of terrorism by Libyan leader Moamar Khadafi.

Controlling arms and explosives can assist in cutting off the munitions of terrorists. In Ireland, for example, the fertilizer commonly in use was very explosive. The solution was to develop less explosive fertilizer. Media self-regulation involves efforts to not glamorize terrorist activity including keeping kidnappings out of the news in order to prevent their spread. Finally, there is a need to maintain public composure and to keep terrorism in perspective. Although the dangers of terrorism are real, public panic and hysteria only feed into the goals of terrorism (Kidder, 1986, p. 17).

Crimes against the government threaten the status quo of society and societal reaction has been quite strong; however, until recently public reaction to crimes by the government has been quite mild. This is partly due to the belief that, since the government makes and enforces the law, it is hard to imagine it also violating the law. In the United States public innocence in this regard appears to have become more jaded since revelations of CIA and FBI wrongdoing and the events of Watergate.

Turk (1982, p. 236) indicates: "Any conception of legal deviance in political policing inevitably clashes with the fact that such organizations are invented to prevent radical political changes . . . national security . . . political and military considerations override any legal or ethical ones." Some secrecy on the part of intelligence agencies is in the public interest. The level of lying and deceit beyond the public interest is difficult to weigh; indeed the data required for such a judgment are not available until after the fact. The danger lies, of course, in the government, the servant of the people, becoming the master—Big Brother knows best.

## The Criminology of Scandal

William Chambliss (1989) in describing "state-organized crime" has indicated that episodes of major political scandal in the United States have been fairly sporadic until the Cold War. David Simon (1996) points out that between 1860 and 1920 the United States experienced two major scandals, Teapot Dome and Credit Mobiliere, involving a major crisis on the federal level. This amounts to roughly one scandal every 50 years. Since the Kennedy assassination of 1963, there have been repeated scandals at the federal level. The subsequent and controversial Kennedy assassination investigation was followed by mistrust regarding U.S. involvement in Vietnam, revelations regarding wrongdoing by the FBI and CIA including illegal experiments on American citizens, assassinations, Watergate, Iran-Contra, the savings and loan debacle, and Iraqgate.

All of these scandals share common characteristics (Simon, 1996; Simon and Hagan, 1995):

1. They were all due to secret actions of the government often involving illegal, unethical, or harmful behavior. They have all taken place since the passage of the National Security Act of 1947, which institutionalized the most secretive aspects of what President Eisenhower termed the military-industrial complex, and C. Wright Mills (1956) called the power elite or higher immorality.
2. All the episodes were the subject of official hearings or investigations which tend to become part of the scandals themselves because of charges of cover-up. The causes of and mysterious events surrounding scandals linger.
3. Such deceit, cover-ups, and lack of satisfying investigations feed serious charges and plots that rival the imagination of the best fiction writers.
4. Many of the participants in these scandals interrelate and turn up in other scandals, and these crimes affect other crimes and deviance as well. CIA involvement with drug trafficker and ex-Panamanian leader Manuel Noriega may have compromised the "War on Drugs."

In the postmodern era something unique has taken place in the American experience (Simon, 1995; Hagan and Simon, 1994, p. 23): the institutionalization of deviant means, namely, secrecy in the name of national security to achieve perceived goals. What is most interesting in examining modern scandals since 1963 is the involvement in some manner of intelligence agencies and, in particular, the CIA and, to a lesser extent, the FBI. Most recently the Oklahoma City bombing was undertaken in part due to right-wing revenge over the Waco and Ruby Ridge, Idaho, confrontations between federal agents and cult and right-wing elements. Most dramatic are the clear links between the World Trade Center bombing and the aborted plan to blow up various Manhattan targets by Islamic fundamentalist fanatics and a "blowback" from CIA training, support, and protection of these groups during and even since the Afghan War. In short, we trained these fanatics.

The Universities of Dawa ("the call") and Jihad ("holy war") in Pakistan were founded in 1985 as Saudi and U.S.-financed "war colleges" (Islamic Sandhursts) for mujahedin then fighting the Soviet invasion of Afghanistan. Their most famous alumnus was "nom de guerre" Ramzi Yousef (an alias, real name Abdul Basit Mahmud Abdul Karim), the mastermind behind the World Trade Center bombing. With the end of the Afghan War, CIA and special forces advisers left; but Abdul Basit and his cohorts, now well trained, launched their "blowback" attacks on infidels worldwide including in the United States. The new Jihadis are believed to have access to more than 500 unaccounted for Stinger antiaircraft missiles which were given to the mujahedin during the Afghan War (Weaver, 1995).

One of the difficulties in dealing with violations of international law is the lack of unanimity in the world community as well as effective enforcement mechanisms. With the end of the Cold War in the early nineties the United Nations began to attempt to assume a larger multilateral role in international peacekeeping. In 1993 over 180 unenforceable resolutions were adopted by the U.N. Security Council, including a demand for the cessation of "ethnic cleansing" in Bosnia and an end to fighting in Somalia. The resolutions were summarily ignored since the United Nations lacked the ability to enforce its decisions. In 1987, the United Nations was running five operations requiring 10,000 soldiers and costing $233 million. By 1993 it was running eighteen peacekeeping operations with 75,000 troops with a price tag of $3 billion. The Clinton administration, which had been struggling with its new role of the world's only superpower, was grappling with defining the United States' role in intervention. The emergent U.S. directive for intervention included:

> . . . *one or a combination of the following—international aggression, a humanitarian disaster requiring urgent action coupled with violence, a sudden and unexpected interruption of established democracy or gross violation of human rights coupled with violence or the threat thereof (Lewis, 1993, p. 9).*

Former political offenders may find that victory for their cause may elevate them to respected leaders. Such was the case with Yasar Arafat (PLO), Menachem Begin (Israel), Lech Walesa (Poland), Vaclav Havel (Czech Republic), and Nelson Mandela (South Africa). Former war criminals Idi Amin (Uganda) or "Papa Doc" Duvalier (Haiti) may be granted political asylum and live out their lives in luxury or, as in the case of accused Nazi war criminals such as Klaus Barbie (France), Adolph

Eichman, Martin Borman, and Joseph Mengele (Germany), hide out in remote areas of South America with the complicity of South American governments. Klaus Barbie, "the Butcher of Lyons," an ex-Gestapo SS commander, was spirited out of Bolivia by the French secret service in 1983 and was convicted in 1987 of crimes against humanity. Adolph Eichman, the head of the Nazi campaign to kill the Jews of Europe, was kidnapped by the Israelis in 1960 and hanged in 1962; while Joseph "the Angel of Death" Mengele, the architect of inhuman experiments in the concentration camps, was believed accidentally drowned in Brazil in 1979. Ex-Nazi Borman was believed still hiding out or dead in Argentina in the nineties. Argentina released "Nazi files" (made available by President Carlos Saul Menem in 1993) revealing over a thousand possible Nazi names of those who had been welcomed by that country after World War II. Argentina had previously fought attempts to search and prosecute these persons (Nash, 1993).

An interesting example of societal reaction to individuals charged with complicity in war crimes is that of Kurt Waldheim, former secretary general of the United Nations and Austrian president. On the eve of the election for the presidency of Austria charges were levied (but never prosecuted) that Waldheim had, as an SS officer during World War II, transmitted orders to Axis troops to shoot Yugoslav partisans, burn their villages, send resistance supporters to concentration camps, and supervised "ethnic cleansing" operations. Despite these charges Austrians, who as a nation have never fully acknowledged their complicity in Hitler's Third Reich, elected Waldheim to the presidency (Rosenbaum and Hoffer, 1994). In 1994 Waldheim was even honored with a decoration by Pope John Paul II (Rosenthal, 1994).

When an authoritarian regime becomes democratic, former torturers are often granted amnesty since the new democracy is fragile and fears alienating the military caste, who at any point could erase civilian rule (Millett, 1994, p. 296). Such was the case in Argentina in the early nineties. Reversion is a continuing concern.

*And the torture never ends, because it is never admitted to, the torturer's famous boast—"no one will ever know, no one will ever hear you, no one will ever find out"—continues to hold true. . . . Amnesty's [Amnesty International's] emblem is a candle in the wind wrapped in barbed wire, the wire encircling, the candle flame bent, but not blown out; maintaining itself (ibid., pp. 300, 305).*

A specter haunts the twenty-first century. The more complex, urban, and industrial and interrelated the global community becomes, the easier it becomes for a small, fanatical minority of the left or right to disrupt, destroy, or terrorize. At the level of collective behavior and social change, dynamic societies can continue to be anticipated to generate new social movements and new demands for change and, depending on the response, new political offenders either as bell-ringers of change or overzealous guardians at the gates.

## EXHIBIT 8.1   Counterterrorism Measures: Preventive, Proactive, and Reactive

*Terrorist Incidents*

During the period 1989–1993, 32 terrorist incidents were recorded in the United States and Puerto Rico. From a regional perspective, the majority of these, 12, or roughly 37.5 percent of the total, occurred in the North Central region of the United States. This was closely followed by 11 incidents, or roughly 34 percent, occurring in Puerto Rico. The Western region recorded seven (in Arizona, Texas, California and Washington State). The remaining two incidents were perpetrated in the Eastern region of the United States. There were no incidents during this time frame in the Southern region.

Bombing attacks (including detonated and undetonated devices, tear gas, pipe and fire bombings) dominated the type of attack during this period. They were responsible for 24 of 32 incidents which occurred. Also included were two cases of malicious destruction of property, one hostile takeover, and five arsons. During this time frame, six deaths and 1,042 injuries occurred, which are all attributed to the bombing of the World Trade Center (WTC).

From 1989–1992, there had been a relatively steady number of terrorist incidents recorded. This number increased slightly in 1993, with 12 incidents recorded. This increase is attributed to the bombing of the WTC in New York City, Skinhead activity on the West Coast, and incidents perpetrated in several Chicago department stores by individuals claiming to represent the Animal Liberation Front.

The years 1992 and 1993 each contained one act of international terrorism.

In April, 1992, the Iranian Mission to the United Nations in New York City was forcibly taken over by members of the Mujahedin-E-Khalq, an Iranian oppositionist group, and in February, 1993, the WTC was bombed. These incidents mark the first acts of international terrorism perpetrated in the United States since the end of 1983.

Consequently, the international terrorist threat in the United States has both changed and increased, as the aura of invincibility against terrorist attacks on U.S. soil has now been challenged. Worldwide political and social events, such as the end of the Cold War, the civil war in the former Yugoslavia, and the Israeli-Palestinian Peace Accord have brought many dramatic changes to the world as Americans looked on. There are those who may use these occurrences as justification to conduct acts of terrorism in the United States or against Americans and U.S. interests overseas, in furtherance of national causes or their own political agendas.

*Suspected Terrorist Incidents*

During the period 1989–1993, the FBI recorded 23 suspected terrorist incidents. There has been a noticeable decline in this statistic over the past five years. There was a high of 16 suspected incidents in 1989; one suspected incident each for the years 1990 and 1991; no suspected incidents in 1992; and two suspected incidents in 1993. The most popular weapon was the use of explosive devices, both detonated and undetonated.

*Continued*

Source: Federal Bureau of Investigation. *Terrorism in the United States,* 1993. Washington, D.C.: Government Printing Office, 1994, excerpts from pp. 17–29.

**EXHIBIT 8.1**    *Continued*

| | Terrorist Incidents | Suspected Terrorist Incidents | Terrorism Preventions | |
|---|---|---|---|---|
| 1989 | 4 | 16 | 7 | Totals: |
| 1990 | 7 | 1 | 5 | Terrorist Incidents: 32 |
| 1991 | 5 | 1 | 4 | Suspected Terrorist Incidents: 20 |
| 1992 | 4 | 0 | 0 | Terrorism Preventions: 23 |
| 1993 | 12 | 2 | 7 | |

Targeted locations included California; Florida; Illinois; New York; and Puerto Rico. Two injuries resulted from these suspected terrorist incidents.

Suspected terrorist incidents are characterized as lacking specific evidence which links these acts to known or suspected terrorist groups; subsequently, these incidents are recorded under this category. Should additional investigative data reveal specific responsibility and attribution for any of these suspected incidents, the classification will be upgraded to a terrorist incident.

### Terrorism Preventions

Twenty-three potential acts of terrorism were prevented during the period 1989–1993. In 1993, seven preventions were recorded. If these attempted attacks had actually been perpetrated, numerous deaths, injuries, and substantial property damage would have resulted. Therefore, the significance of terrorist incident preventions cannot be over-estimated. The FBI's goal is to prevent acts of terrorism before they occur.

The following definitions establish the minimum criteria used by the FBI to determine statistical compilations.

### Terrorism

Terrorism is the unlawful use of force or violence against persons or property to intimidate or coerce a government, the civilian population, or any segment thereof, in furtherance of political or social objectives.

The FBI categorizes two types of terrorism in the United States. Domestic terrorism involves groups or individuals whose terrorist activities are directed at

**EXHIBIT 8.1**  *Continued*

elements of our government or population without foreign direction. International terrorism involves terrorist activity committed by groups or individuals who are foreign-based and/or directed by countries or groups outside the United States, or whose activities transcend national boundaries.

*Terrorist Incident*

A terrorist incident is a violent act, or an act dangerous to human life, in violation of the criminal laws of the United States or of any state, to intimidate or coerce a government, the civilian population, or any segment thereof, in furtherance of political or social objectives.

*Suspected Terrorist Incident*

This is a potential act of terrorism; however, responsibility for the act cannot be attributed to a known or suspected terrorist group. Assessment of the circumstances surrounding that act will determine its inclusion in that category. Also, additional information through investigation can cause a redesignation of a suspected terrorist incident to terrorist incident status.

*Terrorism Prevention*

A documented instance in which a violent act by a known or suspected terrorist group or individual with the means and a proven propensity for violence is successfully interdicted through investigative activity.

*Counterterrorism Investigative Guidelines and Statutory Authority*

Domestic terrorism investigations are conducted in accordance with the "Attorney General Guidelines for General Crimes, Racketeering Enterprises, and Domestic Security/Terrorism Investigations."

International terrorism investigations are conducted in accordance with the "Attorney General Guidelines for FBI Foreign Intelligence Collection and Foreign Counterintelligence Investigations."

While the FBI has been charged with the lead federal agency authority to investigate acts of terrorism in the United States, there is no all-encompassing federal law concerning this issue. The FBI bases its investigative and prosecutive efforts on several existing federal criminal statutes.

Also, due to terrorist attacks against American citizens abroad, Congress passed the Comprehensive Crime Control Act of 1984. Chapter XX of the act deals with hostage taking. Also, the Omnibus Diplomatic Security and Antiterrorism Act of 1986 created a new section of the U.S. Code which expands federal jurisdiction in matters of extraterritoriality to include homicide, conspiracy to commit homicide, or physical violence committed against a U.S. national abroad as part of a terrorist endeavor.

U.S. extraterritorial jurisdiction may be asserted in a foreign country provided there is approval from the host country and close procedural coordination with the U.S. Department of State.

*Threat Analysis/Domestic Groups*

For the first time in the history of the FBI's Counterterrorism Program there were no terrorist incidents perpetrated by Puerto Rican terrorist groups in 1993. Puerto Rican terrorist groups seek independence from the United States. The Puerto Rican independence movement and its violent manifestations have been in existence for several decades.

*Continued*

**EXHIBIT 8.1**   *Continued*

The reason for the absence of Puerto Rican terrorist activity is unknown; however, it is believed to be at least partly attributable to a political plebiscite which was held in Puerto Rico in November, 1993. The plebiscite provided the residents of Puerto Rico with the opportunity to vote in order to determine whether Puerto Rico should continue in commonwealth status, become a state of the United States or become independent. The voters ruled in favor of maintaining the commonwealth status of Puerto Rico.

It is a possibility that Puerto Rican terrorists were waiting for the plebiscite to be completed before conducting terrorist activity. Therefore, due to the outcome of the plebiscite in which voters chose commonwealth status over independence, the issue which guides the independence movement still remains. The potential for terrorist activity by Puerto Rican terrorist groups remains as well.

*Threat Analysis/International Groups*

For the first time since the end of 1983, there have been two acts of international terrorism within two years conducted inside the United States. With the takeover of the Iranian Mission to the United Nations in New York City in 1992, the bombing of the World Trade Center in 1993 and the arrest of eight subjects who were attempting to build bombs that were to target several locations in New York City, also in 1993, the terrorist threat in the United States has changed considerably. These international terrorist incidents and the terrorist incident prevention in New York City have startled Americans into the realization that acts of terrorism can and will occur within our borders.

The most notable development in 1993 was the emergence of international radical fundamentalism both around the world and inside the United States. The bombing of the World Trade Center and the terrorism preventions in New York City are manifestations of this new phenomena. The New York incidents reflect the characteristics of international radical fundamentalists. They are defined as loosely knit groups whose members represent multiple nationalities. They share a motivation to overthrow democratic governments worldwide and to replace them with nonsecular governments.

State sponsors of terrorism such as Iran, Iraq, Libya, Syria, and the Sudan, have insulated themselves from direct support of terrorism in the United States. However, several of the state sponsors of terrorism are supporters of international radical fundamentalists and they have remained quite active in supporting acts of terrorism outside the United States.

The potential terrorist threat posed by subnational terrorist organizations remains. These groups seek the creation of an independent state within existing government boundaries or the revolutionary overthrow of these governments. Subnational groups include FUQRA, a radical fundamentalist group, and Sikh terrorists. The Provisional Irish Republican Army (PIRA), is also considered a subnational terrorist group. PIRA conducts fund-raising activities in the United States it also uses the United States as a safe haven for escaped fugitives and attempts to acquire sophisticated technology here for ultimate use in Northern Ireland.

**EXHIBIT 8.1** *Continued*

*The most notable development in 1993 was the emergence of international radical fundamentalism both around the world and inside the United States.*

Certain developments occurring in 1993 have served to present new challenges to the FBI's Counterterrorism Program. These events include the country of Sudan being added to the state sponsors of terrorism list after review by the U.S. Intelligence Community; the arrest of Sheik Omar Abdel Rahman, a leader to the Al-Gama Al-Islamiyya, an International Radical Fundamentalist group; and the Palestine Liberation Organization-Israeli peace accord. Individuals may use these developments as justification for the perpetration of acts of terrorism. Anti-American sentiment is prevalent throughout the world and will remain so. There will continue to be elements in our society who consider perpetrating acts of terrorism as a legitimate means of furthering their political or social objectives.

### Terrorism Investigations are Preventive, Proactive, and Reactive

On February 26, 1993, the world looked on as the United States became the scene of the most dramatic terrorist attack in its history. In a matter of minutes, the bombing of the World Trade Center in New York City brought international terrorism to America's shores and once again, to the hearts of the American people. Nothing has served to highlight the importance of the FBI's counterterrorism mission more than the stark image of the World Trade Center's Twin Towers on that fateful day.

A recurring factor of terrorism is the use of violence to elicit fear and effect political change, with the world becoming an international staging area for such activity. One disturbing worldwide trend is that during the past ten years, large-scale, indiscriminate acts of violence continue as terrorists set off bombs in highly populated areas. These attacks have occurred aboard airplanes; in airports; office complexes; military barracks; and diplomatic establishments, with flagrant disregard for human life. When senseless, brutal acts of terror-ism occur against the United States, FBI efforts are directed at swiftly pursuing and arresting for prosecution those who commit, or aid and abet those engaged in these criminal acts of terrorism. This is a responsibility the FBI assumes with the greatest urgency when a terrorist attack threatens the physical well-being of Americans or the national security of the United States.

### The FBI's Role

The FBI is the lead agency responsible for combating terrorism within the United States and against U.S. interests throughout the world. The FBI received this mandate in April 1982, under a National Security Decision Directive signed by the President of the United States. It gave the Department of Justice, and through its auspices, the FBI, specific responsibilities for coordinating the federal response to terrorist incidents. In this role, the FBI's mission is two-fold: first, to identify and

*Continued*

---

**EXHIBIT 8.1**    *Continued*

prevent terrorist acts before they occur; and second, to launch an immediate and effective investigative response should an act of terrorism occur.

The response phase involves prompt, effective investigation of criminal acts committed by individual terrorists or terrorist groups against the United States. The investigation of terrorist attacks, culminating in arrests, convictions, and imprisonment, sends a powerful message to terrorists worldwide that the United States will not tolerate acts of international terrorism on its shores or against its citizens.

*The International Terrorist Threat*

As dramatically illustrated by the World Trade Center (WTC) bombing, it would be incorrect to conclude from past counterterrorism successes that the threat of terrorism against the United States has been permanently eradicated. According to U.S. Department of State (USDS) statistics, there were approximately 883 terrorist incidents against Americans from 1989 to 1993. Anti-U.S. attacks accounted for 20 percent, or 88 out of 427, of the terrorist incidents recorded worldwide during 1993. The level of terrorist incidents by international groups against Americans remains a constant counterterrorism challenge facing the United States.

*Proactive Response*

The impact of the World Trade Center bombing, as well as revelations concerning the attempted plot to bomb the United Nations and several other key locations in New York City, has been heavily felt by Americans. Through a heightened proactive response, the FBI aggressively undertakes to identify and interdict the activities of terrorists before they strike. This prevention phase

involves acquiring, through legal means, intelligence information related to groups or individuals who would choose terrorism as a means to threaten or attack Americans, U.S. interests, or foreign nationals within the United States. The information acquired is carefully analyzed, appropriately disseminated, and effectively used to prevent terrorist acts before they occur. The success of these preventions also signals that the United States is a hostile environment for terrorists and further serves as a powerful deterrent against future acts of terrorism.

On June 24, 1993, the FBI thwarted a plot designed to unleash a reign of terror on New York City by bombing several major locations there. The significance of the FBI's interdiction was realized when the perpetrators were apprehended in the process of constructing explosive devices.

*Law Enforcement and Legislative Initiatives*

In 1986, the Vice President's Task Force on Combatting Terrorism released a report which outlined policy recommendations for responding to the threat of terrorism. One of the proposals made in the report was to increase public awareness for the purposes of better informing the American people about the nature of terrorism and the threat it poses to U.S. national security interests. One of the ways the FBI attempts to better inform the American public on the nature of the changing intelligence threat to the United States and U.S. national security interests, is through the Development of Espionage, Counterintelligence, and Counterterrorism Awareness (DECA) program. The DECA program is the public voice and education media for the counterintelligence and counterterrorism program. It

**EXHIBIT 8.1**  *Continued*

attempts to heighten threat awareness within the public, foreign affairs, intelligence, military, and defense contractor communities. Through these endeavors, the FBI works to increase public knowledge regarding potential threats and the need to practice security awareness.

The Vice President's Task Force on Combatting Terrorism served as a catalyst for the emergence of an active and effective counterterrorism community in the United States. This development greatly benefitted the fight against terrorism, including enhanced coordination and cooperation, as well as increased intelligence and information sharing among those agencies and departments tasked with counterterrorism responsibilities. Past successes in the U.S. Government's fight against terrorism are attributable in large part to this coordinated counterterrorism effort.

Congress has also played a vital role in this success by providing the legal tools needed for the FBI to fulfill its counterterrorism mission. While previous statutes enabled the FBI to investigate acts of terrorism inside the United States, legislation enacted by Congress in 1984 and 1986 expanded FBI jurisdiction to include investigation of terrorist acts abroad. The Comprehensive Crime control Act of 1984 created a new section in the U.S. Criminal Code concerning hostage taking. The Omnibus Diplomatic Security and Antiterrorism Act of 1986 established a new violation pertaining to terrorist acts conducted abroad against U.S. nationals.

In addition, the Aviation Security Improvement Act of 1990 ensured the creation of a new cooperative effort between the Federal Aviation Administration and the FBI in developing initiatives to improve aviation security. The cooperative work of these two agencies has led to security enhancements at U.S. domestic airports to ensure the safety of domestic air transportation systems.

*Joint Terrorism Task Forces*

Increased counterterrorism cooperation between various law enforcement agencies has led to the formation of Joint Terrorism Task Forces, composed of federal, state, and local law enforcement officials. These task forces are designed to bring together a coordinated approach to terrorism investigations, while taking advantage of a wide range of law enforcement resources.

Cooperation among U.S. governmental agencies alone is not enough to successfully counter the global nature of the terrorist threat. U.S. authorities have also sought to increase cooperation with friendly foreign nations. Consequently, the United States, under the direction of the USDS, has participated in bilateral meetings and multilateral conferences with many foreign governments in an effort to better combine and exchange information on terrorism-related issues. In addition, incidents of kidnapping, hostage taking, and terrorist attacks against American citizens abroad have involved close cooperative efforts between the FBI, USDS, and host country governments in matters involving U.S. extraterritorial jurisdiction. All of these initiatives have contributed to the U.S. counterterrorism response and promoted the enhancement of worldwide counterterrorism efforts.

Because of U.S. diplomatic involvement in the global political arena and the

*Continued*

**EXHIBIT 8.1** *Continued*

openness of our society and borders at home, the United States remains vulnerable to future acts of international terrorism. With the bombing of the WTC, international terrorism in the United States has entered a new era. In its wake comes the realization that terrorism will not waiver, meaning peaceful nations and innocent civilians will be evermore caught in the cross fire. As the United States moves further into the 1990s, this threat will continue to challenge the FBI.

### Emergence of International Radical Fundamentalism

International radical fundamentalism, a term used to identify terrorists who justify their violent acts through a radical interpretation of their religious beliefs, is a relatively new terrorist phenomenon in the United States. While domestic or indigenous terrorist activity has endured in this country, international terrorist attacks have been limited. Attacks conducted by international terrorists have generally been targeted against traditional enemies, such as Sikh terrorists attacking Indian Government officials inside the United States. Although the United States has been the venue for such attacks, we have rarely been the primary target.

#### Bombing of the World Trade Center

This trend ended, however, on February 26, 1993, with the bombing of the WTC. Notwithstanding the millions of dollars of property damage incurred as a result of that heinous act, hundreds of persons were injured, and six others were killed. One might have surmised that the arrests of the individuals believed responsible for the bombing, a few weeks after the attack, would have deterred such future activity. However, four months later, nine other individuals were arrested conspiring to conduct similar attacks in the New York City area. Thus far, the common thread between these two cases appears to be radical religious interpretations, permeated by a militant religious authority who justifies violence in the name of God.

#### Unique Characteristics

Although devout in their religion, radical fundamentalists reject traditional religious ideologies practiced by the general populace. Instead, they favor a violent propagation of their faith, and believe that the only true course to achieve their objective is the conversion of mankind through violence. Oftentimes the term "jihad" is used to explain terrorist violence conducted by radical fundamentalists. This jihad, however, is not a holy war within oneself, but rather a war against the infidels, or unbelievers, those, like the United States, whom they believe stand in the way of the establishment of radical nonsecular states.

International radical fundamentalists operating inside the United States exhibit traits unlike most other international terrorist organizations. While international terrorist entities are generally homogenous in nature, distrustful of others "outside the fold," radical fundamentalist sects are comprised of various nationalities, oftentimes including historical religious enemies. The convicted perpetrators of the WTC bombing and other radical fundamentalists who reportedly conspired to conduct other attacks in New York, included individuals of several nationalities. They were Egyptian, Jordanian, Iraqi, Palestinian, possible

---

**EXHIBIT 8.1** *Continued*

Pakistani, and Sudanese individuals. Radical fundamentalist sects have seemingly put cultural and religious differences to the wayside, concentrating instead on their shared goal—the spread of their religious beliefs through armed struggle.

Also, while international terrorist groups are generally more structured in nature with established hierarchies, radical fundamentalist groups in the United States have exhibited the ability to come together and operate in an ad hoc manner, which can form and reform depending on the need or desire. That is not to say that there are no leaders within these groups. As with most other terrorist entities, leaders do take hold in these sects and may serve to facilitate needed support for the overall function of the group.

Further, radical fundamentalists operating inside the United States are truly international in the sense that they are known to have transited and operated in several parts of the world, seemingly with little difficulty. Some of these individuals are educated, primarily in the sciences, with careers ranging from taxi cab drivers to engineers. Most derive from the lower classes within their homelands where they have witnessed the struggle between the perceived "oppressed" and their governments. Historically, radical fundamentalists have spawned from and their violence increased as the result of economic and political upheavals in the Middle East and North Africa.

*Future Trends*

The potential for future terrorism emanating from international radical fundamentalists inside the United States exists. Given the present state of global affairs, particularly in the Middle East and the North African countries of Algeria and Egypt and the former Yugoslavia, international radical fundamentalist activity is expected to remain a significant challenge for the U.S. law enforcement community. This is particularly true in the former Yugoslavia, where ethnic and religious populations are reportedly being persecuted and forced from their homes by opposing forces.

# References

Adams, James. *Sellout: Aldrich Ames and the Corruption of the CIA.* New York: Viking, 1995.

Agee, Philip. *Inside the Company: CIA Diary.* New York: Stonehill, 1975.

Allen, Harry E., et al. *Crime and Punishment: An Introduction to Criminology.* New York: The Free Press, 1981.

Alpern, David M., Richard Sandza, and Martin Kasindorf. "The Case of the Missing Spy." *Newsweek,* 21 October 1985, 46.

Anderson, Edward J. "A Study of Industrial Espionage." *Parts I & II, Security Management,* January/March 1977.

Anderson, Jack, and Dale Van Atta. "Reagan Deals with Iranian Torturers," *Erie Morning News,* 23 November 1985, p. 3B.

———. "Human Rights—Iranian Prisons Remain a Horror," *Erie Times-News,* 14 January 1990, p. 3E.

"Animal Rights Group Destroys Mink Research." *The Chronicle of Higher Education,* March 11, 1991, A5.

"As His Backers Protest, Philip Berrigan Is Sentenced to Prison," *The New York Times,* 7 July 1994, p. C20.

Bamford, James. *The Puzzle Palace: Inside the National Security Agency.* New York: Houghton Mifflin, 1982.

Bandow, Doug. "Robert Gates: A Case Worth Investigating," *The Wall Street Journal,* 12 September 1991, p. A19.

Barak, Gregg, ed. *Crimes by the Capitalist State: An Introduction to State Criminality.* Albany, N.Y.: State University of New York Press, 1991.

Barrett, Paul M. "Geneva Conventions: Rules for War," *The Wall Street Journal,* 30 June 1991, p. A3.

Bartholet, Jeffrey. "How Big a Threat is Hamas?" *Newsweek,* 31 October 1994, 37.

———. "A Guaranteed Trip to Heaven." *Newsweek,* 24 April 1995, 42.

Baylor, Timothy. "Informants/Agent Provocateurs—Violators of Trust: One Element in the Tactical Repertoire of Social Control Agents." Paper presented at the American Sociological Association Meetings, Washington, D.C., August 1990.

Bell, Daniel. *The End of Ideology.* Glencoe, Ill.: The Free Press, 1964.

Bergamini, David. *Japan's Imperial Conspiracy.* New York: William Morrow and Company, 1971.

Bernstein, Carl. "Conspiracy Without End: The Legacy of Watergate," *Erie Times-News,* 10 January 1993, p. 3B.

Bittman, Ladislaw. *The Deception Game.* New York: Ballantine, 1981.

———. *KGB Disinformation.* New York: Pergamon, 1985.

Blackstock, Nelson. *Cointelpro: The FBI's Secret War on Political Freedom.* New York: Random House, 1976.

Blackstock, Paul W. *Agents of Deceit: Frauds, Forgeries and Political Intrigue Among Nations.* Chicago: Quadrangle, 1966.

Blakey, G. Robert. "The Mafia and JFK's Murder," *The Washington Post National Weekly Review,* 15–21 November 1993, pp. 23–24

Blakey, G. Robert, and Richard Billing. *The Plot to Kill the President: Organized Crime Assassinated JFK.* New York: New York Times Books, 1981.

Blitzer, Wolf. *Territory of Lies.* New York: Harper and Row, 1989.

Bliven, Naomi. "Books: All the President's Men II." *New Yorker,* 17 June 1991, 113–16.

Bottom, Norman R., Jr., and Robert Gallati. *Industrial Espionage.* Boston: Butterworth, 1984.

Brewton, Pete. *The Mafia, CIA and George Bush.* New York: SPI Books, Shapolsky Publishers, 1992.

Broadwell, William. "Commercial Espionage: The Phenomenon of Information Theft." *Security Administration* 6 (1984): 41–51.

Brown, Richard M. "Historical Patterns of Violence in America." In *Violence in America,* a staff report to the National Commission on the Causes and Prevention of Violence, eds. Hugh D. Graham and Ted R. Gurr, pp. 43–80. New York: New American Library, 1969.

"Cambodia: Pol Pot's Lifeless Zombies." *Time,* 3 December 1979, 55–56.

"Can Moscow Trust Its KGB Spies." *U.S. News and World Report,* 7 October 1985, 14.

Caputi, Jane, and Diana E. H. Russell. "Femicide: Speaking the Unspeakable." *MS.* 1 (September/October 1990), 34–37.

Chambliss, William. *On the Take: From Petty Crooks to Presidents.* 2d ed. Bloomington, Ind.: Indiana University Press, 1988(a).

———. "State-Organized Crime." *Criminology* 27 (1988[b]): 183–208.

———. "State-Organized Crime." *Criminology* 27 (1989): 183–208.

Chambliss, William J., and Robert B. Seidman. *Law and Order and Power.* Reading, Mass.: Addison-Wesley, 1971.

Choate, Pat. *Agents of Influence.* New York: Alfred A. Knopf, 1990.

Clarke, James W. *American Assassins: The Darker Side of Politics.* Princeton, N.J.: Princeton University Press, 1982.

Clinard, Marshall B., and Richard Quinney. *Criminal Behavior Systems: A Typology.* 2d ed. New York: Holt, Rinehart and Winston, 1974.

Clutterbuck, Richard. *Living With Terrorism.* New Rochelle, N.Y.: Arlington House, 1975.

Cohen, Roger. "Ex-Guard for Serbs Tells of Grisly 'Cleansing Camps,'" *The New York Times,* 1 August 1994, pp. A1, A4.

Cohn, Bob. "Weinberger the Scribbler." *Newsweek,* 29 June 1992, 24.

Congressional Research Service. *Human Rights Conditions in Selected Countries and the U. S. Response.* Report prepared for the House Committee on International Relations, 95th Congress, 2d Session. Washington, D.C.: Government Printing Office, 25 July 1978, pp. 10–14.

Cook, Fred J. *Maverick: Fifty Years of Investigative Reporting.* New York: G.P. Putnam's Sons, 1984.

Copeland, Miles. *Beyond Cloak and Dagger: Inside the CIA.* New York: Pinnacle Books, 1974.

Cousins, Norman. "How the U.S. Used Its Citizens as Guinea Pigs." *Saturday Review,* 10 November 1979, 10.

Cressey, Donald R. *Other People's Money: The Social Psychology of Embezzlement.* New York: The Free Press, 1953.

Crittenden, Ann. *Sanctuary: A Story of American Conscience and Law in Collision.* New York: Weidenfeld and Nicolson, 1988.

Danner, Mark. "The Truth of El Mozote." *New Yorker,* 6 December 1993, 50–133.

Darnton, John. "Six Kennedys Join In-Law in Ulster Murder Appeal," *The New York Times,* 24 February 1994, p. A6.

"Death Squads Prey on Rio Street Children." *CJ the Americas* 4 (April–May 1991): 12.

DeKeseredy, Walter S., and Katharine Kelly. "Woman Abuse in University and College Dating Relationships: The Contribution of the Ideology of Familial Patriarchy." *Journal of Human Justice* 4 (Spring 1993): 25–52.

Des Forges, Alison. "Genocide: It's a Fact in Rwanda," *The New York Times,* 11 May 1994, p. A11.

Dobash, R. Emerson, and Russell Dobash. *Violence Against Wives.* New York: The Free Press, 1979.

Dobbs, Michael. "Sacrificed to the Super-power," *The Washington Post National Weekly Edition,* 20–26 September 1993, pp. 13–14.

Donohue, Thomas J. "Nonessential Animal Testing: Luxury Through Brutality." *Networkings,* Fall 7 (1992): 3.

Donovan, Robert. *Assassins.* New York: Harper Brothers, 1952.

Draper, Theodore. *A Very Thin Line: The Iran-Contra Affair.* New York: Hill and Wang, 1991.

Dudney, Robert S. "How Soviets Steal U.S. High Tech Secrets." *U.S. News and World Report,* 12 August 1985, 33–38.

Duffy, Brian. "A Marine and His 'Swallow'." *U.S. News and World Report,* 26 January 1987, 25.

Dye, Thomas R. *Who's Running America.* 4th ed. Englewood Cliffs, N.J.: Prentice-Hall, 1986.

Dye, Thomas R., and Harmon Zeigler. *The Irony of Democracy.* 8th ed. Pacific Grove, Calif.: Brooks Cole, 1990.

"Editorial," *The Wall Street Journal,* 1 October 1991, p. A18.

Elias, Robert. *The Politics of Victimization: Victims, Victimology and Human Rights.* New York: Oxford University Press, 1986.

Emerson, Steven. "The Great Satan Wins One," *The Wall Street Journal,* 25 June 1993, p. A10.

Epstein, Jay. "Edwin Wilson and the CIA: How Badly One Man Hurt Our Nation." *Parade Magazine,* 18 September 1983, 22–24.

Executive Office of Public Safety. *Hate Crime/Hate Incidents in Massachusetts.* 1991 Annual Report. Boston: Department of Public Safety, 1992.

Federal Bureau of Investigation. *Terrorism in the United States: 1982–1992.* Terrorist Research and Analytical Center, Counter-terrorism Section, Intelligence Division. Washington, D.C.: Government Printing Office, 1993.

———. *Terrorism in the United States, 1993.* Washington, D.C.: Government Printing Office, February 1994.

Fisher, Marc, and Phil McCombs. "Going by the Book of Hate," *The Washington Post National Weekly Edition,* 1–7 May 1995, p. 9.

Fonzi, Gaeton. *The Last Investigation.* New York: Thunder's Mouth, 1993.

Fraser, Caroline. "The Raid at Silver Spring." *New Yorker,* 19 April 1993, 66–84.

Fricker, Mary, and Steven Pizzo. "Outlaws at Justice." *Mother Jones,* May/June 1992, 30–38.

Friedman, Alan. *Spider's Web: The Secret History of How the White House Illegally Armed Iraq.* New York: Bantam Books, 1993.

Friedman, Robert I. "The CIA's Jihad." *New York Magazine,* 27 March 1995, 38–47.

Friedrich, Carl J. *The Pathology of Politics.* New York: Harper and Row, 1972.

Friedrichs, David O. "Governmental Crime: Making Sense of the Conceptual Confusion." Paper presented at the Academy of Criminal Justice Sciences Meetings, Pittsburgh, Penn., March 1992.

Garrow, David. *The FBI and Martin Luther King.* New York: W. W. Norton, 1981.

Gejdenson, Sam. "Come Clean on Iraq," *The Washington Post National Weekly Edition,* 26 October 1992, p. 31.

Goulden, Joseph C. *The Death Merchant: The Rise and Fall of Edwin P. Wilson.* New York: Simon and Schuster, 1984.

Gravel, Mike, ed. *The Pentagon Papers.* 4 vols. Boston: Beacon Press, 1971.

Greenberg, Joel. "Palestinian 'Martyrs': Defiant and So Willing," *The New York Times,* 25 January 1995, p. A6.

Greider, William. *Who Will Tell the People.* New York: Simon and Schuster, 1992.

Hacker, Frederick J. *Crusaders, Criminals and Crazies.* New York: W. W. Norton, 1976.

Hagan, Frank E. "Sub Rosa Criminals: Spies as Neglected Criminal Types." *Clandestine Tactics and Technology: A Technical Background Intelligence Service* (International Association of Chiefs of Police) 9, Issue 11 (1986): 1–9.

———. "Espionage as Political Crime: A Typology of Spies." *Journal of Security Administration* 12 (June 1989): 19–36.

———. "From HUD to Iran-Contra: Crimes of the Reagan Era." Paper presented at the American Society of Criminology Meetings, New Orleans, November 1992.

———. *Introduction to Criminology: Theories, Methods and Criminal Behavior.* 3d ed. Chicago: Nelson-Hall, 1994.

———. "The Ames Spy Case and the Typology of Spies." Paper presented at the Academy of Criminal Justice Sciences Meetings, Boston, March 1995a.

———. "Spies." Paper presented at the American Society of Criminology Meetings, Boston, November 1995b.

Hagan, Frank E., and Peter J. Benekos. "The Great Savings and Loan Scandal: An Analysis of the Biggest Financial Fraud in American History." *Journal of Security Administration* 14 (June 1991): 41–64.

Hagan, Frank E., and David R. Simon. "Crimes of the Bush Era." Paper presented at the American Society of Criminology Meetings, Phoenix, October 1993.

―――. "From Inslaw to Iraqgate: Elite Deviance in the Bush Era." Paper presented at the Academy of Criminal Justice Sciences Meetings, Chicago, March 1994.

Halperin, Morton H., et al. *The Lawless State: The Crimes of the U.S. Intelligence Agencies.* New York: Penguin, 1976.

"The Hamas Way of Death," *The New York Times,* 16 April 1993, Op-Ed, p. A6.

Hamm, Mark. *American Skinheads: The Criminology and Control of Hate Crime.* Westport, Conn.: Praeger, 1993.

―――. *Hate Crime: International Perspectives on Causes and Control.* Cincinnati: Anderson, 1994.

Harris, John W., Jr. "Domestic Terrorism in the 1980s." *FBI Law Enforcement Bulletin,* October 1987, 5–13.

Hastings, Donald W. "The Psychiatry of Presidential Assassination." *Journal Lancet* 85 (March 1965): 93–100; (April 1965): 157–62; (May 1965): 189–92; and (July 1965): 294–301.

Henderson, Joel H., and David R. Simon. *Crimes of the Criminal Justice System.* Cincinnati: Anderson, 1994.

Herman, Edward. *The Real Terror Network.* Boston: South End Press, 1983.

Hersh, Seymour. "The Spoils of the Gulf War." *New Yorker,* 6 September 1993, 70–81.

Hofstadter, Richard. *The Paranoid Style in American Politics.* New York: Alfred A. Knopf, 1965.

Holden-Rhodes, Jim, and Peter Lupscha. "Gray Area Phenomena: New Threats and Policy Dilemmas." *CJ International* 9 (January/February 1993): 11–17.

Hosenball, Mark. "What October Surprise?: The 1980 Hostage-Deal Story Still Can't Be Proved." *The Washington Post National Weekly Edition,* 29 April–5 May 1991, pp. 24–25.

Hunter, Edward. *Brain-Washing in Red China.* New York: Vanguard Press, 1951.

Hurst, J. W. "Treason." *Encyclopedia of Crime and Justice.* Edited by S. H. Kadish. New York: The Free Press, vol. 4, 1983, pp. 1559–62.

Hyde, H. Montgomery. *The Atom Bomb Spies.* New York: Ballantine, 1980.

Ignatius, David. "The World's Leading Terrorist." *The Washington Post,* 5 February 1992, p. 6A.

Ingraham, Barton L. *Political Crime in Europe: A Comparative Study of France, Germany and England.* Berkeley, Calif.: University of California Press, 1979.

"Iran-Contra: Who's Next." *Newsweek,* 27 July 1992, 4.

"Iraq: An Accusation of Torture." *Newsweek,* 13 March 1989, 39.

Jacobs, Charles, and Mohamed Athie. "Bought and Sold." *The New York Times,* 13 July 1994, Op-Ed, p. A11.

Jacoby, Tamar, and Robert Parry. "Casey's Domestic 'Covert Op'." *Newsweek,* 12 October 1987, 36.

Jacoby, Tamar, Richard Sandza, and Robert Parry. "Going After Dissidents." *Newsweek,* 8 February 1988, 29.

Japan Yearbook. *Tokyo: Foreign Affairs Association of Japan, 1944.* Cited in Japan's Imperial Conspiracy by David Bergamini. New York: William Morrow and Company, 1971.

"Jewel Thieves Linked to Yugoslavia Civil War," *Erie Morning News,* 23 December 1991, p. 5A.

Johnson, Haynes. *Sleepwalking Through History: America in the Reagan Years.* New York: W. W. Norton, 1991.

"Jury Selection Begins in 'Eco-Terrorism' Trial," *Erie Morning News,* 11 June 1991, p. 5A.

Kapsidelis, Martin. *The Atom Bomb Spies.* New York: Ballantine, 1985.

Karmen, Andrew. "Agents Provocateurs in the Contemporary U.S. Leftist Movement." In *The Criminologist: Crime and the Criminal,* ed. Charles Reasons, pp. 209–25. Pacific Palisades, Calif.: Goodyear Publishing, 1974.

Kelman, Herbert C., and V. Lee Hamilton. *Crimes of Obedience: Toward a Social Psychology of Authority and Responsibility.* New Haven, Conn.: Yale University Press, 1988.

Kenworthy, Tom. "The Hunt for Surprise October," *The Washington Post National Weekly Edition,* 12–18 August 1991, p. 14.

Kessner, Lawrence. *The Spy Next Door.* Westport, Conn.: Arlington House, 1981.

Kettle, Martin. *Sidney Reilly: The True Story of the World's Greatest Spy.* New York: St. Martin's Press, 1984.

Khan, Sadruddin Aga. "War Crimes Without Punishment," *The New York Times,* 8 February 1994, p. A15.

Kidder, Rushworth L. *Connecting Law and Society.* Englewood Cliffs, N.J.: Prentice-Hall, 1983.

———. "Unmasking Terrorism," *Christian Science Monitor Special Report,* 13–21 May 1986, pp. 17–20.

Kirkham, James F. *Assassination and Political Violence.* Washington, D.C.: Government Printing Office, 1969.

Kittrie, Nicholas N., and Eldon D. Wedlock, Jr., eds. *The Tree of Liberty: A Documentary History of Rebellion and Political Crime in America.* Baltimore: Johns Hopkins University Press, 1986.

Klanwatch. "Domestic Terrorists: The KKK in the 'Fifth Era'." *Klanwatch Intelligence Report,* The Southern Poverty Law Center, Montgomery, Ala., 1985, 5–10.

Kneece, Jack. *Family Treason: The Walker Spy Ring Case.* New York: Stein and Day, 1986.

Koppel, Ted. "The Perils of Info-Democracy," *The New York Times,* 1 July 1994, Op-Ed, p. A15.

Krauss, Clifford. "Christopher Picks El Salvador Panel," *The New York Times,* 25 March 1993(a), p. A3.

———. "Senate Lengthens Sentences for Hate Crimes," *The New York Times,* 5 November 1993(b), p. A9.

———. "U.S. Aware of Killings, Worked with Rightists, Paper Suggests," *The New York Times,* 9 November 1993(c), p. A4.

Kuper, Leo. *Genocide: Its Political Use in the Twentieth Century.* New Haven, Conn.: Yale University Press, 1981.

La Franiere, Sharon, and Susan Schmidt. "Accused Spy Ronald Pelton Was Preoccupied with Money," *The Washington Post,* 7 December 1985, pp. A1, A12.

Laqueur, Walter. *The Age of Terrorism.* Boston: Little, Brown, 1987.

Lardner, George, Jr. "A Departing President's Midnight Raid on History," *The Washington Post National Weekly Edition,* 22–28 March 1993, pp. 31–32.

"Law and Order and Abortion Clinics," *The New York Times,* 1 July 1994, p. A14.

Lawler, Philip F. "An Issue This Paper Can't Sidestep," *The Wall Street Journal,* 29 August 1991, p. A11.

Lawrence, Jill. "Feds Used Human Subjects in Radiation Exposure Experiments," *Erie Times News,* 25 October 1988, pp. 1A, 12A.

Ledeen, Michael. *Perilous Statecraft: An Insider's Account of the Iran-Contra Affair.* New York: Charles Scribner's Sons, 1988.

Lemert, Edwin M. "An Isolation and Closure Theory of Naive Check Forgery." *Journal of Criminal Law, Criminology and Police Science* 44 (1953): 296–307.

Lemkin, Raphael. *Axis Rule in Occupied Europe.* Washington, D.C.: Carnegie Endowment for International Peace, 1944.

Lewis, Anthony. "The Whole Truth," *The New York Times,* 9 December 1993, p. A11.

Lewis, Paul. "U.N. Rebukes Myanmar Leaders On Human Rights and Democracy," *The New York Times,* 7 December 1993, p. A5.

Liddy, Gordon. *Will.* New York: Dell, 1981.

Lieberman, Jethro K. *How the Government Breaks the Law.* Baltimore: Penguin, 1984.

Lindsey, Robert. *The Falcon and the Snowman.* New York: Simon and Schuster, 1979.

———. *The Flight of the Falcon.* New York: Simon and Schuster, 1983.

Liston, Robert. *The Dangerous World of Spies and Spying.* New York: Platt and Munk, 1967.

Longmire, Dennis. "Crimes of Power and Opulence: Criminological Researcher's Experience with Taboos." Paper presented at the American Society of Criminology Meetings, Chicago, November 1988.

Maas, Peter. *Killer Spy: The Inside Story of the FBI's Pursuit and Capture of Aldrich Ames, America's Deadliest Spy.* New York: Warner, 1995.

MacDonald, Andres. *The Turner Diaries.* 2d ed. Arlington, Va.: The National Alliance, 1980.

MacFarquhar, Emily. "The War Against Women." *U.S. News and World Report,* 28 March 1994, 42–48.

Maclean, Fitzroy. *Take Nine Spies.* New York: Atheneum, 1978.

Mandela, Nelson. *Long Walk to Freedom: The Autobiography of Nelson Mandela.* Boston: Little, Brown, 1995.

Marchetti, Victor, and John D. Marks. *The CIA and the Cult of Intelligence.* New York: Alfred A. Knopf, 1974.

Marcus, Ruth, and Joe Pichirallo. "Chin Believed Planted in U.S. as a Spy," *The Washington Post,* 6 December 1985, pp. A1, A22.

Marks, John. *The Search for the Manchurian Candidate: The CIA and Mind Control.* New York: Times Books, 1979.

Martin, David W., and John Walcott. *Best Laid Plans: The Inside Story of America's War Against Terrorism.* New York: Harper and Row, 1988.

Martin, John M., James F. Haran, and Anne Romano. "Espionage: A Challenge to Criminology and Criminal Justice." Paper presented at the Academy of Criminal Justice Sciences Meetings, San Francisco, April 1988.

Martin, John M., and Anne T. Romano. *Multinational Crime: Terrorism, Espionage and Arms Trafficking.* Newbury Park, Calif.: Sage, 1992.

Maser, Werner. *Nuremberg: A Nation on Trial.* Trans. Richard Barry. New York: Charles Scribner's Sons, 1979.

Masland, Tom, et al. "Slavery." *Newsweek,* 4 May 1992, 30–38.

Marx, Gary. "External Efforts to Damage or Facilitate Social Movements: Some Patterns, Explanations, Outcomes and Complications." In *The Dynamics of Social Movements,* eds. Mayer N. Zald and John D. McCarthy. Cambridge, Mass.: Winthrop Publishers, 1979.

———. *Undercover: Police Surveillance in America.* Berkeley, Calif.: University of California Press, 1990.

Mayer, Martin. *The Greatest-Ever Bank Robbery: The Collapse of the Savings and Loan Industry.* New York: Charles Scribner's Sons, 1990.

McGrory, Mary. "He Can Run, But He Can't Hide: Dick Thornburgh's No Show in Congress," *The Washington Post National Weekly Edition,* 29 July–4 August 1991, p. 25.

Meier, Kenneth J. *Politics and Bureaucracy: Policy-making in the Fourth Branch of Government.* 2d ed. Monterey, Calif.: Brooks Cole, 1987.

Miller, Nathan. *The Founding Finaglers.* New York: David McKay, 1976.

———. *Stealing From America.* New York: Paragon House, 1992.

Millett, Kate. *The Politics of Cruelty: An Essay on the Literature of Political Imprisonment.* New York: W. W. Norton, 1994.

Mills, C. Wright. *The Power Elite.* New York: Oxford University Press, 1956.

Misner, Gordon E. "Process Barbie: Lyons, and the Nazi Trial." *CJ International* 3 (1987): 3–4, 28–32.

Morganthau, Tom, et al. "Moscow's Prying Eyes." *Newsweek,* 30 September 1985, 3.

Morganthau, Tom, Kim Willenson, and Richard Sandza. "Blue Chip Defector: A KGB 'Biggie' Bolts to the CIA." *Newsweek,* 7 October 1985, 28.

Morley, Christopher, and Louella D. Everett, eds. *The Shorter Bartlett's Familiar Quotations.* New York: Pocket Books, Inc., 1965.

Morrell, David. *The Brotherhood of the Rose.* New York: St Martin's/Marek, 1984.

Mossberg, Walter S. "Pan Am Bombing Probe Takes New Turn as Device Points to Libyan-Based Agents." *The Wall Street Journal,* 11 October 1990, p. A11.

Moyers, Bill. *The Secret Government: The Constitution in Crises.* Cabin John, Md.: Seven Locks Press, 1988.

Moynihan, Daniel P. *Pandaemonium: Ethnicity in International Politics.* New York: Oxford University Press, 1993.

Myers, Gustavus. *The History of Great American Fortunes.* New York: Modern American Library, 1936.

Nash, Nathaniel C. "Argentine Files Show Huge Effort to Harbor Nazis," *The New York Times,* 14 December 1993, p. A3.

National Advisory Committee on Criminal Justice Standards and Goals. *Report of the Task Force on Disorders and Terrorism.* Washington, D.C.: Government Printing Office, 1976.

NBC. "KGB/USA." *American Almanac.* Broadcast 10 October 1985.

Netanyahu, Benjamin. *Terrorism: How the West Can Win.* New York: Farrar, Straus and Giroux, 1986.

Nettler, Gwynn. *Criminal Careers.* Vol. 2. Cincinnati: Anderson, 1982.

"North Freed," *The Wall Street Journal,* 17 September 1991, p. A16.

North, Oliver, with William Novak. *Under Fire: An American Story.* New York: Harper Collins, 1991.

"Nuremberg Principle." *The Nation,* 26 January 1970, 78.

Ogata, R. Craig. "Understanding Corporate Deviance: The Case of Industrial Espionage." *Journal of Security Administration* 6 (January 1984): 17–29.

O'Rourke, P. J. "Piggy Banks." *Rolling Stone,* 24 August 1989, 43.

Orwell, George. *Animal Farm.* New York: Harcourt, Brace, 1954.

————. *1984.* New York: New American Library, 1971.

Paige, Connie. *The Right to Lifers: Who They Are, How They Operate, Where They Get the Money.* New York: Summit Books, 1985.

"Palestinian Organizations." *CJ International* 6 (September–October 1990): 11–18.

"Panel Clears Bush in Probe of Hostage Deal with Iran," *Erie Morning News,* 2 July 1992, p. 2A.

Passas, Nikos. "International Criminal Enterprises and U.S. Interests: Lessons from the BCCI Affair." Paper presented at the National Strategy Information Center Meetings, Washington, D.C., 4 December 1992.

Penkovsky, Oleg. *The Penkovsky Papers.* Edited by Frank Gibney. Garden City, N.Y.: Doubleday, 1965.

"A People's Charter on Human Rights," *The New York Times,* 10 December 1993, p. A18.

Peters, Edward. *Torture.* Oxford: Basil Blackwell, 1985.

Philby, Kim. *My Silent War.* London: MacGibbon and Kee, 1968.

Pincher, Chapman. *Too Secret, Too Long.* New York: St. Martin's Press, 1984.

Pincus, Walter, and George Lardner, Jr. "How Can You Tell Friend from Foe? George Schultz Wanted Nancy Reagan's Help But She Wanted Him Fired," *The Washington Post National Weekly Edition,* 1–7 March 1993, pp. 8–9.

————. "Iran-Contra's Moral for Presidents," *The Washington Post National Weekly Edition,* 7–13 February 1994, p. 23.

Pizzo, Stephen. "Family Values." *Mother Jones,* September/October 1992(a), 28–68.

————. "Loose Change: The First Family." *Mother Jones,* March/April 1992(b), 19–21.

Plate, Thomas, and Andrea Darvi. *Secret Police: The Inside Story of a Network of Terror.* Garden City, N.Y.: Doubleday, 1981.

Ploscowe, M. "Treason." In *Encyclopedia of the Social Sciences,* eds. Edwin R. A. Seligman and Alvin S. Johnson. New York: Macmillan, 1935, vol. 15, pp. 93–96.

Poland, James M. *Understanding Terrorism: Groups, Strategies and Responses.* Englewood Cliffs, N.J.: Prentice-Hall, 1988.

Poponoe, David. *Sociology.* 10th ed. Englewood Cliffs, N.J.: Prentice-Hall, 1995.

Posner, Gerald. *Case Closed: Lee Harvey Oswald and the JFK Assassination.* New York: Random House, 1993.

Proal, Louis. *Political Crime.* Montclair, N.J.: Patterson Smith (originally published in 1898), 1973.

Quinney, Richard C. *The Social Reality of Crime.* Boston: Little, Brown, 1970.

Regan, Tom. *All That Dwell Therein: Animal Rights and Environmental Ethics.* Berkeley, Calif.: University of California Press, 1982.

Report of the Congressional Committee Investigating the Iran-Contra Affair, with Supplemental, Minority and Additional Views. Washington, D.C.: Government Printing Office, 1987.

Rockefeller Commission. *The Rockefeller Report to the President by the Commission on CIA Activities.* Washington, D.C.: Government Printing Office, 1975.

Rockwell, Beth. "School of Dictators," *Erie Morning News,* 15 August 1994, p. 6A.

Roebuck, Julian, and S. C. Weeber. *Political Crime in the United States.* New York: Praeger, 1978.

Ronelaugh, John. *The Agency: The Rise and Decline of the CIA: From Wild Bill Donovan to William Casey.* New York: Simon and Schuster, 1986.

Rosenbaum, David E. "True to Form: Life Styles of the Infamous and Venal," *New York Times,* 5 June 1994, p. 4E.

Rosenbaum, Eli M., and William Hoffer. *Betrayal: The Untold Story of the Kurt Waldheim Investigation and Cover-Up.* New York: St. Martin's Press, 1994.

Rosenberg, Tina. "Terror, Tribunals and the Truth: A U.N. Report Puts the Spotlight on El Salvador's Civil War," *The Washington Post National Weekly Edition,* 22–28 March 1993, pp. 23–24.

Rosenthal, A. M. "The Pope's Knight," *The New York Times,* 12 August 1994, p. A15.

———. "Jihad in America," *The New York Times,* 3 February 1995, p. A15.

Ross, Jeffrey I. "Structural Causes of Oppositional Political Terrorism: Towards a Causal Model." *Journal of Peace Research* 30, 3 (1993): 317–329.

———. *Controlling State Crime.* Hamden, Conn.: Garland Publishing, 1994.

Ross, Shelley. *Fall From Grace: Sex, Scandal and Corruption in American Politics from 1702 to the Present.* New York: Ballantine Books, 1988.

Rushdie, Salman. "Simple Truths and Apostles of Death," *The New York Times,* 14 July 1994, Op-Ed, p. A15.

———. *The Satanic Verses.* New York: Viking Penguin, 1989.

Safire, William. "Iraqgate Giveaway," *The New York Times,* 20 May 1993(a), p. A13.

———. "Is the Fix In?," *The New York Times,* 9 September 1993(b), p. A15.

———. "Beware of 'Proactive'," *The New York Times,* 8 May 1995, p. A13.

Sagarin, Edward. "Introduction" to Louis Proal's *Political Crime.* Montclair, N.J.: Patterson Smith, 1973.

Sapp, Allen B. "Rationalizations for Domestic Violence: An Analysis of The Secret Army . . . Wenn Alle Bruder Schweigen." Center for Criminal Justice Research, Central Missouri State University, March 1986.

Satchell, Michael. "The Just War Never Ends." *U.S. News and World Report,* 19 December 1988, 31–38.

Satchell, Michael, Gillian Sanford, and Rene Riley. "Why the Secrets Slip Out." *U.S. News and World Report,* 1 June 1987, 20–22.

Schafer, Stephen. "The Concept of the Political Criminal." *Journal of Criminal Law, Criminology and Police Science* 62 (Spring 1971): 380–387.

———. *The Political Criminal: The Problems of Morality and Crime.* New York: The Free Press, 1974.

Scheflin, Alan W., and Edward M. Opton, Jr. *The Mind Manipulators.* New York: Paddington Press, 1978.

Schlesinger, Arthur M., Jr. *The Imperial Presidency.* Boston: Houghton Mifflin, 1973.

———. *The Cycles of American History.* Boston: Houghton Mifflin, 1986.

Schmid, Alex P., and Janny de Graaf. *Violence as Communication: Insurgent Terrorism and the Western News Media.* Beverly Hills, Calif.: Sage, 1982.

Schur, Edwin M. *The Politics of Deviance.* Englewood Cliffs, N.J.: Prentice-Hall, 1980.

Sciolino, Elaine. "A Budding Scandal, In Brief: A Primer on the BNL Affair," *The New York Times,* 18 October 1992, p. E4.

————. "State Department Says China Has Failed to Improve Human Rights Record," *The New York Times,* 12 January 1994, p. A1.

Scott, Peter D. *Deep Politics and the Death of JFK.* Berkeley, Calif.: University of California Press, 1993.

Seale, Patrick. *Abu Nidal: Gun for Hire.* New York: Random House, 1992.

"The Secret Army . . . Wenn Alle Bruders Schweigen," (anonymous). Fowlerville, Mich.: followers of the Way, 1985.

"The Secrets of South Africa's Hit Squad." *Newsweek,* 25 November 1989, 56.

Sederberg, Peter C. *Terrorist Myths: Illusions, Rhetoric and Reality.* Englewood Cliffs, N.J.: Prentice-Hall, 1989.

Shapiro, Joseph, et al. "An Epidemic of Fear and Loathing." *U.S. News and World Report,* 8 May 1995, 37–44.

Sharansky, Natan. *Fear No Evil.* New York: Random House, 1988.

"Signers Vow to Defy Immigration Law." *National Catholic Reporter,* 24 February 1989, 6.

Simon, David R. "Reagan Era Corruption and the Prophecy of C. Wright Mills," unpublished paper. 1992.

————. "Criminology and the Kennedy Assassination." *Quarterly Journal of Ideology* (Autumn 1993): 15–26.

————. *Social Problems: The Sociological Imagination.* New York: McGraw-Hill, 1995.

————. *Elite Deviance.* 5th ed. Boston: Allyn and Bacon, 1996.

Simon, David R., and Stanley D. Eitzen. *Elite Deviance.* 4th ed. Boston: Allyn and Bacon, 1993.

Simon, David R., and Frank Hagan. "The Criminology of Scandal." Paper presented at the Academy of Criminal Justice Sciences Meetings, Boston, March 1995.

Simpson, John, and Jana Bennett. *The Disappeared and the Mothers of the Plaza.* New York: St. Martin's Press, 1985.

Singer, Mark. "Quaylegate," *The New York Times,* 16 October 1992, p. A17.

Skolnick, Jerome H. *The Politics of Protest: The Skolnick Report to the National Commission on the Causes and Prevention of Violence.* New York: Ballantine Books, 1969.

Smith, Bradley F. *Reaching Judgment at Nuremberg.* New York: Basic Books, 1977.

Sterling, Claire. *The Terror Network: The Secret War of International Terrorism.* New York: Holt, Rinehart and Winston, 1981.

Stone, L. A. "I Spy a Myth." *Security Management* (October 1991): 28–32.

Styron, Rose. "Justice Depraved," *The New York Times,* 23 February 1994, p. A17.

Summers, Anthony. *Conspiracy.* New York: McGraw-Hill, 1980.

Thomas, Charles W., and John R. Hepburn. *Crime, Criminal Law and Criminology.* Dubuque, Iowa: William C. Brown, 1983.

Thomas, Evan, et al. "Deadly Mole." *Newsweek,* 7 March 1994, 20–31.

Thompson, J. W., and S. K. Padover. *Secret Diplomacy: Espionage and Cryptography 1500–1815.* 2d ed. New York: Frederick Ungar, 1963.

Tomsho, Robert. *The American Sanctuary Movement.* Austin, Tex.: Texas Monthly Press, 1987.

Truell, Peter, and Larry Gurwin. *False Profits: The Inside Story of BCCI, The World's Most Corrupt Financial Empire.* Boston: Houghton Mifflin, 1992.

Tunnell, Kenneth D., ed. *Political Crime in Contemporary America: A Critical Approach.* New York: Garland Press, 1993.

Turk, Austin T. *Criminality and the Legal Order.* Chicago: Rand McNally, 1969.

——. *Political Criminality: The Defiance and Defense of Authority.* Beverly Hills, Calif.: Sage, 1982.

Turner, Stansfield. *Secrecy and Democracy: The CIA in Transition.* New York: Houghton Mifflin, 1985(a).

——. "Why Americans Become Kremlin Agents." *U.S. News and World Report,* 12 August 1985(b), 32.

"2 Tell of Radiation Experiments on Them," *The New York Times,* 14 January 1994, p. A12.

Tzu, Sun. *The Art of War.* Trans. Samuel D. Griffith. New York: Oxford University Press, 1963.

Unger, Craig. "Let's Go to the Tapes on the Mystery of October Surprise," *The Washington Post National Weekly Edition,* 25–31 May 1992, p. 25.

United Nations. *Convention Against Torture.* New York: United Nations, 1984.

U.S. Department of State. *Country Reports on Human Rights Practices for 1993.* Report to the House Committee on Foreign Affairs and the Senate Committee on Foreign Relations. Washington, D.C.: Government Printing Office, February 1994.

Vice President's Task Force. *Report on the Vice President's Task Force on Combatting Terrorism.* Washington, D.C.: Government Printing Office, 1986.

Volkman, Ernest. *Warriors of the Night: Spies, Soldiers and American Intelligence.* New York: W. B. Saunders, 1985.

Waas, Murray, and Craig Unger. "In the Loop: Bush's Secret Mission." *New Yorker,* 2 November 1992, 64–83.

Wade, Worth. *Industrial Espionage and the Mis-Use of Trade Secrets.* Ardmore, Penn.: Advance House, 1965.

Walker, Douglas, et al. "How Ames Fooled the CIA." *Newsweek,* 9 May 1994, 25–26.

Walsh, Lawrence E. *Final Report of the Independent Counsel for Iran-Contra Matters.* 3 vols. Washington, D.C.: Government Printing Office, 18 January 1994.

"Walsh's Hostage: Review and Outlook," *The Wall Street Journal,* 18 June 1992, p. A16.

Ward, Dick. "Gray Area Phenomena: The Changing Nature of Organized Crime and Terrorism." *CJ International* 11 (March–April 1995): 1, 18.

Warren Commission. *Report of the President's Commission on the Assassination of President Kennedy.* Washington, D.C.: Government Printing Office, 1964.

Watson, Russell, et al. "America's Nuclear Secret." *Newsweek,* 27 December 1993, 14–18.

Weaver, Mary Anne. "Children of the Jihad." *New Yorker,* 12 June 1995, 40–47.

Weiner, Tim. "Blowback: From the Afghan Battlefield." *New York Times Magazine,* 13 March 1994a, 52–55.

——. "Agency Chief Pledges to Overhaul Fraternity Atmosphere at the CIA," *The New York Times,* 19 July 1994b, pp. A1, A10.

Weiner, Tim, David Johnston, and Neil A. Lewis. *Betrayal: The Story of Aldrich Ames, An American Spy.* New York: Random House, 1995.

West, Nigel. *The Circus: MI5 Operations 1945–1972.* New York: Stein and Day, 1983.

Westin, Alan F. *Whistle Blowing: Loyalty and Dissent in the Corporation.* New York: McGraw-Hill, 1981.

Whitaker, Mark, et al. "The Forgotten: Prisoners of Conscience." *Newsweek,* 14 February 1983, 40–55.

Wiggins, Michael E. "The Turner Diaries: Blueprint for Right-Wing Extremist Violence." Center for Criminal Justice Research, Central Missouri State University, 1986.

Wilkenson, Paul. *Political Terrorism.* New York: Wiley, 1976.

Williams, Marjorie. "Getting a Grip (or Losing It) on Iran-Contra," *The Washington Post National Weekly Edition,* 30 September–6 October 1991, pp. 11–12.

Wines, Michael. "Ex-CIA Official Says U.S. Ignores Syrian Terror," *The New York Times,* 21 December 1990, p. A7.

Wise, David. *Nightmover: How Aldrich Ames Sold the CIA to the KGB for $4.6 Million.* New York: Harper Collins, 1995.

Wise, David, and T. B. Ross. *The Espionage Establishment.* New York: Bantam, 1968.

Witt, Howard. "CIA Sued for Attempt at Brainwashing," *Erie Daily Times,* 3 October 1988, p. 2A.

Wolf, J. B. "Enforcement Terrorism." *Police Studies* 3 (1981): 45–54.

Woodward, Bob. *Veil: The Secret War of the CIA: 1981–1987.* New York: Simon and Schuster, 1987.

Wrone, David R., and Russell S. Nelson, Jr. *Who's the Savage: A Documentary History of the Mistreatment of the Native North Americans.* Greenwich, Conn.: Fawcett Premier Books, 1973.

Wu, Harry. "China's Gulag," *The New York Times,* 4 February 1994, p. A15.

Wynne, Greville. *Contact on Gorky Street.* New York: Atheneum, 1967.

# Author Index

# Subject Index